EFFICACY & ONCOLOGY SAS: INTERVIEW PREP

100 VITAL QUESTIONS AND ANSWERS

SHIVA RAVINDRA

Made with ♥ on the Notion Press Platform
www.notionpress.com

*Welcome to "**Clinical SAS Efficacy & Oncology Q&A Interview Prep**"*

Introduction

*My name is **Shivaravindra**, and I have 15+ years of experience in Clinical SAS.
I have worked on numerous end-to-end projects, extensively involving SDTM, ADaM,
and TFL.*

In today's competitive job market, many SAS programmers find themselves well-versed in programming but lacking in-depth knowledge of specific domains such as oncology and efficacy. This gap in understanding often becomes a significant barrier, making it challenging to crack interviews and secure positions that require specialized expertise.

This book aims to bridge that gap by providing comprehensive coverage of key concepts in clinical SAS programming, with a particular focus on oncology and efficacy. Whether you're a fresher or a seasoned professional with over 10 years of experience, this book is designed to enhance your understanding and prepare you thoroughly for interviews in this niche field.

Why This Book?

Understanding the Challenge: Many SAS programmers struggle to grasp the intricate details of oncology and efficacy, which are crucial for clinical trials and research. This book addresses these challenges head-on, offering detailed explanations and practical insights.

Comprehensive Coverage: From foundational concepts to advanced topics, this book covers a wide range of subjects relevant to clinical SAS programming in oncology. Each concept is explained in detail, ensuring you gain a deep and thorough understanding.

Interview-Focused: The content is specifically tailored to help you succeed in interviews. We include a wide variety of questions and answers that you are likely to encounter, along with detailed explanations to help you understand the reasoning behind each answer.

For All Experience Levels: Whether you're just starting your career or have years of experience, this book is designed to be valuable to you. Freshers will find it an excellent resource for building a strong foundation, while experienced candidates can use it to refine their knowledge and stay updated with the latest industry standards.

What to Expect

- **Detailed Explanations:** Each concept is broken down into simple, easy-to-understand language, with examples to illustrate key points.
- **Practical Insights:** Learn from real-world examples and scenarios that are commonly encountered in clinical trials and oncology research.
- **Extensive Q&A:** A comprehensive collection of interview questions and answers, ranging from basic to advanced levels, to help you prepare effectively.
- **Tips and Tricks:** Useful strategies and tips to help you tackle interview questions confidently and efficiently.

This book is your guide to mastering the intricacies of clinical SAS programming in oncology. By the end of this journey, you will be well-equipped with the knowledge and confidence to excel in your interviews and advance your career in this specialized field.

Let's embark on this journey together, and take a significant step towards your career growth and success in clinical SAS oncology.

"Embrace the challenges, learn from every experience, and persist with determination; your success in clinical SAS oncology awaits."

Contents

Contents

Contents

*To my beloved wife, **Ramya** ,*

Your unwavering love, encouragement, and support have been my guiding light throughout this journey. This book is a testament to your constant belief in me and your endless patience as I pursued my passion.

Thank you for standing by my side, inspiring me to reach new heights, and making every moment together a cherished memory.

This book is dedicated to you with all my love and gratitude.

CHAPTER I

What is the oncology therapeutic area?

Cancer is a disease characterized by the uncontrolled growth and spread of abnormal cells in the body. These cells can invade and damage normal tissues and organs, potentially leading to serious health problems and, if untreated, can be life-threatening.

The *oncology therapeutic area* refers to a specialized field within medicine focused on the study, diagnosis, treatment, and management of **cancer**. It encompasses various cancers affecting different parts of the body and involves multiple treatment modalities and research to improve patient outcomes.

Key Aspects of the Oncology Therapeutic Area:

Types of Cancer:

Example: Breast cancer, lung cancer, prostate cancer, colorectal cancer, etc.

Diagnosis and Screening:

Example: Mammograms for breast cancer screening, colonoscopies for colorectal cancer detection, and PSA tests for prostate cancer screening.

Treatment Modalities:

Surgery: Removing tumors surgically, such as a lumpectomy for breast cancer.

Chemotherapy: Using drugs to kill cancer cells, like doxorubicin for various cancers.

Radiation Therapy: Using high-energy radiation to target and destroy cancer cells, often used in brain cancer.

Immunotherapy: Enhancing the body's immune system to fight cancer, such as using checkpoint inhibitors like pembrolizumab for melanoma.

Targeted Therapy: Drugs designed to target specific genetic mutations in cancer cells, like imatinib for chronic myeloid leukemia (CML).

Supportive Care and Palliative Care:

Example: Managing symptoms and side effects of cancer treatment, providing pain relief, and addressing psychological needs of patients.

Research and Clinical Trials:

Example: Investigating new cancer treatments, understanding cancer biology, and developing innovative therapies through clinical trials.

Multidisciplinary Approach:

Example: Collaborative care involving oncologists, radiologists, pathologists, surgeons, and other specialists to provide comprehensive treatment plans.

Patient Education and Advocacy:

Example: Educating patients about their diagnosis, treatment options, and supporting them through their cancer journey.

CHAPTER II

Can you explain the role of oncology-specific SDTM domains in clinical trials?

SDTM domains are TU,TR and RS

In every oncology study, subjects undergo various imaging methods such as MRI, CT scans, and X-rays to detect the presence of cancer tumors in the body.

This process is known as **Identification**.

1. **Identification of Tumors:**

- **Target Lesions:** Tumors with measurable diameters.
- **Non-Target Lesions:** Tumors with non-measurable diameters.

2. **Measurement of Tumors:**

- Tumors are measured at different time points, such as Visit 1, Visit 2, etc.
- This step is called **Measurement**.

Measurements follow the RECIST guidelines:

- **RECIST Definition:** RECIST (Response Evaluation Criteria in Solid Tumors) provides standardized criteria for measuring tumor response.
- **Guidelines:**
- A maximum of 5 target lesions are selected per patient, with no more than 2 lesions per organ.
- Target lesions are labeled as T01, T02, etc.
- Non-target lesions are labeled as NT01, NT02, etc.
- **Measurement Criteria:**
- **Target Lesions:** Diameter and sum of diameters.
- **Non-Target Lesions:** Presence or absence.

3. **Assessment of Tumor Response:**

- Tumor responses are evaluated based on the measurements.
- This step is called **Assessment**.
- **Response Classification:**
- **Target Response:** Based on target lesions.
- **Non-Target Response:** Based on non-target lesions.
- **Overall Response:** Combined response of target and non-target tumors.

4. **SDTM Domains for Tumor Data:**

- **Identification Information:
    Stored in the SDTM **TU (Tumor Identification)** domain.
- **TULINKID Variable:** Stores the unique number of the tumor.
- **RESULT Variable:** Indicates target or non-target information.

- **Measurement Information:
    Stored in the SDTM **TR (Tumor Response)** domain.
- **RESULT Variable:** Contains diameter or sum of diameters.
- **Response Information:** Stored in the SDTM **RS (Response)** domain.
- **Response Variable:** Captures target, non-target, or overall response information.

The RS domain records responses categorized as **Complete Response (CR), Partial Response (PR), Progressive Disease (PD), and Stable Disease (SD).**

Target lesions

length diameter tumor >10mm
max 5, max 2 per organ
short axis lymph node >15mm
Determine SLD sum of length diameters

Response Evaluation Criteria Ii
Solid Tumors (RECIST)

Non-target lesions

lesions <10mm
non-measurable like pleural fluid, ascites,
lymphangitis

Lesions are abnormal changes in an organ or in tissue due to injury or disease.

Identification of Tumors

IDENTIFY TUMORS

TULNKID	TUTESTCD	TUTEST	TUORRES
NT01	TUMIDENT	Tumor Identification	NON-TARGET
NT02	TUMIDENT	Tumor Identification	NON-TARGET
NT03	TUMIDENT	Tumor Identification	NON-TARGET
NT04	TUMIDENT	Tumor Identification	NON-TARGET
NT05	TUMIDENT	Tumor Identification	NON-TARGET
NT06	TUMIDENT	Tumor Identification	NON-TARGET
NT07	TUMIDENT	Tumor Identification	NON-TARGET
NT08	TUMIDENT	Tumor Identification	NON-TARGET
NT09	TUMIDENT	Tumor Identification	NON-TARGET
NT10	TUMIDENT	Tumor Identification	NON-TARGET
T01	TUMIDENT	Tumor Identification	TARGET
T02	TUMIDENT	Tumor Identification	TARGET
T03	TUMIDENT	Tumor Identification	TARGET
NT01	TUMIDENT	Tumor Identification	NON-TARGET
NT02	TUMIDENT	Tumor Identification	NON-TARGET
NT03	TUMIDENT	Tumor Identification	NON-TARGET
NT04	TUMIDENT	Tumor Identification	NON-TARGET
NT05	TUMIDENT	Tumor Identification	NON-TARGET
NT06	TUMIDENT	Tumor Identification	NON-TARGET
NT07	TUMIDENT	Tumor Identification	NON-TARGET
NT08	TUMIDENT	Tumor Identification	NON-TARGET
NT09	TUMIDENT	Tumor Identification	NON-TARGET
NT10	TUMIDENT	Tumor Identification	NON-TARGET

IDENTIFY TUMORS

TULOC	TUMETHOD
SMALL BREAST MASS AND INFEROLATERAL ASPECT OF LEFT BREAST	CONTRAST ENHANCED CT SCAN
ENHANCING LESIONS IN THE MEDIAL ASPECT OF THE LEFT BREAST	CONTRAST ENHANCED CT SCAN
LEFT RIB CAGE/FLANK SUBCUTANEOUS #1	CLINICAL EVALUATION
LEFT RIB CAGE/FLANK SUBCUTANEOUS #3	CLINICAL EVALUATION
LEFT RIB CAGE/FLANK SUBCUTANEOUS #5	CLINICAL EVALUATION
LEFT RIB CAGE/FLANK SUBCUTANEOUS #6	CLINICAL EVALUATION
LEFT RIB CAGE/SUBCUTANEOUS #7	CLINICAL EVALUATION
LEFT RIB CAGE/SUBCUTANEOUS #8	CLINICAL EVALUATION
LEFT RIB CAGE/SUBCUTANEOUS #9	CLINICAL EVALUATION
LEFT RIB CAGE/FLANK SUBCUTANEOUS #10 (IL #3)	CLINICAL EVALUATION
MASS WITHIN INFERIOR LATERAL LEFT BREAST	CONTRAST ENHANCED CT SCAN
LEFT RIB CAGE/FLANK SUBCUTANEOUS #2 (IL #1)	CLINICAL EVALUATION
LEFT RIB CAGE/FLANK SUBCUTANEOUS #4 (IL #2)	CLINICAL EVALUATION
SMALL BREAST MASS AND INFEROLATERAL ASPECT OF LEFT BREAST	CONTRAST ENHANCED CT SCAN
ENHANCING LESIONS IN THE MEDIAL ASPECT OF THE LEFT BREAST	CONTRAST ENHANCED CT SCAN
LEFT RIB CAGE/FLANK SUBCUTANEOUS #1	CLINICAL EVALUATION
LEFT RIB CAGE/FLANK SUBCUTANEOUS #3	CLINICAL EVALUATION
LEFT RIB CAGE/FLANK SUBCUTANEOUS #5	CLINICAL EVALUATION
LEFT RIB CAGE/FLANK SUBCUTANEOUS #6	CLINICAL EVALUATION
LEFT RIB CAGE/SUBCUTANEOUS #7	CLINICAL EVALUATION
LEFT RIB CAGE/SUBCUTANEOUS #8	CLINICAL EVALUATION
LEFT RIB CAGE/SUBCUTANEOUS #9	CLINICAL EVALUATION

MEASURE TUMORS TR

TRGRPID	TRLNKID	TRTESTCD	TRTEST	TRORRES	TRORRESU
TARGET	T01	LDIAM	Longest Diameter	5	mm
TARGET	T02	LDIAM	Longest Diameter	12	mm
TARGET	T03	LDIAM	Longest Diameter	12	mm
TARGET	T04	LDIAM	Longest Diameter		
TARGET	T05	LDIAM	Longest Diameter		
TARGET		SUMLDIAM	Sum of Longest Diameter	29	mm
NON-TARGET	NT01	TUMSTATE	Tumor State	PRESENT	

MEASURE TUMORS TR

	TRGRPID	TRLNKID	TRTESTCD	TRTEST	TRORRES
7	TARGET		SUMLDIAM	Sum of Longest Diameter	29
3	NON-TARGET	NT01	TUMSTATE	Tumor State	PRESENT
3	NON-TARGET	NT02	TUMSTATE	Tumor State	PRESENT
]	NON-TARGET	NT03	TUMSTATE	Tumor State	PRESENT
1	NON-TARGET	NT04	TUMSTATE	Tumor State	PRESENT
2	NON-TARGET	NT05	TUMSTATE	Tumor State	PRESENT
3	NON-TARGET	NT06	TUMSTATE	Tumor State	PRESENT
4	NON-TARGET	NT07	TUMSTATE	Tumor State	PRESENT
5	NON-TARGET	NT08	TUMSTATE	Tumor State	PRESENT
5	NON-TARGET	NT09	TUMSTATE	Tumor State	PRESENT
7	NON-TARGET	NT10	TUMSTATE	Tumor State	PRESENT
3	TARGET	T01	LDIAM	Longest Diameter	NON EVALUABLE
3	TARGET	T02	LDIAM	Longest Diameter	12
	NON-TARGET	NT01	TUMSTATE	Tumor State	PRESENT
	NON-TARGET	NT02	TUMSTATE	Tumor State	UNABLE TO EVALUATE
	NON-TARGET	NT03	TUMSTATE	Tumor State	UNABLE TO EVALUATE
	NON-TARGET	NT04	TUMSTATE	Tumor State	UNABLE TO EVALUATE
	NON-TARGET	NT05	TUMSTATE	Tumor State	UNABLE TO EVALUATE
	NON-TARGET	NT06	TUMSTATE	Tumor State	UNABLE TO EVALUATE
	NON-TARGET	NT07	TUMSTATE	Tumor State	UNABLE TO EVALUATE
	NON-TARGET	NT08	TUMSTATE	Tumor State	UNABLE TO EVALUATE
	TARGET	T01	LDIAM	Longest Diameter	22

ACCESS RESPONSE RS

USUBJID	RSSEQ	RSGRPID	RSTESTCD	RSTEST	RSCAT	RSORRES		RSS
MMSC 2023-01-101001	5	NON-TARGET	OVRLNTR	Overall Non-target Response		Not Evaluated	NE	
MMSC 2023-01-101001	7	TARGET	OVRLTRG	Overall Target Response		Not Evaluated	NE	
MMSC 2023-01-101002	4	NON-TARGET	OVRLNTR	Overall Non-target Response		Not Evaluated	NE	
MMSC 2023-01-101002	6	TARGET	OVRLTRG	Overall Target Response		Not Evaluated	NE	
MMSC 2023-01-101003	5	NON-TARGET	OVRLNTR	Overall Non-target Response		Non-Complete Response/Non-Progressive Disease	SD	
MMSC 2023-01-101003	7	TARGET	OVRLTRG	Overall Target Response		Stable Disease	SD	
MMSC 2023-01-101006	2	NON-TARGET	OVRLNTR	Overall Non-target Response		Non-Complete Response/Non-Progressive Disease	SD	
MMSC 2023-01-101006	4	TARGET	OVRLTRG	Overall Target Response		Stable Disease	SD	
MMSC 2023-01-101007	5	NON-TARGET	OVRLNTR	Overall Non-target Response		Progressive Disease	PD	
MMSC 2023-01-101007	7	TARGET	OVRLTRG	Overall Target Response		Stable Disease	SD	

CHAPTER III

Step-by-Step Guide to Evaluating Efficacy in Oncology ADaMs, Dataset by Dataset

1. **Study Protocol**:
- Every clinical trial necessitates a comprehensive protocol outlining study objectives and procedures.
- Protocols in oncology trials specify efficacy endpoints crucial for assessing treatment outcomes.
    2. **Statistical Analysis Plan (SAP)**:
- The SAP offers a detailed roadmap for analyzing data collected during the trial.
- It includes descriptions of efficacy endpoints, their derivation methods, and rules for censoring.
- The SAP ensures consistency in data analysis and interpretation across different datasets.
    3. **Tables-Listings-Graphics (TLG) Shells**:
- TLG shells are templates outlining the structure and format for presenting trial results.
- These shells accompany the SAP, providing clear guidelines on how efficacy parameters and other study outcomes should be presented.
- TLG shells aid in standardizing the presentation of results across various datasets and trial sites.
    4. **Common Efficacy Endpoints in Oncology**:
- Overall Survival (OS): Measures the duration from treatment initiation to death from any cause.
- Time to Progression (TTP): Tracks the time from treatment initiation to disease progression.
- Progression-Free Survival (PFS): Measures the time from treatment initiation to disease progression or death.
- Objective Response Rate (ORR): Evaluates the proportion of patients with tumor size reduction or disappearance following treatment.
- Note: Most oncology efficacy endpoints involve censoring to account for patients who haven't experienced the event of interest. However, ORR and some others may not require censoring.

By adhering to these protocols, plans, and templates, oncology trials maintain rigor and consistency in evaluating treatment efficacy and presenting results across diverse datasets.
    1. **SDTM Domains for Data Collection**:
- CDISC (Clinical Data Interchange Standards Consortium) has established a standard data structure known as the Study Data Tabulation Model (SDTM) for organizing clinical trial data.
- The SDTM Implementation Guide (IG) outlines this standard, which includes specific domains for capturing tumor-related information.
    2. **Tumor Package**:
- Within the SDTM, the tumor package comprises three key domains: TU, TR, and RS.
- Each domain serves a distinct purpose in representing the data collected during clinical trials involving tumor lesions and disease response.
    3. **Tumor Identification (TU) Domain**:
- The TU domain stores data that uniquely identifies tumors tracked throughout the study duration.
- It serves as a reference for identifying specific tumors and linking them to subsequent assessments.
    4. **Tumor Results (TR) Domain**:
- The TR domain contains detailed information about tumors identified in the TU domain.
- This includes quantitative measurements (e.g., lesion diameter for solid tumors) and qualitative assessments (e.g., evaluation of non-target or new lesions).
- Measurements are recorded at baseline and subsequent timepoints to facilitate response evaluations.
- For solid tumors, the TR domain also includes the summation of diameters of target lesions, aiding in the assessment of treatment response.

5. **Disease Response (RS) Domain**:
- The RS domain holds the results of response evaluations conducted at different timepoints.
- These evaluations are derived from data collected in the TU and TR domains, providing a comprehensive overview of disease response over time.

By adhering to SDTM standards and utilizing these specific domains, clinical trials can effectively capture and organize tumor-related data, facilitating analysis and interpretation of treatment response in oncology research.

1. **ADaM Datasets Requirements**:
- The design of analysis datasets in clinical trials is driven by scientific and medical objectives.
- The purpose of Analysis Data Model (ADaM) is to provide a framework for analyzing data while ensuring clear communication of trial aspects from data collection to analysis to results.

2. **Key Principles**:
- ADaM datasets serve as the authoritative source for all data derivations used in statistical analyses.
- They incorporate both derived and collected data, allowing for analysis with minimal additional programming.
- Standardized analysis datasets and metadata enhance communication, transparency, and understanding of data lineage for reviewers and recipients.

3. **Analysis-Ready Datasets**:
- Analysis datasets should be accompanied by metadata and be analysis-ready.
- They should have a structure and content facilitating statistical analysis with minimal programming, often achieved through a "one proc away" approach.

4. **Survival Analysis**:
- Survival analysis methods are commonly used to study the occurrence and timing of events in clinical studies.
- Survival data may involve censored observations where the event of interest hasn't occurred for all subjects by the end of the observation period.
- ADaM standards recommend using Time-to-Event Variables to capture censoring status, date of censoring, and reasons for censoring.
- This structured approach supports widely used time-to-event analysis methods such as Kaplan-Meier Estimation and Cox Proportional Hazard Model.

By adhering to ADaM standards and incorporating these requirements, clinical trials ensure clear communication, transparency, and robust analysis of data, enhancing the validity and reliability of study results.

Analysis Dataset ADTR (Tumor Results)

1. **Overview**:
- The ADaM dataset ADTR is designed to resemble the SDTM domain TR.
- It contains one observation per subject per timepoint per tumor per response assessment criteria per evaluator.

2. **Baseline and New Lesions**:
- Baseline lesions (Target and Non-Target) are identified at screening.
- New lesions reported post-baseline are stored in the TU domain and represented in ADTR by two records:
- Date/timepoint of initial appearance.
- Date/timepoint of unequivocal assessment.

3. **New Lesion Parameters**:
- Because the initial appearance of a new lesion may differ from the unequivocal assessment, two parameters for New Lesion are recommended.
- Suggested parameters (if using RECIST ver 1.1) include:
- 'Longest Diameter (mm)'
- 'Short Axis Diameter (mm)'
- 'Tumor State - Non-Target Lesion'
- 'Tumor State - New Lesion - Initial Appearance'
- 'Tumor State - New Lesion - Unequivocal Assessment'

4. **Target Lesion Information**:
- The SDTM domain TR also records the sum of diameters of target lesions at each timepoint.
- This timepoint-level information is preferably stored in the ADaM dataset ADTRS.

5. **Example of ADTR**:
- For detailed examples of ADTR dataset structure, please refer to Appendix 1.

By following these guidelines, the ADTR dataset effectively captures detailed tumor results, ensuring robust and clear data for analysis in oncology clinical trials.

Analysis Dataset ADTRS (Timepoint Responses)

1. **Purpose**:
- ADTRS contains timepoint level results, with one observation per subject per timepoint per parameter per response assessment criteria per evaluator.

2. **Possible Parameters**:
- 'Timepoint Sum of Target Lesion Diameters: Lymph Nodes (mm)'
- 'Timepoint Sum of Target Lesion Diameters: Non-Lymph Nodes (mm)'
- 'Timepoint Sum of all Target Lesion Diameters (mm)'
- 'Timepoint Target Lesions Response'
- 'Timepoint Non-Target Lesions Response'
- 'Initial Appearance of New Lesions'
- 'Timepoint Overall Response'

3. **Parameter Qualifiers**:
- Information about evaluators, which cannot be included as qualifiers in the BDS structure, is integrated into the parameters (e.g., "Timepoint Overall Response by Independent Reviewer").

4. **Result Variables**:
- For numeric results, use the variable AVAL.
- For character results, use the variable AVALC.

5. **Analysis Flags (ANLzzFL)**:
- Analysis flags indicate which observations are included in or excluded from future analyses.
- Flags are sequentially numbered (e.g., ANL01FL) and defined based on the SAP methodology.
- Examples of when to exclude evaluations:
- After the start of new anti-cancer treatment.
- After a specified number of days post last dose date.
- After more than one missing adequate assessment.
- After the initial response of PD (Progressive Disease).
- ANL01FL = "Y" for records included in the main analysis based on SAP censoring rules.

6. **Sensitivity Analyses**:
- Additional analysis flags are created for sensitivity analyses with different censoring rules.
- Examples:
- ANL02FL for analyses including timepoints after more than one missing adequate assessment.
- ANL03FL for analyses using Immune-Related Response Evaluation Criteria.

7. **Responder Flags**:
- Flags to identify the first occurrence of a confirmed response (Complete Response 'CR' or Partial Response 'PR').
- Based on SAP criteria for confirmation of response:
- For sequences like {'SD', 'PR', 'SD', 'SD', 'PR', 'PR'}, the fifth evaluation is flagged.
- For sequences like {'SD', 'PR', 'PD'}, no records are flagged as 'PR' is not confirmed.

8. **Percent Change from Baseline (PCHG)**:
- Derived for the parameter 'Timepoint Sum of all Target Lesion Diameters (mm)' at each post-baseline timepoint.
- Used in ADEF (Analysis Dataset for Efficacy) to calculate the Percent Change in Sum of Target Lesion Diameters

from Baseline to Post-baseline Nadir.
- Useful for visualizations like waterfall plots.

Analysis Dataset ADEF

1. **Purpose**:
- The ADEF dataset contains derived efficacy parameters where censoring is irrelevant.
- Structured as one observation per subject per subject-level parameter per response assessment criteria per evaluator.

2. **Parameter Qualifiers**:
- Qualifiers such as evaluator information are included in the parameter names (e.g., "Best Overall Response by Independent Reviewer").

3. **Common Subject-Level Parameters**:
- 'Best Overall Response' (BOR)
- 'Percent Change in Sum of Target Lesion Diameters from Baseline to Post-baseline Nadir'

4. **Data Derivation**:
- BOR is derived for all intent-to-treat subjects.
- Percent Change in Sum of Target Lesion Diameters is derived for subjects with baseline and at least one post-baseline measurement, marked with the corresponding analysis flag in ADTRS.
- Values for these parameters are stored in variables AVAL (numeric) or AVALC (character).

5. **BOR Derivation**:
- The derivation algorithm for BOR is specified in the SAP.
- Multiple BOR parameters may be included if calculated with and without response confirmation or using different evaluation criteria.
- BOR is essential for deriving Objective Response Rate (ORR), a common efficacy endpoint.
- ADTRS cannot substitute for ADEF in BOR derivation due to potential differences in post-baseline evaluations and confirmation requirements.

6. **Evaluation Criteria and Parameters**:
- Multiple parameters for 'Percent Change in Sum of Target Lesion Diameters from Baseline to Post-baseline Nadir' may be included, one per evaluation criteria.
- Disease Control Rate (DCR), an exploratory endpoint, is calculated using BOR values.

7. **Custom Flags**:
- **EFORFL (Objective Response Flag)**: Indicates if a subject has achieved an objective response.
- **EFDCFL (Disease Control Flag)**: Indicates if a subject has achieved disease control.
- These flags are populated only for the BOR parameter.

8. **Additional Variable**:
- **BORDESC (Best Overall Response Description)**: Provides rationale for assigning BOR (e.g., 'Confirmed CR', 'Unconfirmed PR', 'Early SD').

9. **Clinical Benefit Flag (EFCBFL)**:
- This flag is included in the ADTTE dataset instead of ADEF, with the explanation provided in the subsequent section.

By adhering to these guidelines, the ADEF dataset effectively captures and communicates key efficacy parameters, ensuring clear and accurate analysis of clinical trial data.

Analysis Dataset ADTTE

1. **Purpose**:
- ADTTE contains efficacy parameters requiring censoring, which are crucial in oncology clinical trials.
- Structured as one observation per subject per time-to-event subject-level parameter per response assessment criteria per evaluator.

2. **Parameter Qualifiers**:
- Qualifiers such as evaluator information are included in the parameter names (e.g., "Progression Free Survival

(months) by Investigator").

    3. **Common Time-to-Event Parameters**:
- "Overall Survival Time (Months)"
- "Progression Free Survival Time (Months)"
- "Duration of Response (Months)"

    4. **Parameter Derivation**:
- "Overall Survival Time" and "Progression Free Survival Time" are derived for all intent-to-treat subjects.
- "Duration of Response" is derived only for subjects with BOR of 'CR' or 'PR' in ADEF (subjects with EFORFL value of 'Y' in ADEF).
- Multiple parameters can be included to accommodate different evaluation criteria or sensitivity analysis rules.
- Values of these parameters are stored in variables AVAL and CNSR (Censor), as per CDISC guidance "ADaM Basic Data Structure for Time-to-Event Analysis. Version 1.0".

    5. **Additional Key Variables**:
- **ADT**: Analysis Date
- **STARTDT**: Time to Event Origin Date for Subject
- **EVNTDESC**: Event or Censoring Description
- **CNSDTDSC**: Censor Date Description

    6. **Algorithm for Derivation**:
- The specific derivation algorithms for these parameters should be detailed in the SAP.

    7. **Custom Flags for Clinical Benefit Rate (CBR)**:
- **EFDUSDFL (Durable SD Flag)**: Created for subjects with BOR of 'SD' and a duration of SD $\geq$ xx weeks (defined by protocol and SAP).
- **EFCBFL (Clinical Benefit Flag)**: Marked 'Y' if the subject has ADEF.EFORFL of 'Y' or EFDUSDFL of 'Y'.

    8. **Durable Stable Disease (SD)**:
- Durable SD is declared for subjects with BOR of 'SD' and the duration of SD is treated as a time-to-event concept using the same PFS censoring rule.
- Duration of SD equals the progression-free survival time for subjects with a BOR of SD.
- EFDUSDFL is created only for subjects with BOR of 'SD'.

    By following these guidelines, the ADTTE dataset effectively captures time-to-event data, ensuring accurate and transparent analysis of key efficacy endpoints in oncology clinical trials.

Conclusion

    1. **Techniques and References**:
- This paper outlines techniques for deriving and storing all required subject-level efficacy parameters in oncology clinical trials.
- Reference documents include the Study Protocol, SAP, TLG shells, and CDISC ADaM Guidance.

    2. **Censoring Considerations**:
- The methods ensure proper handling of parameters regardless of the need for censoring.

    3. **Dataset Creation Sequence**:
- Follow the specified order for creating ADaM datasets for efficacy:
- **ADTR**: Tumor Results
- **ADTRS**: Timepoint Responses
- **ADEF**: Derived Efficacy Parameters
- **ADTTE**: Time-to-Event Data
- Each dataset builds on the results of the previous one.

    4. **Analysis and Occurrences Flags**:
- The article details the establishment of analysis and occurrence flags in ADTRS.
- These flags assist in selecting the needed timepoint evaluations using different response criteria.

5. **Flexibility of Criteria**:
- The methodologies can be adapted to any tumor-specific evaluation criteria, not limited to RECIST criteria.

By adhering to these guidelines and leveraging the described techniques, researchers can ensure the accurate and efficient derivation and storage of subject-level efficacy parameters, facilitating robust analysis and transparent reporting in oncology clinical trials.

The SDTM TR and TU domains are used as the source data for tumor assessments. Each new lesion is recorded with two separate entries: one for the initial appearance and another for the unequivocal assessment. All assessments are based on independent imaging reviews according to RECIST 1.1 guidelines. Optional variables such as EVAL, EVALID, ACPTFL, and CRIT can be employed for other assessments, including those conducted by investigators, and to apply different criteria.

By utilizing these SDTM domains and optional variables, tumor assessments can be captured and analyzed comprehensively and accurately.

USUBJID (Unique Subject Identifier)	ATPT (Analysis Timepoint)	TRLNKID (Link ID)	PARAM (Parameter)	ADT (Analysis Date)	AVAL (Analysis Value)	AVALC (Analysis Value (C))	EVAL (Evaluator)	EVALID (Evaluator Specified)	ACPTFL (Accepted Record Flag)	CRIT (Criterion)
1111	SCREENING	TNL1	Longest Diameter (mm)	2017-01-01	20		INDEP.	READER1	Y	RECIST1.1
1111	SCREENING	TL1	Short Axis Diameter (mm)	2017-01-02	15		INDEP.	READER1	Y	RECIST1.1
1111	SCREENING	NT1	Tumor State - Non-Target Lesion	2017-01-01		Present	INDEP.	READER1	Y	RECIST1.1
1111	WEEK 6	TNL1	Longest Diameter (mm)	2017-02-15	18		INDEP.	READER1	Y	RECIST1.1
1111	WEEK 6	TL1	Short Axis Diameter (mm)	2017-02-15	13		INDEP.	READER1	Y	RECIST1.1
1111	WEEK 6	NT1	Tumor State - Non-Target Lesion	2017-02-16		Present	INDEP.	READER1	Y	RECIST1.1
1111	WEEK 6	NEW1	Tumor State - New Lesion - Initial Appearance	2017-02-16		Yes	INDEP.	READER1	Y	RECIST1.1
1111	WEEK 12	TNL1	Longest Diameter (mm)	2017-04-01	0		INDEP.	READER1	Y	RECIST1.1
1111	WEEK 12	TL1	Short Axis Diameter (mm)	2017-04-01	17		INDEP.	READER1	Y	RECIST1.1
1111	WEEK 12	NT1	Tumor State - Non-Target Lesion	2017-03-31		Absent	INDEP.	READER1	Y	RECIST1.1
1111	WEEK 12	NEW1	Tumor State - New Lesion - Unequivocal Assessment	2017-03-31		Present	INDEP.	READER1	Y	RECIST1.1
1111	SCREENING	TNL1	Longest Diameter (mm)	2017-01-01	21		INDEP.	READER2		RECIST1.1
1111	SCREENING	TL1	Short Axis Diameter (mm)	2017-01-02	16		INDEP.	READER2		RECIST1.1
1111	SCREENING	NT1	Tumor State - Non-Target Lesion	2017-01-01		Present	INDEP.	READER2		RECIST1.1
1111	WEEK 6	TNL1	Longest Diameter (mm)	2017-02-15	20		INDEP.	READER2		RECIST1.1
1111	WEEK 6	TL1	Short Axis Diameter (mm)	2017-02-15	15		INDEP.	READER2		RECIST1.1
1111	WEEK 6	NT1	Tumor State - Non-Target Lesion	2017-02-16		Present	INDEP.	READER2		RECIST1.1
1111	WEEK 12	TNL1	Longest Diameter (mm)	2017-04-01	0		INDEP.	READER2		RECIST1.1
1111	WEEK 12	TL1	Short Axis Diameter (mm)	2017-04-01	10		INDEP.	READER2		RECIST1.1
1111	WEEK 12	NT1	Tumor State - Non-Target Lesion	2017-03-31		Absent	INDEP.	READER2		RECIST1.1

ADTR DATASET

According to the protocol, the subject should be evaluated once every six weeks. However, the subject missed more than one assessment between the Week 6 and Week 24 evaluations. As a result, the timepoint evaluation from Week 24 (2017-09-20) cannot be marked with Analysis Flag 01, and the '1st Occurrence of Response' Flag (ANL51FL) cannot be assigned to this timepoint, even if the Timepoint Overall Response is 'PR'.

For sensitivity analysis, flags ANL02FL and ANL52FL are used to include timepoint evaluations that occurred after more than one missed adequate assessment. Thus, the Timepoint Overall Response of 'PR' on 2017-09-20 is marked with ANL52FL. Additionally, variables such as ACPTFL and CRIT from the ADTR example can be added to ADTRS for different tumor assessments and criteria. Since qualifiers (like information about Evaluator) are not allowed in the BDS structure, this information is incorporated into the parameters.

USUBJID (Unique Subject Identifier)	ATPT (Analysis Timepoint)	PARAM (Parameter)	ADT (Analysis Date)	AVAL (Analysis Value)	AVALC (Analysis Value (C))	PCHG (Percent Change from Baseline)	ANL01FL (Analysis Flag 01)	ANL51FL (1st Occur of Response Flag)	ANL02FL (Analysis Flag 02)	ANL52FL (1st Occur of Response – Sensitivity Flag)
2222	SCREENING	Timepoint Sum of all Target Lesion Diameters (mm) by Investigator	2017-04-01	50			Y		Y	
2222	WEEK 6	Timepoint Sum of all Target Lesion Diameters (mm) by Investigator	2017-05-15	40		-20.0	Y		Y	
2222	WEEK 6	Timepoint Target Lesions Response by Investigator	2017-05-15		SD		Y		Y	
2222	WEEK 6	Timepoint Non-Target Lesions Response by Investigator	2017-05-15		Non-CR / Non-PD		Y		Y	
2222	WEEK 6	Initial Appearance of New Lesions by Investigator	2017-05-15		No		Y		Y	
2222	WEEK 6	Timepoint Overall Response	2017-05-15		SD		Y		Y	
2222	WEEK 24	Timepoint Sum of all Target Lesion Diameters (mm) by Investigator	2017-09-20	30		-40.0			Y	
2222	WEEK 24	Timepoint Target Lesions Response by Investigator	2017-09-20		PR				Y	
2222	WEEK 24	Timepoint Non-Target Lesions Response by Investigator	2017-09-20		Non-CR / Non-PD				Y	
2222	WEEK 24	Initial Appearance of New Lesions by Investigator	2017-09-20		No				Y	
2222	WEEK 24	Timepoint Overall Response by Investigator	2017-09-20		PR				Y	Y

ADTRS DATASET

Following the previous example of ADTRS where two analysis flags were used, the EFORFL and EFDCFL flags are generated for each parameter of BOR. The variables EVAL and CRIT can be added to ADEF to account for different tumor assessments and criteria. However, acceptance flags (ACPTFL) are not needed in ADEF as only the accepted independent imaging review records are used. Since qualifiers like information about the Evaluator are not allowed in the BDS structure, this information is now incorporated into the parameters.

USUBJID (Unique Subject Identifier)	PARAM (Parameter)	AVAL (Analysis Value)	AVALC (Analysis Value (C))	BORDESC (Best Overall Response Description)	EFORFL (Objective Response Flag)	EFDCFL (Disease Control Flag)
2222	Best Overall Response by Investigator		SD	Observed SD		Y
2222	Best Overall Response – Sensitivity Analysis by Investigator		PR	Observed PR	Y	Y
2222	Percent Change in Sum of Target Lesion Diameters from Baseline to Post-baseline Nadir by Investigator	-20.0				
2222	Percent Change in Sum of Target Lesion Diameters from Baseline to Post-baseline Nadir - Sensitivity Analysis by Investigator	-40.0				

ADEF DATASET

USUBJID (Unique Subject Identifier)	PARAM (Parameter)	AVAL (Analysis Value)	CNSR (Censor)	STARTDT (Time to Event Origin Date for Subject)	ADT (Analysis Date)	EVNTDESC (Event or Censoring Description)	CNSDTDSC (Censor Date Description)	EFDUSDFL (Durable SD Flag)	EFCBFL (Clinical Benefit Flag)
2222	Overall Survival (months)	18.23	1	2017-04-04	2018-10-10	No Death at Time of Data Cut-off	Last Known Alive Date		
2222	Progression Free Survival (months) by Investigator	1.38	1	2017-04-04	2017-05-15	More than one missing adequate assessment'	Date of the Last Adequate Overall Tumor Assessment by SAP		
2222	Progression Free Survival – Sensitivity Analysis (months) by Investigator	5.59	1	2017-04-04	2017-09-20	No Death or PD at Time of Data Cut-off	Date of the Last Adequate Overall Tumor Assessment by requirements of Sensitivity Analysis		Y
2222	Duration of Response – Sensitivity Analysis (months) by Investigator	0.03	1	2017-09-20	2017-09-20	No Death or PD at Time of Data Cut-off	Date of the Last Adequate Overall Tumor Assessment by requirements of Sensitivity Analysis		

ADTTE DATASET

CHAPTER IV

Endpoints in oncology clinical trials

Endpoints in Cancer Clinical Trials

When we study new treatments for cancer, we measure their success using different endpoints. Here are the main ones:

1. **Overall Survival (OS):**

This is the time from the start of the trial until the patient dies, no matter the cause. For example, if a patient joins the trial and lives for five years before passing away, their OS is five years.

2. **Progression-Free Survival (PFS):**

This measures the time from the start of the trial until the cancer gets worse or the patient dies. If a patient's cancer worsens after three years but they die after four years, we consider the three-year mark for PFS.

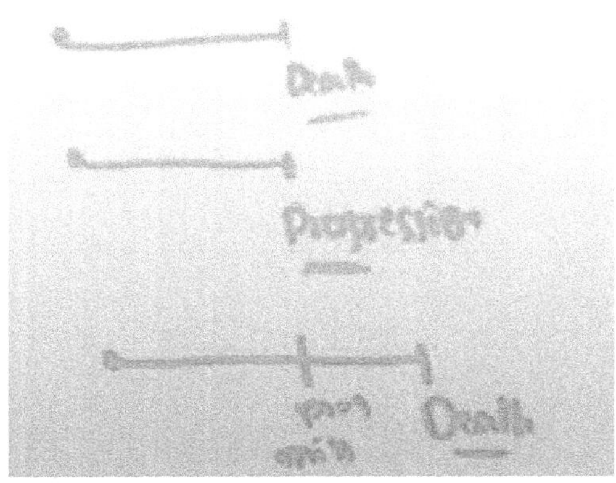

PFS

3. **Time to Progression (TTP):**

This is the time from the start of the trial until the cancer gets worse. If the cancer hasn't worsened but the patient dies, we don't count the death for TTP.

4. **Disease-Free Survival (DFS):**

This is the time from when the cancer is completely gone to when it comes back or a new cancer appears. For example, if a patient's cancer is gone and then returns after two years, their DFS is two years.

5. **Objective Response Rate:**

This measures how many patients have a significant shrinkage of their cancer. It includes:
- **Complete Response (CR):** Cancer completely disappears.
- **Partial Response (PR):** Cancer shrinks but doesn't disappear.
- **Progressive Disease (PD):** Cancer gets worse.
- **Stable Disease (SD):** Cancer doesn't get better or worse.

6. #### Best Overall Response (BOR)

The **best response** recorded from the **start of treatment until disease progression or recurrence**, assessed by the investigator using RECIST 1.1 criteria.

Response categories include
Complete Response (CR),
Partial Response (PR),
Stable Disease (SD),

Not Evaluable (NE),
and Progressive Disease (PD).

BOR requires confirmation of CR and PR responses at least 4 weeks after initial scans, and SD must be observed for at least 5 weeks from the start of treatment.

7.#### Duration of Response (DOR)

The length of time from the **first confirmed objective response (CR or PR)** to the first documentation of **disease progression or death** from any cause.

For patients without progression or death, DOR is censored at the last tumor assessment date.

If there is no tumor assessment after the last response date, DOR is censored at the date of response plus one day.

Differences Between PFS and TTP:

- **PFS (Progression-Free Survival):** Time from the start of the trial to either cancer **progression or death**. Both events are considered.

- **TTP (Time to Progression):** Time from the start of the trial to only cancer progression. **Death is not considered** unless it happens after progression.

For instance, if a patient joins a trial and their cancer gets worse after two years, their TTP is two years. If they die after three years without cancer progression, their TTP is still counted as two years. However, for PFS, if they die after three years without progression, the PFS would be three years.

CHAPTER V

What are the most recent oncology projects titles you've worked on?

Project-01: Study Title

- **Title**:
An Open-label Phase 1b Study of ORIC-101 in Combination with Anticancer Therapy in Patients with **Advanced or Metastatic Solid Tumors**

- **Question**: What are Advanced or Metastatic Solid Tumors?
Explanation:
- **Advanced Solid Tumors**: Cancers that have grown extensively and may not be confined to their site of origin.
- **Metastatic Solid Tumors**: Cancers that have spread from their original site to other parts of the body.

Project-02: Study Title

- **Title**:
Phase 1 Trial of Intralesional Immunotherapy with IFx-Hu2.0 Vaccine in Patients with **Advanced Merkel Cell Carcinoma or Cutaneous Squamous Cell Carcinoma**
- **Explanation**:
- **Advanced Merkel Cell Carcinoma**: A rare, aggressive skin cancer that has progressed significantly and may have spread to other parts of the body.
- **Cutaneous Squamous Cell Carcinoma**: A common form of skin cancer that originates in the squamous cells of the skin and can become advanced, potentially spreading to other areas.

Project-03: Study Title

- **Title**:
A Phase-2 Open-Label Multi-Centre Study of Single Agent Enzastaurin in Patients with *Relapsed Cutaneous T-cell Lymphoma*
- **Explanation**:
- **Relapsed Cutaneous T-cell Lymphoma**: A type of cancer that affects the T-cells of the skin and has returned after a period of remission.

Project-04: Study Title

- **Title**:
A Phase 2 Randomized Study of Relatlimab plus Nivolumab in Combination with Chemotherapy vs. Nivolumab in Combination with Chemotherapy as First Line Treatment for Participants with *Stage IV or Recurrent Non-small Cell Lung Cancer (NSCLC)*
- **Explanation**:
- **Stage IV Non-small Cell Lung Cancer (NSCLC)**: The most advanced stage of lung cancer where the disease has spread to other parts of the body.
- **Recurrent Non-small Cell Lung Cancer (NSCLC)**: Lung cancer that has returned after treatment.

Project-05: Study Title

Phase I Dose Escalation Study of the Safety, Tolerability, Pharmacokinetics, and Pharmacodynamic Properties of Oral AT-406 in Combination with Daunorubicin and Cytarabine in Patients with Poor-risk, Acute Myelogenous Leukemia (AML)

CHAPTER VI

What are the most recent oncology projects Objetives you've worked on?

Project-01: Study Title

Title: An Open-label Phase 1b Study of ORIC-101 in Combination with Anticancer Therapy in Patients with Advanced or Metastatic Solid Tumors

Primary Objective

- **Objective**: To identify the **dose of ORIC-101 that is safe**, tolerable, and provides target therapeutic exposure in combination with anticancer therapy.

Secondary Objectives

- **Objective 1**: To characterize the pharmacokinetic (PK) profile of ORIC-101, its metabolites, and the combination agent(s) when used with anticancer therapy.
- **Objective 2**: To characterize the multi-cycle safety profile of ORIC-101 in combination with anticancer therapy.
- **Objective 3**: To evaluate the antitumor activity of ORIC-101 in combination with anticancer therapy.

Exploratory Objectives

- **Objective 1**: To evaluate the level of glucocorticoid receptor (GR) expression in archival tumor tissue from patients with solid tumors.
- **Objective 2**: To evaluate pharmacodynamic (PD) biomarkers associated with ORIC-101 in combination with anticancer therapy.
- **Objective 3**: To evaluate potential predictive biomarkers of ORIC-101 efficacy in combination with anticancer therapy.

Project-02: Study Title

Title: Phase 1 Trial of Intralesional Immunotherapy with IFx-Hu2.0 Vaccine in Patients with Advanced Merkel Cell Carcinoma or Cutaneous Squamous Cell Carcinoma

Primary Objective

- **Objective**: To assess the **safety** of vaccinating with intralesional IFx-Hu2.0 therapy in patients with Merkel cell carcinoma (MCC) or cutaneous squamous cell carcinoma (cSCC).

Secondary Objectives

- **Objective 1**: To assess the feasibility of administering IFx-Hu2.0.
- **Objective 2**: To evaluate the preliminary efficacy of IFx-Hu2.0.

Exploratory Objective

- **Objective**: To evaluate the immune response through biomarkers.

Project-03: Study Title

Title: A Phase-2 Open-Label Multi-Centre Study of Single Agent Enzastaurin in Patients with Relapsed Cutaneous T-cell Lymphoma

Primary Objective

- **Objective**: To determine the **overall objective tumor response rate** of Enzastaurin in patients with relapsed cutaneous T-cell lymphoma (CTCL).
- **Focus**: Assess the response of tumors specifically in patients with relapsed mycosis fungoides or cutaneous T-cell lymphoma to the treatment with Enzastaurin.
- **Measurement**: The response rate will be determined by evaluating the reduction in tumor size or stabilization of tumor growth using standardized criteria such as RECIST.
- **Response Rate**: Reported as the percentage of patients who achieve a complete response (CR) or partial response (PR) out of the total number of patients evaluated.

- **Example**: If a treatment regimen achieves a response rate of 40%, it means that 40% of patients experienced either a complete or partial response to the treatment.

Secondary Objectives
- **Objective 1**: To assess the length and intensity of exposure to the study medication.
- **Objective 2**: To monitor and record adverse events.
- **Objective 3**: To conduct physical examinations.
- **Objective 4**: To measure vital signs.
- **Objective 5**: To perform laboratory tests.
- **Objective 6**: To conduct electrocardiograms (ECGs).
- **Objective 7**: To assess patients using the Eastern Cooperative Oncology Group (ECOG) performance status.

Explanation
- **Mycosis Fungoides**: A type of cutaneous T-cell lymphoma (CTCL).
- **mSWAT (Modified Severity Weighted Assessment Tool)**: A scoring system used to evaluate the severity and extent of skin involvement in patients with mycosis fungoides. It is a modified version of the Severity Weighted Assessment Tool (SWAT), specifically designed for mycosis fungoides.

Project-04: Study Title

Title: A Phase 3 Study to Evaluate the Efficacy and Safety of BMS-986213 Compared to Nivolumab Monotherapy in Patients with Previously Untreated, Unresectable, or Metastatic Melanoma

Primary Objective
- **Objective**: To assess the progression-free survival (PFS) of BMS-986213 compared to nivolumab monotherapy.

Study Details
1. **Participants**: Individuals diagnosed with previously untreated, unresectable, or metastatic melanoma.
2. **Evaluation Method**: Progression-free survival will be evaluated through a Blinded Independent Central Review (BICR) following RECIST v1.1 guidelines.
3. **Definition of PFS**: The duration between randomization and the earliest documented progression of the disease or death from any cause, whichever occurs first.

Secondary Objective
- **Objective**: To compare the overall survival (OS) of BMS-986213 to nivolumab monotherapy in participants with previously untreated, unresectable, or metastatic melanoma.

Safety Objective
- **Objective**: To assess the overall safety and tolerability of BMS-986213 and nivolumab monotherapy.
- **Measures**: Incidence of adverse events (AEs), serious adverse events (SAEs), adverse events leading to discontinuation of treatment, death, and laboratory abnormalities.

Project-05: Study Title

Primary Objective:

Safety and Tolerability: Assess the safety and tolerability of oral AT-406.

Maximum Tolerated Dose (MTD): Determine the maximum tolerated dose of oral AT-406 when administered in combination with daunorubicin and cytarabine in patients with Acute Myeloid Leukemia (AML).

Secondary Objectives:

Pharmacokinetic Profile: Determine the pharmacokinetic profile of AT-406, daunorubicin, and cytarabine to investigate potential drug-drug interactions.

Pharmacodynamic Profile: Determine the pharmacodynamic profile of oral AT-406.

Response Rate: Determine the response rate, including:

Complete Response (CR)

Complete Response Incomplete (CRi)

Partial Response (PR)

Relapse-Free Survival (RFS): Estimate the relapse-free survival.

Overall Survival (OS): Estimate the overall survival.
Cytogenetic Response Rate: Estimate the cytogenetic response rate.
<u>Exploratory Objectives:</u>
Biomarkers: Determine the biomarkers associated with response in AML.

CHAPTER VII

What are the most recent oncology projects end–points you've worked on?

Project-01:
    Title: An Open-label Phase 1b Study of ORIC-101 in Combination with Anticancer Therapy in Patients with Advanced or Metastatic Solid Tumors
    ### Efficacy Analyses
    #### Overview
Three key *efficacy endpoints* and corresponding statistical methods are detailed for analyzing study results.
    #### Tumor Scan Dates
- When tumor scan dates span multiple study days for a scheduled visit:
- Latest imaging date used for response or stable disease (SD).
- Earliest imaging date used for progression-free survival (PFS).
    #### Best Overall Response (BOR)
- **Definition**: BOR is derived from the overall tumor visit responses as assessed by the investigator based on RECIST 1.1 criteria.
- Best response recorded from the start of treatment until disease progression/recurrence.
- Response categories: Complete Response (CR), Partial Response (PR), Stable Disease (SD), Not Evaluable (NE), and Progressive Disease (PD).
- If CR or PR is not confirmed and SD is less than 4 weeks, BOR will be NE.
- **Confirmation Requirements**:
- CR and PR responses must be confirmed at least 4 weeks after initial scans.
- SD must be observed at least 5 weeks from the date of the first study treatment.
- **Study-Specific BOR Criteria **:
- CR at first time point and CR at subsequent time point = BOR: CR.
- CR at first time point and PR, SD, or PD at subsequent time point = BOR depends on whether the minimum duration for SD was met.
- PR at first time point and CR at subsequent time point = BOR: PR.
- PR at first time point and PR, SD, or PD at subsequent time point = BOR depends on SD duration.
- NE at first and subsequent time points = BOR: NE.
- If initial CR is later found to be PR, BOR should be revised to PR.
- **SD Duration**:
- Minimum of 5 weeks to qualify as BOR.
    #### Duration of Response (DOR)
- **Calculation**: Measured in months for confirmed responders (CR or PR).
- DOR is from the date of the first **objective response** to the **first documentation** of disease progression or death.
- For patients without progression or death, DOR is censored at the last tumor assessment date.
- If no tumor assessment after the last response date, DOR is censored at the response date + 1 day.
    #### Progression-Free Survival (PFS)
- **Calculation**: Time in months from the first dose of study therapy to disease progression or death.
- **Censoring**:
- Alive without progression or death at the time of analysis: censored at the most recent progression-free observation date.
- New cancer therapy before progression: censored at the last disease assessment before the new therapy.

- Without progression or death: censored at the last evaluable disease assessment.
- No disease assessment: censored at the date of the first study treatment.
- PD or death after multiple missed/invalid assessments: censored at the last valid tumor assessment before the missed/invalid assessment.
- **Summary**: PFS summarized using 25th percentile, median, 75th percentile, 95% confidence intervals, and Kaplan-Meier graphical methods.

Overall Survival (OS)
- **Calculation**: Time in months from the first dose of study therapy to death or the date of last follow-up.
- **Censoring**:
- Patients not dead: censored at the last known alive date.
- Withdrawn or lost to follow-up: censored at the date of last contact or last data point collected.
- **Summary**: OS summarized using 25th percentile, median, 75th percentile, 95% confidence intervals, and Kaplan-Meier graphical methods.
- **Additional Data**: Number and percentage of patients who died, were lost to follow-up, or survived will be summarized.

Project-02: Study Title

Title: Phase 1 Trial of Intralesional Immunotherapy with IFx-Hu2.0 Vaccine in Patients with Advanced Merkel Cell Carcinoma or Cutaneous Squamous Cell Carcinoma

Study Endpoints

Primary Endpoint
- **Safety**: Defined as the absence of **dose-limiting toxicities (DLTs)**.
- **Criteria**: Absence of any grade 3-5 treatment-related adverse events (AEs) per Common Terminology Criteria for Adverse Events (CTCAE) v5.0.
- **Time Frame**: From the first injection (Day 1) to final follow-up (Day 28, 35, or 42, depending on dosing schedule) ± 7 days.

Secondary Endpoints
- **Feasibility**: Defined as study completion by ≥80% of patients (i.e., 16 out of 20) in the per-protocol analysis.
- **Preliminary Treatment Response**: Measured by the Overall Response Rate (ORR).

Exploratory Endpoint
- **Tumor-Specific Immune Response**: Measured by laboratory tests of correlative studies.

Project-03: Study Title

Title: A Phase-2 Open-Label Multi-Centre Study of Single Agent Enzastaurin in Patients with Relapsed Cutaneous T-cell Lymphoma

Primary Endpoint

ORR:

Objective1:

To determine the **Overall Objective Tumor Response Rate** of ENZASTAURIN in patients with Relapsed Cutaneous T-cell Lymphoma.

Explanation: This endpoint aims to assess the response of tumors specifically in patients with relapsed micosis fungoides or cutaneous T-cell lymphoma to treatment with ENZASTAURIN.

The response rate will be determined by evaluating the reduction in tumor size or stabilization of tumor growth using standardized criteria such as RECIST.

Additionally, the **modified Severity Weighted Assessment Tool (mSWAT) scoring system** will be utilized to assess the severity and extent of skin involvement in patients with micosis fungoides.

This tool provides a comprehensive evaluation of skin lesions and their characteristics, including the number of patches, plaques, or tumors.

Objective2:

To evaluate the **Sezary cell count** and its correlation with treatment response, disease progression, and therapeutic decisions in patients with Sezary Syndrome.

Explanation: This endpoint involves utilizing **both lymphocytometry and flow cytometry** to provide quantitative data on the percentage of Sezary cells in the blood, which is an essential parameter for the diagnosis and monitoring of Sezary syndrome. Monitoring changes in the Sezary cell count over time will enable the assessment of treatment response and disease progression. Additionally, it will help guide therapeutic decisions by providing insights into the effectiveness of treatment regimens and the need for adjustments or alternative approaches.

- **Objective3:

To assess the **response rate as the percentage** of patients achieving a complete response (CR) or partial response (PR) out of the total number of patients evaluated.

- **Explanation**: This endpoint involves calculating the response rate by determining the proportion of patients who achieve a complete response (CR) or partial response (PR) to the treatment regimen out of the total number of patients evaluated. A complete response indicates the disappearance of all target lesions, while a partial response signifies at least a 30% decrease in the sum of the longest diameter of target lesions. This assessment provides valuable information on the efficacy of the treatment in inducing tumor regression or stabilization in the patient population under investigation.

The response rate (RR) can be calculated using the following formula:

$$RR = \left(\frac{\text{Number of patients achieving CR} + \text{Number of patients achieving PR}}{\text{Total number of patients evaluated}} \right) \times 100$$

Where:

- Number of patients achieving CR: The count of patients who achieve a complete response.

- Number of patients achieving PR: The count of patients who achieve a partial response.

- Total number of patients evaluated: The total number of patients assessed for treatment response.

Project-04

Endpoints for Study

"A Phase 3 Study to Evaluate the Efficacy and Safety of BMS-986213 Compared to Nivolumab Monotherapy in Patients with Previously Untreated, Unresectable, or Metastatic Melanoma"

Primary Endpoint

- **Progression-Free Survival (PFS) Assessment**:
- **Objective**: To evaluate the PFS of BMS-986213 compared to nivolumab monotherapy.
- **Method**: PFS will be assessed through a Blinded Independent Central Review (BICR) following RECIST v1.1 guidelines.
- **Definition**: Duration between randomization and the earliest documented progression of the disease or death from any cause, whichever occurs first.

Secondary Endpoint

- **Overall Survival (OS) Comparison**:
- **Objective**: To compare the OS of BMS-986213 to nivolumab monotherapy in participants with previously

untreated, unresectable, or metastatic melanoma.

Safety Endpoint

- **Overall Safety and Tolerability Assessment**:
- **Objective**: To assess the overall safety and tolerability of BMS-986213 and nivolumab monotherapy.
- **Measures**: Evaluation of the incidence of adverse events (AEs), serious adverse events (SAEs), adverse events leading to treatment discontinuation, death, and laboratory abnormalities.

CHAPTER VIII

What are the most recent oncology projects Study design you've worked on?

Project-01

Trial Design and Study Procedures:

- **Study Type:** Open-label, uncontrolled, multi-center, dose-finding study.
- **Patient Population:** Patients with advanced solid tumors.
- **Treatment Plan:**
- Patients will be treated with ORIC-101 initially in combination with nab-paclitaxel until disease progression, unacceptable toxicity, or meeting other stopping criteria.
- Additional dose-finding cohorts with various other agents may be evaluated through protocol amendments.
- **Dose and Schedule Selection:** The recommended phase 2 dose (RP2D) and schedule will be chosen from safe and well-tolerated doses and schedules, considering preliminary PK and/or PD data.
    Treatments and Assignment:
    - **Investigational Product:** ORIC-101 administered in combination with nab-paclitaxel.
- **Administration Schedule:** Evaluation of intermittent and continuous administration of ORIC-101 once daily in 28-day cycles using a traditional 3 + 3 design.
    ORIC-101 Dosing and Administration:
    - **Administration Schedule:** Intermittent (5 days on, 2 days off) followed by continuous administration.
- **Starting Dose Level:** 80 mg intermittent (Dose Level 1A).
- **Administration:** ORIC-101 dispensed on Day 1 of each cycle and administered once per day for 5 or 7 days.
    Nab-paclitaxel Dosing and Administration:
    - **Initial Dose:** 100 mg/m2 weekly for 3 weeks every 28 days.
- **Adjusted Dose:** 75 mg/m2 on Days 1, 8, and 15 in combination with 80 mg ORIC-101.
    Dose Finding and Stopping Rules:
    - **Design:** Traditional 3 + 3 design.
- **Safety Review:** SRC reviews safety data after 3 or 6 evaluable patients complete the first cycle.
- **Determination of MTD and RP2D:** Based on safety data review by investigators, medical monitor, and sponsor.
    Definition of DLT:
    - **Criteria:** Events listed in SAP occurring within 28 days after the first dose and considered possibly related to study treatment.
    Sample Size Determination:
    - **Approximate Sample Size:** 30-42 enrolled, evaluable patients.
- **Objective:** Determine **safe and tolerable dose** and initial estimates of therapy's antitumor activity rather than statistical power calculations.

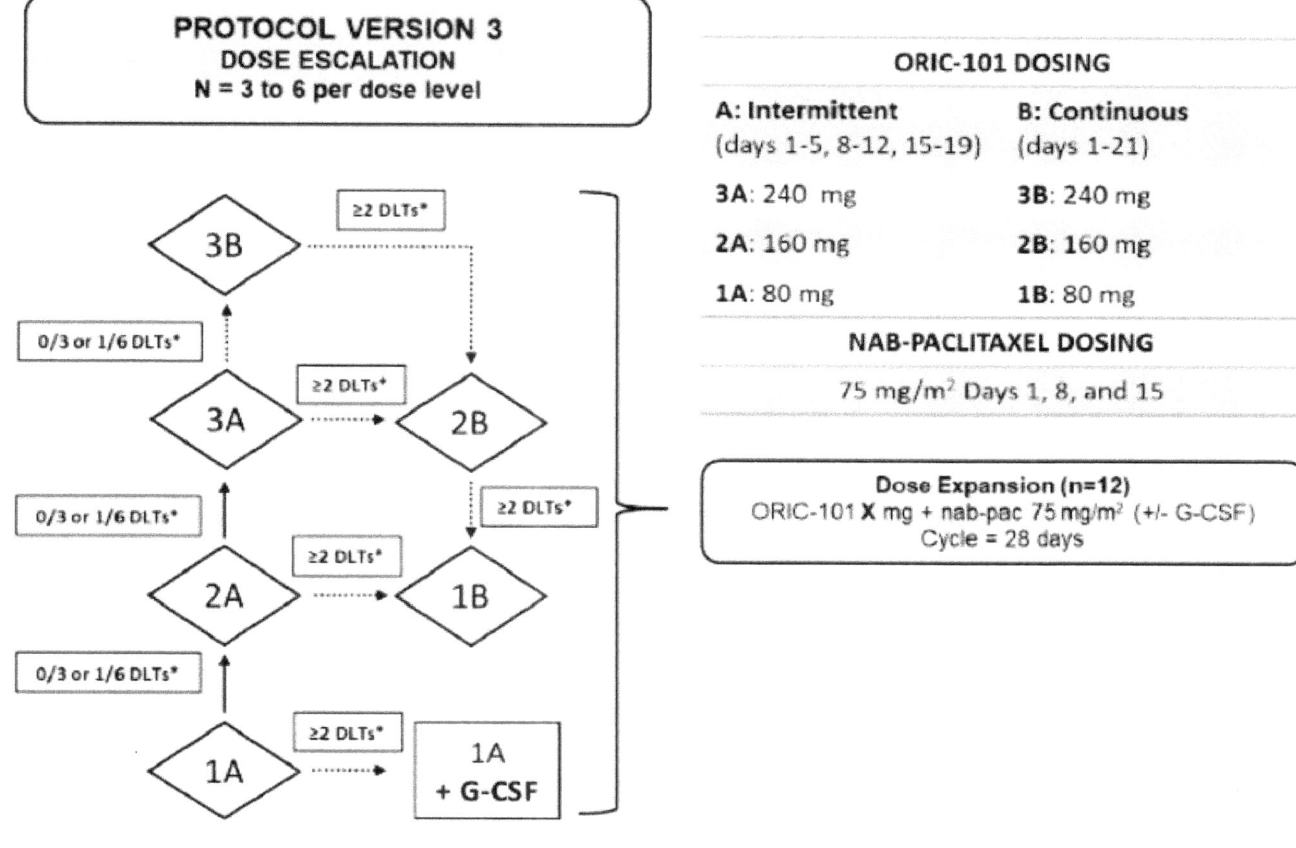

Project-02

Design:

- **Patient Eligibility:** Approximately twenty adult patients (≥18 years of age) with histologically confirmed Merkel cell carcinoma (MCC) or cutaneous squamous cell carcinoma (cSCC) with accessible lesions.
- **Enrollment:** A total of 20 patients across both indications will be enrolled.
- **Treatment:** Patients will receive IFx-Hu2.0 as a monotherapy at up to three time points.
- **Dosing:** Depending on the number of accessible lesions, a patient could receive up to three doses across three lesions (one dose per lesion).
- **Maximum Lesions:** The maximum number of lesions injected at any time point under this protocol is three lesions.
- **Study Objective:** Primarily a safety study designed to evaluate IFx-Hu2.0 monotherapy.
- **Purpose:** Provide foundational evidence for supporting further investigation of IFx-Hu2.0 + anti-PD-1 combination therapy for patients with advanced MCC or cSCC.

Project-03

Simon's Two-Stage Design:

- **Purpose:** A study design used in early-phase clinical trials, especially in oncology, to evaluate the efficacy of a new treatment.
- **Objective:** Determine if a treatment exhibits sufficient promise to justify further investigation in larger trials.
- **Stage 1:**
- **Number of Subjects:** Initially enroll 25 subjects.

- **Criteria:** Evaluate responses after a specified duration (e.g., at least 4 weeks or 28 days).
- **Response Threshold:** If a predefined number of responses (e.g., 7 confirmed responses) are observed at Stage 1, proceed to Stage 2.
- **Stage 2:**
- **Additional Subjects:** Enroll an additional 55 subjects to reach a total of 80.
- **Confirmation:** Confirm the initial observations and assess further responses.
- **Outcome:** Based on the cumulative responses observed across both stages, determine whether the treatment demonstrates efficacy warranting further investigation or not.

Project-04

Study Design Schematic:
   - **Phase 2:**
- **Number of Participants:** N = 400
- **Treatment Assignment:** Randomized 1:1
- **Treatment Regimens:**
- BMS-986213b IV Q4W (Fixed-dose combination relatlimab/nivolumab)
- Nivolumab IV Q4W (Nivolumab monotherapy)
- **Patient Criteria:**
- Previously untreated for unresectable or metastatic melanoma
- Tissue available for biomarker analyses
- **Stratification Factors:**
- OPD-L1 status
- LAG-3 status
- BRAF status
- AJCC M stage
- **Safety Lead-in Evaluation:** Conducted on the first (up to) 18 participants.
- **Interim Analysis Decision Point:**
- Conducted to assess trial progress and potential modifications.
- **Phase 3:**
- **Number of Participants:** N = 700d
- Consisting of the 400 subjects from Phase 2 and an additional 300 from the Phase 3 part of the trial.
- **Treatment Regimens:** Similar to Phase 2.
- **Dosing Information:**
- BMS-986213b (Relatlimab/nivolumab) dosing:
- For adults: relatlimab 160 mg/nivolumab 480 mg.
- Adolescents 24 kg and < 40 kg: Dosing based on weight.
- Nivolumab monotherapy dosing:
- For adults: 480 mg.
- Adolescents ≥40 kg and < 40 kg: Dosing based on weight.

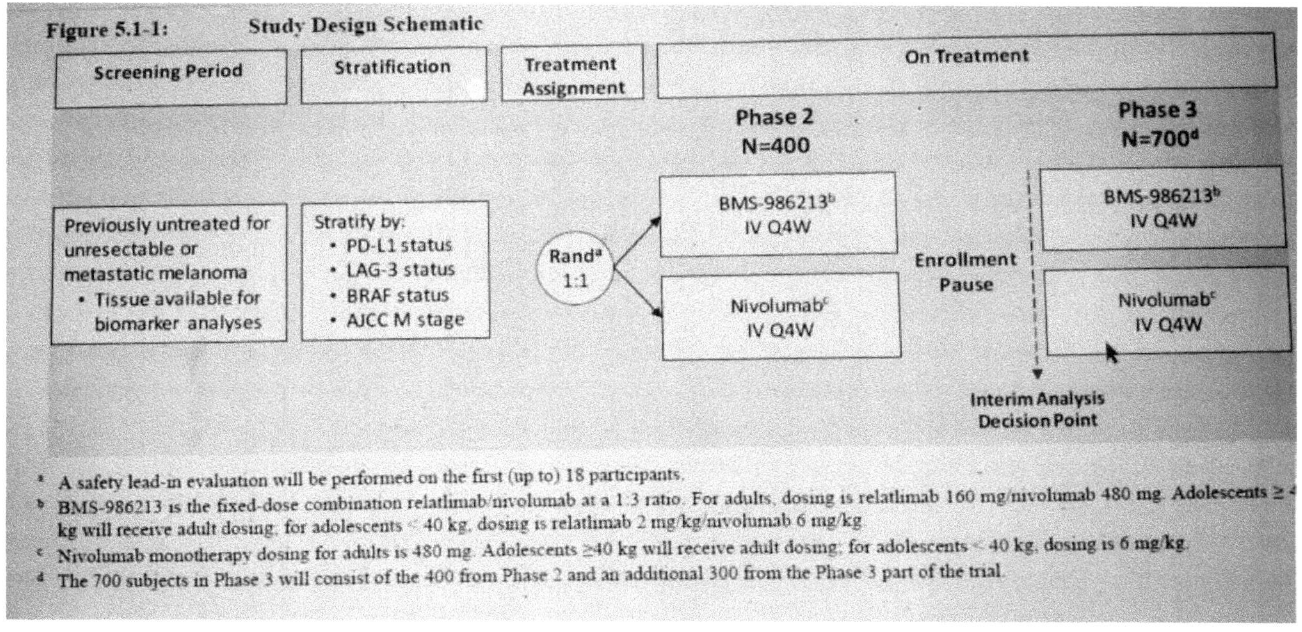

Project-05

1. **Study Design**:
- Open-label, phase 1 trial
- Conducted at multiple centers

2. **Objective**:
- Determine the maximum tolerated dose (MTD) of oral AT-406 in combination with daunorubicin and cytarabine
- Targeting patients with poor-risk AML

3. **Sites and Patient Enrollment**:
- Approximately 7 investigational sites in the United States
- Aimed to enroll a total of 60 patients

4. **Cohort Structure**:
- Patients grouped into sequential cohorts
- Each cohort comprised up to 12 patients, with evaluation of 6 patients
- Purpose: Determine the MTD of AT-406

5. **Dose Escalation and Administration**:
- Escalation during the induction cycle
- AT-406 not given in consolidation cycles
- Administration:
- AT-406 orally for 1-5 days (or 1-3 days)
- Daunorubicin intravenously at 90 mg/m2 for 1-3 days
- Cytarabine intravenously at 100 mg/m2 via continuous infusion for 1-7 days

6. **Management of Persistent AML**:
- Patients needing re-induction post-therapy withdrawal from the study

- Replaced if necessary to ensure sufficient observation for dose-limiting toxicity (DLT)
- Aim: Assess at least 3 patients at each dose level through DLT observation period.

CHAPTER IX

Parameters Derived in ADRS

Project-01

PARAM	Last Disease Assessment Censored at First PD by Investigator
PARAMCD	LSTAC
PARCAT1	Tumor Response
PARCAT2	Investigator
PARCAT3	Recist 1.1
AVAL	- Set to 1 if [ADRS.AVALC]='CR' - Set to 2 if [ADRS.AVALC]='PR' - Set to 3 if [ADRS.AVALC]='SD' - Set to 4 if [ADRS.AVALC]='NON-CR/NON-PD' - Set to 6 if [ADRS.AVALC]='PD' - Otherwise, set to null
AVALC	- Using the last observations from ADRS: - Where [ADRS.PARAMCD]='OVR' - And [ADRS.ANL01FL]='Y' - And [ADRS.ADT] is a valid date on or after the first treatment date [ADSL.TRTSDT] and up to and including the first observation indicating progression ([ADRS.AVALC]='PD') - And [ADRS.AVALC] is 'CR', 'PR', 'SD', 'NON-CR/NON-PD', 'PD' - Set to [ADRS.AVALC] if such an observation exists - Otherwise, set to null for all other subjects in ADSL **Example:** - If the last valid observation before progression is 'PR', then AVALC is set to 'PR'. - If there is no valid observation, AVALC is set to null.

ADT	- Using the last observations from ADRS: - Where [ADRS.PARAMCD]='OVR' - And [ADRS.ANL01FL]='Y' - And [ADRS.ADT] is a valid date on or after the first treatment date [ADSL.TRTSDT] for non-randomized studies or randomization date [ADSL.RANDDT] for randomized studies - And up to and including the first observation indicating progression ([ADRS.AVALC]='PD') - And [ADRS.AVALC] is 'CR', 'PR', 'SD', 'NON-CR/NON-PD', 'PD' - Set to [ADRS.ADT] if such an observation exists - Otherwise, set to null for all other subjects **Example:** - If the last valid observation date before progression is '2023-05-01', then ADT is set to '2023-05-01'. - If there is no valid observation date, ADT is set to null.
ANL01FL	- Set to 'Y'
SRCDOM	- Set to null
SRCVAR	- Set to null
SRCSEQ	- Set to null
Population	- All subjects

Parameter-02 Information

- **PARAM:** *Best Confirmed Overall Response by Investigator*
- **PARAMCD:** *BOR*
- **PARCAT1:** *Tumor Response*
- **PARCAT2:** *Investigator*
- **PARCAT3:** *Recist 1.1*
- **Population:** *All subjects*
- **ANL01FL:** *Set to 'Y'*
- **SRCDOM:** *Set to null*
- **SRCVAR:** *Set to null*
- **SRCSEQ:** *Set to null*

AVAL Calculation
Set `AVAL` to:
1. **1** if `ADRS.AVALC = 'CR'`
2. **2** if `ADRS.AVALC = 'PR'`
3. **3** if `ADRS.AVALC = 'SD'`
4. **4** if `ADRS.AVALC = 'NON-CR/NON-PD'`
5. **5** if `ADRS.AVALC = 'NE'`
6. **6** if `ADRS.AVALC = 'PD'`
7. **null** if none of the above conditions are met
AVALC Calculation
Using observations from ADRS, where:
- `ADRS.PARAMCD = 'OVR'`

- `ADRS.ANL01FL = 'Y'`
- `ADRS.ADT` is a valid date
- `ADRS.AVALC` is 'CR', 'PR', 'SD', 'NON-CR/NON-PD', 'PD', or 'NE'
  Set `ADRS.AVALC` to:
  *1. **CR***
- If `ADRS.AVALC = 'CR'` on each of two overall response assessments ≥ 4 weeks apart, with:
- No other overall response assessment in between, or
- The tumor overall response assessments between these two assessments can be CR (single or multiple assessments) and a maximum of 1 NE.

*2. **PR***
- If the subject had two overall response assessments ≥ 4 weeks apart, with the first being `ADRS.AVALC = 'PR'` and the other being `ADRS.AVALC = 'PR'` or 'CR', with:
- If the initial is PR: CR (single or multiple assessments) and a maximum of 1 NE.
- If the initial is PR and the confirmatory is PR: PR (single or multiple assessments) and a maximum of 1 NE.
- If the initial is PR and the confirmatory is CR: PR (single or multiple assessments) or CR (single or multiple assessments) but CR must not be followed by PR during the confirmation period, and a maximum of 1 NE.

*3. **SD***
- If there exists an observation where `ADRS.AVALC = 'CR'`, 'PR', or 'SD' and `ADRS.ADT` is at least 5 weeks after the first treatment date (`ADSL.TRTSDT`).

*4. **NON-CR/NON-PD***
- If there exists an observation where `ADRS.AVALC = 'NON-CR/NON-PD'` and `ADRS.ADT` is at least 5 weeks after the first treatment date (`ADSL.TRTSDT`).

*5. **PD***
- If there exists an observation where `ADRS.AVALC = 'PD'`.

*6. **NE***
- If there exists an observation where `ADRS.AVALC = 'NE'`, or if the subject has only `ADRS.AVALC = 'CR'`, 'PR', 'SD', or 'NON-CR/NON-PD' less than 5 weeks after the first treatment date (`ADSL.TRTSDT`).

*7. **Null***
- If none of the above conditions are met, including all other subjects in ADSL.

ADT Calculation
  Set `ADT` to:
- The first analysis date `[ADRS.ADT]` where the condition for `ADRS.AVALC = 'CR'`, 'PR', 'SD', 'NON-CR/NON-PD', 'PD', or 'NE' is fulfilled.
- Null if `ADRS.AVALC` is null.

Parameter-03 Information

- **PARAM:** *Confirmed Response by Investigator*
- **PARAMCD:** *CRSP*
- **PARCAT1:** *Tumor Response*
- **PARCAT2:** *Investigator*
- **PARCAT3:** *Recist 1.1*
- **Population:** *All subjects*
- **ANL01FL:** *Set to 'Y'*
- **SRCDOM:** *Set to null*
- **SRCVAR:** *Set to null*
- **SRCSEQ:** *Set to null*

AVAL Calculation

Set `AVAL` to:

1. **1** if `ADRS.AVALC = 'Y'`
2. **0** if `ADRS.AVALC = 'N'`

Examples:
- If `ADRS.AVALC = 'Y'`, then `AVAL` is set to 1.
- If `ADRS.AVALC = 'N'`, then `AVAL` is set to 0.

AVALC Calculation

Using observations from ADRS, where:

- `ADRS.PARAMCD = 'OVR'`
- `ADRS.ANL01FL = 'Y'`
- `ADRS.ADT` is a valid date
- `ADRS.AVALC` is 'CR', 'PR', 'SD', 'NON-CR/NON-PD', 'PD', or 'NE'
- On or after the first treatment date (`ADSL.TRTSDT`) and up to and including the first observation indicating progression (`ADRS.AVALC = 'PD'`)

Set `ADRS.AVALC` to:

1. **Y**
- If `ADRS.AVALC = 'CR'` on each of two overall response assessments ≥ 4 weeks apart, or
- If the subject had two overall response assessments ≥ 4 weeks apart, with the first being `ADRS.AVALC = 'PR'` and the other being `ADRS.AVALC = 'PR'` or 'CR', with:
- No other overall response assessment in between, or
- The tumor overall response assessments between these two assessments can be:
- If the initial is CR: CR (single or multiple assessments) and a maximum of 1 NE.
- If the initial is PR and the confirmatory is PR: PR (single or multiple assessments) and a maximum of 1 NE.
- If the initial is PR and the confirmatory is CR: PR (single or multiple assessments) and CR (single or multiple assessments) but CR must not be followed by PR during the confirmation period, and/or a maximum of 1 NE.
2. **N**
- Including all other subjects in ADSL

Examples:
- **Y**: If a subject has 'CR' assessments on January 1st and February 5th, with no other assessments in between, or only 'CR' and a maximum of 1 'NE' in between, `ADRS.AVALC` is set to 'Y'.
- **N**: If a subject does not meet the criteria for 'Y', `ADRS.AVALC` is set to 'N'.

ADT Calculation

Set `ADT` to:

- The first analysis date `[ADRS.ADT]` where the condition for `ADRS.AVALC = 'Y'` is fulfilled.
- Null if `ADRS.AVALC = 'N'`.

Examples:
- If `ADRS.AVALC` is 'Y' and the first valid `ADRS.ADT` is March 1st, then `ADT` is set to March 1st.
- If `ADRS.AVALC` is 'N', then `ADT` is set to null.

Parameter-04 Information

- ***PARAM:*** *Last Disease Assessment by Investigator*
- ***PARAMCD:*** *LSTA*
- ***PARCAT1:*** *Tumor Response*
- ***PARCAT2:*** *Investigator*
- ***PARCAT3:*** *Recist 1.1*
- ***Population:*** *All subjects*
- ***ANL01FL:*** *Set to 'Y'*
- ***SRCDOM:*** *Set to null*
- ***SRCVAR:*** *Set to null*
- ***SRCSEQ:*** *Set to null*

AVAL Calculation
Set `AVAL` to:
1. **1** if `ADRS.AVALC = 'CR'`
2. **2** if `ADRS.AVALC = 'PR'`
3. **3** if `ADRS.AVALC = 'SD'`
4. **4** if `ADRS.AVALC = 'NON-CR/NON-PD'`
5. **5** if `ADRS.AVALC = 'NE'`
6. **6** if `ADRS.AVALC = 'PD'`
7. **null** if none of the above conditions are met
    Examples:
- If `ADRS.AVALC = 'CR'`, then `AVAL` is set to 1.
- If `ADRS.AVALC = 'PR'`, then `AVAL` is set to 2.
- If `ADRS.AVALC = 'SD'`, then `AVAL` is set to 3.
- If `ADRS.AVALC = 'NON-CR/NON-PD'`, then `AVAL` is set to 4.
- If `ADRS.AVALC = 'NE'`, then `AVAL` is set to 5.
- If `ADRS.AVALC = 'PD'`, then `AVAL` is set to 6.
- If `ADRS.AVALC` does not meet any of the above conditions, then `AVAL` is set to null.

AVALC Calculation
Set `ADRS.AVALC` to:
- The last `ADRS.AVALC` on or after the first treatment date (`ADRS.ADT >= ADSL.TRTSDT`) where:
- `ADRS.PARAMCD = 'OVR'`
- `ADRS.AVALC` is 'CR', 'PR', 'SD', 'NON-CR/NON-PD', 'NE', or 'PD'
- `ADRS.ANL01FL = 'Y'`
- If there is no such observation, set to null for all other subjects in ADSL.
    Examples:
- **CR**: If the last valid `ADRS.AVALC` is 'CR' after the first treatment date, then `ADRS.AVALC` is set to 'CR'.
- **PR**: If the last valid `ADRS.AVALC` is 'PR' after the first treatment date, then `ADRS.AVALC` is set to 'PR'.
- **SD**: If the last valid `ADRS.AVALC` is 'SD' after the first treatment date, then `ADRS.AVALC` is set to 'SD'.
- **NON-CR/NON-PD**: If the last valid `ADRS.AVALC` is 'NON-CR/NON-PD' after the first treatment date, then `ADRS.AVALC` is set to 'NON-CR/NON-PD'.

- **NE**: If the last valid `ADRS.AVALC` is 'NE' after the first treatment date, then `ADRS.AVALC` is set to 'NE'.
- **PD**: If the last valid `ADRS.AVALC` is 'PD' after the first treatment date, then `ADRS.AVALC` is set to 'PD'.
- **Null**: If no valid `ADRS.AVALC` meets the criteria, then `ADRS.AVALC` is set to null.

ADT Calculation

Set `ADT` to:
- The last analysis date (`ADRS.ADT`) on or after the first treatment date (`ADRS.ADT >= ADSL.TRTSDT`) where:
- `ADRS.PARAMCD = 'OVR'`
- `ADRS.AVALC` is 'CR', 'PR', 'SD', 'NON-CR/NON-PD', 'NE', or 'PD'
- `ADRS.ANL01FL = 'Y'`
- If there is no such observation, set to null for all other subjects.
  Examples:
- **Date Example**: If the last valid `ADRS.ADT` is April 15th after the first treatment date, then `ADT` is set to April 15th.
- **Null**: If no valid `ADRS.ADT` meets the criteria, then `ADT` is set to null.

Parameter-05 Information

- **PARAM:** *Overall Response by Investigator*
- **PARAMCD:** *OVR*
- **PARCAT1:** *Tumor Response*
- **PARCAT2:** *Investigator*
- **PARCAT3:** *Recist 1.1*
- **Population:** *Include all observations from RS*
- **ANL01FL:** *See criteria below*
- **SRCDOM:** *RS*
- **SRCVAR:** *RSSTRESC*
- **SRCSEQ:** *RSSEQ*

AVAL Calculation

Set `AVAL` to:
1. **1** if `ADRS.AVALC = 'CR'`
2. **2** if `ADRS.AVALC = 'PR'`
3. **3** if `ADRS.AVALC = 'SD'`
4. **4** if `ADRS.AVALC = 'NON-CR/NON-PD'`
5. **5** if `ADRS.AVALC = 'NE'`
6. **6** if `ADRS.AVALC = 'PD'`
7. **null** if none of the above conditions are met
   Examples:
- If `ADRS.AVALC = 'CR'`, then `AVAL` is set to 1.
- If `ADRS.AVALC = 'PR'`, then `AVAL` is set to 2.
- If `ADRS.AVALC = 'SD'`, then `AVAL` is set to 3.
- If `ADRS.AVALC = 'NON-CR/NON-PD'`, then `AVAL` is set to 4.
- If `ADRS.AVALC = 'NE'`, then `AVAL` is set to 5.
- If `ADRS.AVALC = 'PD'`, then `AVAL` is set to 6.
- If `ADRS.AVALC` does not meet any of the above conditions, then `AVAL` is set to null.

AVALC Calculation

Set `ADRS.AVALC` to:
- The response assessment result in standard format `[RS.RSSTRESC]`, for the overall response parameter `[RS.RSTESTCD]='OVRLRESP'`, from the investigator `[RS.RSEVAL]='INVESTIGATOR'`.
    Examples:
- If the overall response assessment is 'Complete Response (CR)', then `ADRS.AVALC` is set to 'CR'.
- If the overall response assessment is 'Partial Response (PR)', then `ADRS.AVALC` is set to 'PR'.
ADT Calculation
    Set `ADT` to:
-    The date of response assessment `[RS.RSDTC]`, for the overall response parameter `[RS.RSTESTCD]='OVRLRESP'`, from the investigator `[RS.RSEVAL]='INVESTIGATOR'` converted to numeric date.
- If the day is missing and `[ADRS.AVALC]` is 'CR' or 'PR', the day is imputed as the last day of the month.
- If the day is missing and `[ADRS.AVALC]` is not 'CR' or 'PR', the day is imputed as '01'.
- Missing month and year are not imputed.
    Examples:
- If `[RS.RSDTC]` is '2023-05-15', then `ADT` is set to '2023-05-15'.
- If `[RS.RSDTC]` is '2023-05' and `[ADRS.AVALC]` is 'CR', then `ADT` is set to '2023-05-31'.
- If `[RS.RSDTC]` is '2023-05' and `[ADRS.AVALC]` is 'PD', then `ADT` is set to '2023-05-01'.
ANL01FL Calculation
    Set `ANL01FL` to:
- **null** if `[ADRS.AVALC]` is not 'PD', 'NE', 'NON-CR/NON-PD', 'SD', 'PR', or 'CR' (e.g., 'NA' = not available, 'ND' = not done, or null).
- **'Y'** if there is only one observation per subject `[ADRS.USUBJID]` and date `[ADRS.ADT]`.
- **'Y'** for the observation with the worst analysis result `[ADRS.AVALC]` where:
- The order from worst to best is 'PD', 'NE', 'NON-CR/NON-PD', 'SD', 'PR', 'CR'.
- If the worst result is not unique, select the observation with the highest `[RS.RSSEQ]`.
- **null** otherwise.
    Examples:
- If there is only one observation for a subject on a specific date and the result is 'PR', `ANL01FL` is set to 'Y'.
- If there are multiple observations for a subject on a specific date and the results are 'PR' and 'SD', `ANL01FL` is set to 'Y' for the 'SD' observation.
- If `[ADRS.AVALC]` is 'NA', `ANL01FL` is set to null.

Parameter-06 Information

Cancer Therapy
- **PARAM:** Cancer Therapy
- **PARAMCD:** CNCRTRP
- **PARCAT1:** Reference Event
- **AVAL Calculation:** Set to 1 if `[ADRS.AVALC] = 'Y'`, else set to 0 if `[ADRS.AVALC] = 'N'`.
- **ANL01FL Calculation:** Set to 'Y' if `[PR.PRCAT] = 'ANTICANCER RADIOTHERAPY'` where `[PR.PRSTDTC]` is not missing and after the first treatment date `[ADSL.TRTSDT]`, else set to 'N' for all other subjects in ADSL.
- **ADT Calculation:** Set to the date of `[ADSL.DTHDTC]` converted to numeric. No imputation for partial or missing date performed.
- **Population:** All subjects

Parameter-07 Information

Death
- **PARAM:** Death

- **PARAMCD:** DEATH
- **PARCAT1:** Reference Event
- **AVAL Calculation:** Set to 1 if `[ADRS.AVALC] = 'Y'`, else set to 0 if `[ADRS.AVALC] = 'N'`.
- **ANL01FL Calculation:** Set to 'Y' if `[ADSL.DTHDTC]` is not missing or partial, else set to 'N' for all other subjects in ADSL.
- **ADT Calculation:** Set to the date of `[ADSL.DTHDTC]` converted to numeric. No imputation for partial or missing date performed.
- **Population:** All subjects

Parameter-08 Information
Disease Progression by Investigator
- **PARAM:** Disease Progression by Investigator
- **PARAMCD:** PD
- **PARCAT1:** Tumor Response
- **PARCAT2:** Investigator
- **PARCAT3:** Recist 1.1
- **AVAL Calculation:** Set to 1 if `[ADRS.AVALC] = 'Y'`, else set to 0 if `[ADRS.AVALC] = 'N'`.
- **ANL01FL Calculation:** Using observations from ADRS, set to 'Y' if there is an observation with `[ADRS.AVALC] = 'PD'`, else set to 'N' for all other subjects in ADSL.
- **ADT Calculation:** Set to the earliest analysis date `[ADRS.ADT]` or `[ADSL.PROGDT]`, where the condition for `[ADRS.AVALC] = 'Y'` is fulfilled. Else set to null if `[ADRS.AVALC] = 'N'`.
- **Population:** All subjects

Parameter-09 Information
Longest Diameter (mm)
- **PARAM:** Longest Diameter (mm)
- **PARAMCD:** LDIAM
- **PARCAT1:** Tumor Identification
- **PARCAT2:** Investigator
- **AVAL Calculation:** Set to the longest diameter `[TR.TRSTRESN]` where `[TR.TRTESTCD] = 'LDIAM'`.
- **AVALC Calculation:** Set to the longest diameter `[TR.TRSTRESC]` where `[TR.TRTESTCD] = 'LDIAM'`.
- **ADT Calculation:** Set to the corresponding date of assessment `[TR.TRDTC]`.
- **ANL01FL:** Set to 'Y'.
- **SRCDOM:** TR
- **SRCVAR:** TRSTRESC
- **SRCSEQ:** Set to corresponding sequence number `[TR.TRSEQ]`.
- **Population:** All subjects with the longest diameter measures

Project-02

Dataset Variables
- **PARAM:** Parameter
- If `ADRS.PARAMCD='OVRLTRG'` then PARAM='**Target Lesion Response**';
- Else if `ADRS.PARAMCD='OVRLNTRG'` then PARAM='**Non-Target Lesion Response**';
- Else if `ADRS.PARAMCD='OVRLRESP'` then PARAM='**Overall Response**';
- Else PARAM=`RS.RSTEST`.

- **PARAMCD:** Parameter Code
- Set to `RS.RSTESTCD`.

- **AVALC:** Analysis Value (Character)
- Set to `RS.RSORRES`.
  - **AVAL:** Analysis Value
- If `RS.RSSTRESC='CR'` then AVAL=1;
- Else if `RS.RSSTRESC='PR'` then AVAL=2;
- Else if `RS.RSSTRESC` in ('SD', 'Non-CR/Non-PD') then AVAL=3;
- Else if `RS.RSSTRESC='PD'` then AVAL=4;
- Else if `RS.RSSTRESC='NE'` then AVAL=5;
- Else if `RS.RSSTRESC='NA'` then AVAL=6.

CHAPTER X

Parameters Derived in ADTTE

Project-01

Parameter-01 Information

- **PARAM:** Duration of Response by Investigator
- **PARAMCD:** DOR
- **PARCAT1:** Time to Event
- **PARCAT2 (optional):** Investigator
- **PARCAT3 (optional):** Recist 1.1
- **Population:**
    All subjects having a record in ADRS, where `[ADRS.PARAMCD]='CRSP'` and `[ADRS.AVALC]='Y'` and `[ADRS.ANL01FL]='Y'`
- **ADT:** Set to "ADT"
- **STARTDT:** Set to `[ADRS.ADT]` when `[ADRS.PARAMCD] ='CRSP'` and `[ADRS.AVALC]='Y'` and `[ADRS.ANL01FL]='Y'`
- **CNSR:** Set to null
- **EVNTDESC:
    ** Set to "Disease Progression" if there is an observation in ADRS, where `[ADRS.PARAMCD]='PD'` and `[ADRS.ANL01FL]='Y'`.
    Else set to "**Death**" if there is an observation in ADRS, where `[ADRS.PARAMCD]='DEATH'` and `[ADRS.ANL01FL]='Y'`.
    Else set to "**Last Tumor Assessment**" if there is an observation in ADRS, where `[ADRS.PARAMCD]='LSTA'` and `[ADRS.AVALC]` is not null and `[ADRS.ANL01FL]='Y'`.
    Else set to "Confirmed Response plus 1".
- **ANL01FL:** Set to null
- **SRCDOM:** Set to "ADRS"
- **SRCVAR:** Set to "ADT"
- **SRCSEQ:** Set to `[ADRS.ASEQ]` where `[ADRS.PARAMCD]= 'PD'` (if subject experiences disease progression), else set to `[ADRS.ASEQ]` where `[ADRS.PARAMCD]= 'DEATH'` (if subject dies), else set to `[ADRS.ASEQ]` where `[ADRS.PARAMCD]= 'LSTA'` (if subject is censored on last tumor assessment), else leave missing.
    ### Calculation Details
    - **AVAL Calculation:**
- Set to PD date `[ADRS.ADT]` if there is an observation in ADRS, where `[ADRS.PARAMCD]='PD'` and `[ADRS.AVALC]='Y'` and `[ADRS.ANL01FL]='Y'`.
- Else set to Death date `[ADRS.ADT]` if there is an observation in ADRS, where `[ADRS.PARAMCD]='DEATH'` and `[ADRS.AVALC]='Y'` and `[ADRS.ANL01FL]='Y'`.
- Else set to Last Tumor Assessment date `[ADRS.ADT]` where `[ADRS.PARAMCD]='LSTA'` and `[ADRS.AVALC]` is not null and `[ADRS.ANL01FL]='Y'`.
- Else set to date of response `[ADTTE.STARTDT] + 1 day`.
    - **STARTDT Calculation:**
- Set to `[ADRS.ADT]` when `[ADRS.PARAMCD] ='CRSP'` and `[ADRS.AVALC]='Y'` and `[ADRS.ANL01FL]='Y'`.

- **CNSR Calculation:**
- Set to 0 if PD or death occurred, else set to 1.
    - **EVNTDESC Calculation:**
- Set to "Disease Progression" if there is an observation in ADRS, where `[ADRS.PARAMCD]='PD'` and `[ADRS.ANL01FL]='Y'`.
- Else set to "Death" if there is an observation in ADRS, where `[ADRS.PARAMCD]='DEATH'` and `[ADRS.ANL01FL]='Y'`.
- Else set to "Last Tumor Assessment" if there is an observation in ADRS, where `[ADRS.PARAMCD]='LSTA'` and `[ADRS.AVALC]` is not null and `[ADRS.ANL01FL]='Y'`.
- Else set to "Confirmed Response plus 1".

Parameter-02 Information

- **PARAM:** Earliest Contributing Event to Progression Free Survival by Investigator
- **PARAMCD:** PFS
- **PARCAT1:** Time to Event
- **PARCAT2** (optional):** Investigator
- **PARCAT3** (optional):** Recist 1.1
- **Population:** All subjects with non-missing `[ADSL.TRTSDT]`
- **ADT:** Set to "ADT" if `[ADTTE.CNSR]=0` or `[ADTTE.EVNTDESC]='Last Tumor Assessment'`, else set to "TRTSDT".
- **STARTDT:** Set to "Date of First Exposure to Treatment [ADSL.TRTSDT]".
- **CNSR:** Set to 0 if PD or death occurred, else set to 1.
- **EVNTDESC:** Set to "Disease Progression" if there is an observation in ADRS, where `[ADRS.PARAMCD]='PD'` and `[ADRS.AVALC]='Y'` and `[ADRS.ANL01FL]='Y'`. Else set to "Death" if there is an observation in ADRS, where `[ADRS.PARAMCD]='DEATH'` and `[ADRS.AVALC]='Y'` and `[ADRS.ANL01FL]='Y'`. Else set to "Last Tumor Assessment" if there is an observation in ADRS, where `[ADRS.PARAMCD]='LSTA'` and `[ADRS.ANL01FL]='Y'`. Otherwise set to "Treatment Start" where `[ADTTE.ADT]` is set to `[ADSL.TRTSDT]`.
- **ANL01FL:** Set to null
- **SRCDOM:** Set to "ADRS" if `[ADTTE.CNSR]=0` or `[ADTTE.EVNTDESC]='Last Tumor Assessment'`, else set to "ADSL".
- **SRCVAR:** Set to "ADT" if `[ADTTE.CNSR]=0` or `[ADTTE.EVNTDESC]='Last Tumor Assessment'`, else set to "TRTSDT".
- **SRCSEQ:** Set to `[ADRS.ASEQ]` where `[ADRS.PARAMCD]= 'PD'` (if subject experiences disease progression), else set to `[ADRS.ASEQ]` where `[ADRS.PARAMCD]= 'DEATH'` (if subject dies), else set to `[ADRS.ASEQ]` where `[ADRS.PARAMCD]= 'LSTA'` (if subject is censored on last tumor assessment), else set to null.
    ### Calculation Details
    - **ADT Calculation:**
- Set to tumor assessment date `[ADRS.ADT]` where `[ADRS.PARAMCD]='LSTAC'` if PD or death happen after more than one consecutive missed/invalid tumor assessment (`[ADRS.ADT]` where `[ADRS.PARAMCD]='OVR'` and `[ADRS.AVALC]='NE'`).
- Else set to cancer therapy date `[ADRS.ADT]` where `[ADRS.PARAMCD]='CNCRTRP'` and `[ADRS.AVALC]='Y'` and `[ADRS.ANL01FL]='Y'` if cancer therapy start date is before PD date `[ADRS.ADT]` where `[ADRS.PARAMCD]='PD'`.
- Else set to PD date `[ADRS.ADT]` if there is an observation in ADRS, where `[ADRS.PARAMCD]='PD'` and `[ADRS.AVALC]='Y'` and `[ADRS.ANL01FL]='Y'`.
- Else set to Death date `[ADRS.ADT]` if there is an observation in ADRS, where `[ADRS.PARAMCD]='DEATH'` and `[ADRS.AVALC]='Y'` and `[ADRS.ANL01FL]='Y'`.

- Else set to Last Tumor Assessment date `[ADRS.ADT]` if there is an observation in ADRS, where `[ADRS.PARAMCD]='LSTA'` and `[ADRS.ANL01FL]='Y'`.
- Otherwise set to Time to Event Origin Date `[ADTTE.STARTDT]`.
   - **STARTDT Calculation:**
- Set to "Date of First Exposure to Treatment [ADSL.TRTSDT]".
   - **CNSR Calculation:**
- Set to 0 if PD or death occurred, else set to 1.
   - **EVNTDESC Calculation:**
- Set to "Disease Progression" if there is an observation in ADRS, where `[ADRS.PARAMCD]='PD'` and `[ADRS.AVALC]='Y'` and `[ADRS.ANL01FL]='Y'`.
- Else set to "Death" if there is an observation in ADRS, where `[ADRS.PARAMCD]='DEATH'` and `[ADRS.AVALC]='Y'` and `[ADRS.ANL01FL]='Y'`.
- Else set to "Last Tumor Assessment" if there is an observation in ADRS, where `[ADRS.PARAMCD]='LSTA'` and `[ADRS.ANL01FL]='Y'`.
- Otherwise set to "Treatment Start" where `[ADTTE.ADT]` is set to `[ADSL.TRTSDT]`.
   - **SRCDOM Calculation:**
- Set to "ADRS" if `[ADTTE.CNSR]=0` or `[ADTTE.EVNTDESC]='Last Tumor Assessment'`, else set to "ADSL".
   - **SRCVAR Calculation:**
- Set to "ADT" if `[ADTTE.CNSR]=0`

Parameter -03 Information

- **PARAM:** Overall Survival
- **PARAMCD:** OS
- **PARCAT1:** Time to Event
- **PARCAT2** (optional):** Not specified
- **PARCAT3** (optional):** Not specified
- **Population:** All subjects with non-missing `[ADSL.TRTSDT]`
- **ADT:** Set to "ADT" if `[ADTTE.CNSR]=0` and if there is an observation in ADRS, where `[ADRS.PARAMCD]='DEATH'` and `[ADRS.AVALC]='Y'` and `[ADRS.ANL01FL]='Y'`. Else set to "LSTALVDT" if Last Known to be Alive Date `[ADSL.LSTALVDT]` is post Time to Event Origin Date `[ADTTE.STARTDT]`, Otherwise set to "TRTSDT".
- **STARTDT:** Set to Date of First Exposure to Treatment `[ADSL.TRTSDT]`.
- **CNSR:** Set to 0 if death occurred, else set to 1.
- **EVNTDESC:** Set to "Death" if subject died `[ADRS.PARAMCD]='DEATH'` and `[ADRS.AVALC]='Y'` and `[ADRS.ANL01FL]='Y'`. Otherwise set to "Alive".
- **CNSDTDSC:** For censored records set to "Last Contact" where `[ADTTE.ADT]` is set to `[ADSL.LSTALVDT]`, Otherwise set to "Treatment Start" where `[ADTTE.ADT]` is set to `[ADSL.TRTSDT]`.
- **SRCDOM:** Set to "ADRS" if `[ADTTE.CNSR]=0`, Else set to "ADSL".
- **SRCVAR:** Set to "ADT" if `[ADTTE.CNSR]=0` and if there is an observation in ADRS, where `[ADRS.PARAMCD]='DEATH'` and `[ADRS.AVALC]='Y'` and `[ADRS.ANL01FL]='Y'`, Else set to "LSTALVDT" if Last Known to be Alive Date `[ADSL.LSTALVDT]` is post Time to Event Origin Date `[ADTTE.STARTDT]`, Otherwise set to "TRTSDT".
- **SRCSEQ:** Set to `[ADRS.ASEQ]` where `[ADRS.PARAMCD]= 'DEATH'`, Else set to null.
   ### Calculation Details
   - **ADT Calculation:**
- Set to Death date `[ADRS.ADT]` if there is an observation in ADRS, where `[ADRS.PARAMCD]='DEATH'` and `[ADRS.AVALC]='Y'` and `[ADRS.ANL01FL]='Y'`.
- Else set to Last Known to be Alive Date `[ADSL.LSTALVDT]` if this date is post Time to Event Origin Date `[ADTTE.STARTDT]`.

- Otherwise set to Time to Event Origin Date `[ADTTE.STARTDT]`.
  - **STARTDT Calculation:**
- Set to Date of First Exposure to Treatment `[ADSL.TRTSDT]`.
  - **CNSR Calculation:**
- Set to 0 if death occurred, else set to 1.
  - **EVNTDESC Calculation:**
- Set to "Death" if subject died `[ADRS.PARAMCD]='DEATH'` and `[ADRS.AVALC]='Y'` and `[ADRS.ANL01FL]='Y'`.
- Otherwise set to "Alive".
  - **CNSDTDSC Calculation:**
- For censored records set to "Last Contact" where `[ADTTE.ADT]` is set to `[ADSL.LSTALVDT]`.
- Otherwise set to "Treatment Start" where `[ADTTE.ADT]` is set to `[ADSL.TRTSDT]`.
  - **SRCDOM Calculation:**
- Set to "ADRS" if `[ADTTE.CNSR]=0`, Else set to "ADSL".
  - **SRCVAR Calculation:**
- Set to "ADT" if `[ADTTE.CNSR]=0` and if there is an observation in ADRS, where `[ADRS.PARAMCD]='DEATH'` and `[ADRS.AVALC]='Y'` and `[ADRS.ANL01FL]='Y'`.
- Else set to "LSTALVDT" if Last Known to be Alive Date `[ADSL.LSTALVDT]` is post Time to Event Origin Date `[ADTTE.STARTDT]`.
- Otherwise set to "TRTSDT".

CHAPTER XI

Tumor Identification Data in the TU Domain

In clinical trials, the TU domain is used to store data related to the identification of tumors. This includes information on how and where tumors were identified, as well as details about their measurement and classification. Here's a breakdown of the key variables used in the TU domain:

Key Variables in TU Domain:
- **Study Name (STUDYID):** The identifier for the study.
- **Subject Number (USUBJID):** The unique identifier for each subject in the study.
- **Date of Scan (TUDTC):** The date when the scan was performed.
- **Scan Method (TUMETHOD):** The method used to identify the tumor, such as CT scan, X-ray, MRI, ultrasound, etc.
- **Tumor Identifier (TULINKID):** A unique identifier for each tumor, with each row representing a different tumor. Examples include T01, T02 for target lesions, and NT01, NT02 for non-target lesions.
- **Location (TULOC):** The location of the tumor in the body, such as pancreas, lung, kidney, esophagus, etc.
- **Laterality (TULAT):** Indicates the side of the body affected by the tumor (left or right).
- **Tumor Type (TUORRES):** Specifies whether the tumor is a target lesion (measurable) or a non-target lesion (non-measurable).
- **Evaluator (TUEVAL):** Indicates who evaluated the tumor, such as an investigator, central reading facility, oncologist, or radiologist. This can also account for multiple evaluators.

Additional Variables:
- **Study Visit Number (VISITNUM):** The visit number during the study when the scan was performed.
- **Study Visit (VISIT):** The visit name or identifier.
- **Epoch (EPOCH):** The phase or stage of the study during which the scan was performed.
- **Study Day (VISITDY):** The day of the study when the visit occurred.
- **Tumor Test Code (TUTESTCD):** The test code used to classify the type of test performed.

Tumor Identification Methods:
Tumors can be identified using various imaging techniques, including:
- **CT Scan:** A detailed imaging method that creates cross-sectional images of the body.
- **X-ray:** A basic imaging technique used to view structures inside the body.
- **MRI (Magnetic Resonance Imaging):** A technique that uses magnetic fields and radio waves to create detailed images.
- **Ultrasound:** An imaging method that uses sound waves to create images of the inside of the body.
- **PET Scan (Positron Emission Tomography):** A type of imaging that shows how tissues and organs are functioning.

Tumor Locations:
Tumors can be located in various parts of the body, such as:
- **Pancreas**
- **Lung**
- **Kidney**
- **Esophagus**
- **Liver**
- **Brain**
- **Breast**

Tumor Types:

- **Measurable Target Lesions:** Tumors that can be measured accurately, typically used to assess response to treatment.
- **Non-measurable Non-Target Lesions:** Tumors that cannot be measured accurately but are still monitored for changes.

By collecting and organizing this data, researchers can track the progression and response of tumors to treatment over time, providing crucial insights into the effectiveness of new cancer therapies.

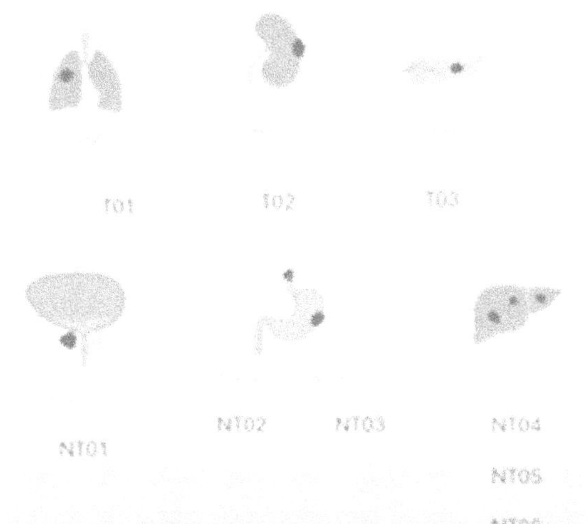

- Study
- Subject
- Date of scan
- Scan method
- Tumor Identifier?
- Location?
- Laterality (side)?
- Tumor type (result)
- Who evaluated?
- Evaluator id

- STUDYID
- USUBJID
- TUDTC
- TUMETHOD
- TULNKID
- TULOC
- TULAT
- TUORRES/TUSTRESC
- TUEVAL
- TUEVALID

TU

CHAPTER XII

SDTM variables in TR domain

In clinical trials, tumor assessments and measurements are stored in the TR domain. This domain captures detailed information about the size and status of both target and non-target lesions. Here's an overview of the key variables and their roles:

Key Variables in the TR Domain:
  - **Study Name (STUDYID):** The identifier for the study.
- **Subject Number (USUBJID):** The unique identifier for each subject in the study.
- **Scan Status (TRSTAT):** Indicates whether the scan was performed. If not, the reason is stored in **TRREASND**.
- **Date of Scan (TRDTC):** The date when the scan was performed.
- **Scan Method (TRMETHOD):** The method used for the scan, such as CT scan, X-ray, MRI, etc.
- **Tumor Identifier (TRLINKID):** A unique identifier for each tumor, with target lesions named T01, T02, etc., and non-target lesions named NT01, NT02, etc.
- **Tumor Measurement (TRORRES/TRSTRESC):** For target lesions, this is the measurement of the tumor diameter. For non-target lesions, it indicates the presence or absence of the tumor.
- **TRORRES:** Original result.
- **TRSTRESC:** Standardized result.
- **Numeric Result (TRSTRESN):** The numeric value of the measurement.
- **Character Result (TRSTRESC):** The character value of the result.
- **Units (TRORRESU/TRSTRESU):** The units for the measurement.
- **Evaluator (TREVAL):** Indicates who evaluated the scan results, such as an investigator or a central oncologist.
- **Evaluator ID (TREVAID):** The identifier for the evaluator.
- **Related Visit Information:**
- **Visit Number (VISITNUM):** The visit number during the study when the scan was performed.
- **Visit Name (VISIT):** The visit identifier or name.
- **Epoch (EPOCH):** The phase or stage of the study during which the scan was performed.
- **Study Day (TRDY):** The day of the study when the visit occurred.
- **Test Code (TRTESTCD):** Describes the type of test performed, such as DIAMETER for target lesions or TUMSTATE for tumor status (presence/absence).

Definitions and Examples:
  - **Target Lesions:** These are measurable tumors. Each target lesion is assigned an identifier like T01, T02, and so on. The size of these lesions is recorded as a diameter in units like millimeters or centimeters. For example, a lesion measured as T01 might have a diameter of 25 mm.
- **Non-Target Lesions:** These are non-measurable tumors. Each non-target lesion is assigned an identifier like NT01, NT02, etc. Instead of a precise measurement, the presence or absence of these lesions is recorded. For example, NT01 might be marked as "Present" or "Absent."

Example Data Entry:
  Here's an example of how data might be recorded in the TR domain:

Variable	**Value**
STUDYID	STUDY123
USUBJID	001
TRSTAT	Performed
TRREASND	(blank)

TRDTC	2023-05-22
TRMETHOD	CT Scan
TRLINKID	T01
TRORRES	30
TRSTRESC	30
TRSTRESN	30
TRORRESU	mm
TRSTRESU	mm
TREVAL	Investigator
TREVAID	INV001
VISITNUM	1
VISIT	Baseline
EPOCH	Screening
TRDY	1
TRTESTCD	DIAMETER

This structured data helps in systematically tracking and evaluating the progression of tumors in clinical trials.

Target Lesions (measure diameters)
- T01
- T02
- T03

Non-target lesions (check presence)
- NT01
- NT02
- ..
- NT06

- Study
- Subject
- Scan performed?
  - If not, reason
- Date of scan
- Scan method
- Tumor Identifier
- Tumor measurement
- Who evaluated?
- Evaluator id

- STUDYID
- USUBJID
- TRSTAT
  - TRREASND
- TRDTC
- TRMETHOD
- TRLNKID
- TRORRES/TRSTRESC
- TREVAL
- TREVALID

TRDTC – TRDY, VISITNUM, VISIT, VISITDY, EPOCH

TRORRES – TRORRESU, TRSTRESC, TRSTRESN, TRSTRESU

TR

CHAPTER XIII

SDTM variables in RS domain

<u>Response of Tumor Information in the RS Domain</u>

The RS (Response) domain in SDTM captures information about the response of tumors to treatment, including target lesions, non-target lesions, and overall tumor assessment. Here are the key variables used in the RS domain:

Key Variables in the RS Domain:

- **Study Name (STUDYID):** The identifier for the study.
- **Subject Number (USUBJID):** The unique identifier for each subject in the study.
- **Date of Scan (RSDTC):** The date when the scan or assessment was performed.
- **Response Test Code (RSTESTCD):** Indicates the type of response being assessed:
- **TRGRESP:** Target lesion response.
- **NTRGRESP:** Non-target lesion response.
- **OVRLRESP:** Overall response.
- **Response Test (RSTEST):** Describes the response being assessed (e.g., response of target, non-target, or overall tumors).
- **Response (RSORRES):** The observed response, which can be categories such as CR (Complete Response), PR (Partial Response), PD (Progressive Disease), SD (Stable Disease), etc.
- **Evaluator (RSEVAL):** Indicates who evaluated the response, such as an investigator or a central oncologist.
- **Evaluator ID (RSEVALID):** The identifier for the evaluator, useful if there are multiple evaluators.
- **Related Visit Information:**
- **Visit Number (VISITNUM):** The visit number during the study when the response was assessed.
- **Visit Name (VISIT):** The visit identifier or name.
- **Epoch (EPOCH):** The phase or stage of the study during which the response was assessed.
- **Study Day (VISITDY):** The day of the study when the visit occurred.
- **Standardized Numeric Result (RSSTRESN):** Numeric value of the standardized response result.
- **Standardized Character Result (RSSTRESC):** Character value of the standardized response result.

Definitions and Examples:

- **Target Lesion Response (TRGRESP):** Evaluates the response of measurable target lesions. For example, if a target lesion shrinks significantly, it might be recorded as PR (Partial Response).
- **Non-Target Lesion Response (NTRGRESP):** Evaluates the response of non-measurable non-target lesions, typically noting presence or absence of progression.
- **Overall Response (OVRLRESP):** Combines the responses of both target and non-target lesions to provide an overall assessment of the tumor status.

Example Data Entry:

Here's an example of how data might be recorded in the RS domain:

Variable	**Value**
STUDYID	STUDY123
USUBJID	001
RSDTC	2023-05-22
RSTESTCD	TRGRESP
RSTEST	Target Lesion Response
RSORRES	PR
RSEVAL	Investigator
RSEVALID	INV001

VISITNUM	1
VISIT	Baseline
EPOCH	Screening
VISITDY	1
RSSTRESN	(numeric result if applicable)
RSSTRESC	PR

In this example, the response of the target lesions was evaluated on the date specified, and the result was recorded as a Partial Response (PR). This structured data allows for consistent tracking and assessment of tumor responses in clinical trials.

mpact on
- Target Lesions
- Non-target lesions
- Overall

- Study   STUDYID
- Subject   USUBJID
- Date of scan   RSDTC
- Response of   RSTESTCD/RSTEST
- Response   RSORRES/RSSTRESC
- Who evaluated?   RSEVAL
- Evaluator id   RSEVALID

RSDTC – RSDY, VISITNUM, VISIT, VISITDY, EPOCH

RSORRES –RSSTRESC, RSSTRESN

RS

CHAPTER XIV

ADTTE Time to death – Overall survival

"Time to Death," often referred to as "Overall Survival" (OS) in clinical trials, measures the duration from the start of treatment until death from any cause.

It is a critical endpoint in many oncology studies, as it directly reflects the treatment's effectiveness in prolonging the lives of patients.

Time to Death Analysis Variables and Derivations

Variable	Label	Logic/Derivation
STARTDT	Time-to-Event Origin Date for Subject	Set to `TRTSDT` (Treatment Start Date)
PARAM	Parameter	Create a parameter named "Time to Death (Days)" for all safety subjects present in ADSL.
PARAMCD	Parameter Code	Set to `T2DEATH` when `PARAM` is "Time to Death (Days)".

ADT	Analysis Date	- For subjects who died on the study (`ADSLDTHDT` not null) after treatment start:
		  Populate using `ADSLDTHDT`.
		 - For subjects who did not die on the study (`ADSLDTHDT` is null):
		  Populate with `ADSLEOT`.

CNSR	Censoring Indicator	- For subjects who died on the study (`ADSLDTHDT` not null) after treatment start:
		  Set to `0`.
		 - For subjects who did not die on the study (`ADSLDTHDT` is null):
		  Set to `1`.

AVAL	Analysis Value	Set to `ADT - STARTDT + 1`.

EVNTDESC	Event or Censoring Description	- For subjects who died on the study (`ADSLDTHDT` not null) after treatment start:
		  Set to "Death".
		 - For subjects who did not die on the study (`ADSLDTHDT` is null):
		  Set to the end of study reason (`ADSLDCSREAS`).

ADTTE T2DEATH parameter specs

Example Data Entry

Variable	Value
STARTDT	2023-01-01
PARAM	Time to Death (Days)
PARAMCD	T2DEATH
ADT	2023-06-15 (if `ADSLDTHDT` not null) / 2023-12-31 (if `ADSLDTHDT` null)
CNSR	0 (if died on study) / 1 (if not)
AVAL	166 (calculated as `ADT - STARTDT + 1` if `STARTDT` is 2023-01-01)
EVNTDESC	Death / End of study reason (e.g., "Completed", "Withdrawn")

This display box format presents the key variables and their derivation logic clearly, ensuring a comprehensive understanding of the time-to-event analysis for subjects in the study.

CHAPTER XV

Censoring Indicator (CNSR) in Oncology Studies

The censoring indicator (CNSR) is a crucial variable in oncology studies, especially in survival analysis.

It indicates whether the *event of interest* (e.g., death, progression) was observed during the study or if the data were censored.

Censoring occurs when the event has not happened for a subject during the study period or the subject was lost to follow-up. Here's how CNSR is typically used in different contexts:

General Definition

CNSR = 0: The event of interest (e.g., death, progression) occurred.

CNSR = 1: The event of interest did not occur (data are censored).

Study Type	CNSR = 0 (Event Observed)	CNSR = 1 (Censored)
Overall Survival (OS)	Subject died.	Subject alive at last follow-up or lost to follow-up before death.
Progression-Free Survival (PFS)	Subject experienced disease progression or died.	Subject did not experience progression or death by study end or lost to follow-up before progression.
Time to Progression (TTP)	Subject experienced disease progression.	Subject did not experience progression by study end or died without prior progression.
Disease-Free Survival (DFS)	Subject experienced disease recurrence or died.	Subject did not experience recurrence or death by study end.

CHAPTER XVI

Best Overall Response

Definition of Best Overall Response

The best overall response in oncology clinical trials refers to ***the most favorable outcome observed*** after treatment, considering the responses of both target and non-target lesions, as well as the presence of any new lesions. It provides a comprehensive evaluation of treatment effectiveness.

Criteria for Best Overall Response

1. **Complete Response (CR)**:
- Complete disappearance of all target and non-target lesions.
- No new lesions.
    2. **Partial Response (PR)**:
- At least a 30% decrease in the sum of diameters of target lesions compared to baseline.
- Persistence of one or more non-target lesions not qualifying for PD.
- No new lesions.
    3. **Stable Disease (SD)**:
- Neither sufficient shrinkage to qualify for PR nor sufficient increase to qualify for PD.
- No new lesions.
    4. **Progressive Disease (PD)**:
- Appearance of one or more new lesions.
- At least a 20% increase in the sum of diameters of target lesions.
- Unequivocal progression of existing non-target lesions.

Best Overall Response	Criteria
Complete Response (CR)	Disappearance of all target and non-target lesions; no new lesions.
Partial Response (PR)	≥30% decrease in sum of diameters of target lesions from baseline; persistence of one or more non-target lesions not qualifying for PD; no new lesions.
Stable Disease (SD)	Neither sufficient shrinkage to qualify for PR nor sufficient increase to qualify for PD; no new lesions.
Progressive Disease (PD)	≥20% increase in sum of diameters of target lesions or unequivocal progression of existing non-target lesions; or appearance of one or more new lesions.

BOR

Example Scenario:

Consider a patient enrolled in an oncology clinical trial for breast cancer. Here's how the best overall response would be assessed over the course of treatment:
    - **Baseline Assessment**:
- Target Lesions: Presence of measurable tumors in the breast and nearby lymph nodes.
- Non-Target Lesions: Some non-measurable lesions in the liver.

- No new lesions.
    - **During Treatment**:
- After several cycles of chemotherapy, the target lesions in the breast and lymph nodes shrink significantly, meeting the criteria for PR.
- Non-target lesions in the liver show no significant change.
- No new lesions are detected.
    - **Assessment after Completion of Treatment**:
- Final evaluation reveals complete disappearance of all target and non-target lesions.
- No new lesions are observed.
- The patient meets the criteria for Complete Response (CR).
    #### Summary:
In this example, the patient's best overall response to treatment is categorized as Complete Response (CR), indicating a favorable outcome with the complete disappearance of all detectable tumors. This demonstrates the efficacy of the treatment in achieving a significant therapeutic response.

CHAPTER XVII

Dose-limiting toxicities (DLTs)

Dose-Limiting Toxicities (DLTs)
Definition
- **Dose-Limiting Toxicities (DLTs)**: Specific side effects or adverse reactions of a drug that are severe enough to prevent an increase in dose or level of that drug. These toxicities are used to determine the maximum tolerated dose (MTD) during clinical trials, particularly in oncology.
Criteria
- DLTs are typically defined as grade 3-5 adverse events according to the Common Terminology Criteria for Adverse Events (CTCAE) v5.0, which occur within a predefined timeframe (e.g., from the first injection to a certain follow-up period).
Example in Oncology
- **Example**: In a clinical trial for a new chemotherapy drug, a DLT might be severe neutropenia (a significant drop in white blood cell count) that persists for more than a week, or a grade 4 thrombocytopenia (very low platelet count) that poses a high risk of bleeding. Another example could be a grade 3 or higher non-hematologic toxicity such as severe diarrhea, neuropathy, or liver enzyme elevations.

- **Specific Case**: In a trial for an investigational cancer drug, a patient may experience grade 3 diarrhea, which leads to dehydration and requires hospitalization. This adverse event would be classified as a DLT because it significantly impacts the patient's health and necessitates a dose adjustment or discontinuation of the drug.

CHAPTER XVIII

Overall Response Rate/Objective Response Rate (ORR)

Definition
- **Overall Response Rate (ORR)**: A measure used in clinical trials to evaluate the efficacy of a treatment, particularly in oncology. ORR is defined as the proportion of patients who achieve a predefined amount of tumor shrinkage (objective response) for a specified duration.
    #### Components
- **Complete Response (CR)**: The disappearance of all target lesions.
- **Partial Response (PR)**: At least a 30% decrease in the sum of the diameters of target lesions, taking as reference the baseline sum diameters.
    #### Calculation
- ORR is calculated as the sum of patients with Complete Response (CR) and Partial Response (PR) divided by the total number of patients in the study.
    #### Example
- **Example**: In a clinical trial with 100 patients, if 10 patients achieve a Complete Response (CR) and 30 patients achieve a Partial Response (PR), the ORR would be (10 + 30) / 100 = 40%. This means that 40% of the patients experienced significant tumor shrinkage as a result of the treatment.
    #### Significance
- ORR is a key indicator of a treatment's antitumor activity and is often used in early-phase clinical trials to provide a preliminary assessment of efficacy. It helps in determining whether a treatment warrants further investigation in larger, more definitive trials.

CHAPTER XIX

Varibales in ADTR

Dataset Variables
   - **ADTR:**
- **PARAM:** Parameter
- Set to `TR.TRTEST` concatenated with number of lesion from `TR.TRLNKID` and with units `TR.TRSTRESU` in brackets. For each record with `TR.TRTEST='Sum of Diameter'`, derive two records with `PARAM='Sum of Diameter Change from Nadir'` and `'Sum of Diameter Percent Change from Nadir'`.

- **PARAMCD:** Parameter Code
- Set to `TR.TRTESTCD` concatenated with number of lesion from `TR.TRLNKID`. For derived records, code PARAM as `'SDMCHG'` and `'SDMPCHG'`.

- **PARCAT1:** Parameter Category 1
- Set to `TR.TRGRPID`.

- **PARAMTYP:** Parameter Type
- Set to `'DERIVED'` for derived parameters.

- **AVAL:** Analysis Value
- Set to `TR.TRSTRESN` for non-derived parameters. Set to `ADTR.AVAL - (nadir value)` for `'SDMCHG'` where nadir is the lowest value prior to the visit. Set to `100*(ADTR.AVAL - nadir)/nadir` for `'SDMPCHG'`. Do not derive parameters for baseline.

- **AVALC:** Analysis Value (Character)
- Set to `TR.TRSTRESC` for character results.

- **BASE:** Baseline Value
- Set to `ADTR.AVAL` where `ADTR.ABLFL = 'Y'`.

- **CHG:** Change from Baseline
- Set to `ADTR.AVAL - ADTR.BASE` for post-baseline records.

- **PCHG:** Percent Change from Baseline
- Set to `100*(ADTR.AVAL - ADTR.BASE)/ADTR.BASE` for post-baseline records.

- **ABLFL:** Baseline Record Flag
- Set to Y for the last non-missing record before or on the first dose date (`TRTSDT`). Defined only for `PARAMCD='SUMDIAM'`.

CHAPTER XX

Censoring Guidelines for Overall Survival (OS) and Progression–Free Survival (PFS) as Endpoints

1. In the time-to-event ADaM dataset, event occurrence or censoring is tracked by the variable CNSR, where CNSR = 0 denotes events, and CNSR > 0 signifies censored records.

2. The date of the event or censoring is recorded in the ADT variable.

3. AVAL variable calculates the time to event or censoring from the origin. The typical formula for AVAL computation is (ADT [Date of Event/Censoring] - randomization date + 1).

4. It's crucial to document confirmation criteria and pre-defined time windows for confirmatory scans.

Derivation of CNSR and AVAL

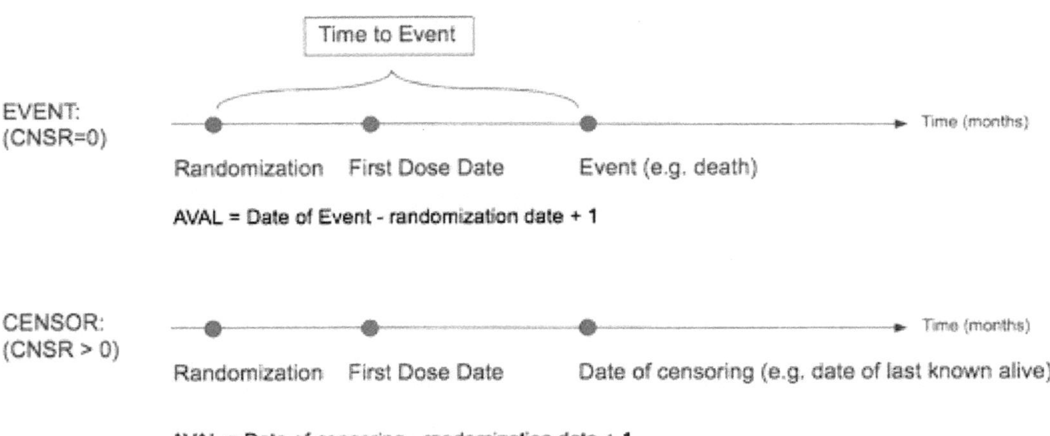

5. AVAL is computed using the analysis date in months: (ADT - RANDDT + 1) divided by 30.4375.

SUBJID	PARAM	PARAMCD	RANDDT	ADT	AVAL	CNSR	EVNTDESC	EVNDTDSC
101	Time to Overall Survival	OS	2018-02-06	2018-12-02	9.85	0	Dead	Date of Death
102	Time to Overall Survival	OS	2018-02-11	2018-08-26	6.47	1	Alive	Date of Last Known Alive
103	Time to Overall Survival	OS	2018-02-13	2018-09-23	7.32	1	Lost to Follow-up	Date of Last Known Alive
104	Time to Overall Survival	OS	2018-02-22	2018-12-21	9.95	1	Dead after Analysis Cutoff	Analysis Cutoff Date

CHAPTER XXI

Special statistical analysis for efficacy

1. **Log-rank test**: This statistical test is employed to compare the overall survival (OS) or progression-free survival (PFS) between two treatment groups in oncology trials.

2. **Kaplan-Meier curve**: A graphical representation of survival distribution across different treatment groups, providing an intuitive visualization of survival probabilities over time. The 50th percentile of Kaplan-Meier estimates serves as an estimate of the median duration (the time when half of the patients are event-free) for time-to-event endpoints.

3. **Reverse Kaplan-Meier**: This method involves reversing events such that loss-to-follow-up instances are considered as "events," while actual outcome events are treated as "censored." It is used to estimate the median follow-up time.

4. **Cox regression**: A statistical technique used to estimate and compare survival experiences between two treatment groups. Hazard ratio (HR) is typically calculated with Cox regression, representing the relative risk of experiencing an event of interest between the groups.

5. **Binomial test of binary proportion**: This test, along with its confidence interval (Exact CI or normal approximation), is utilized to compare the proportion of subjects free of events or to assess differences in response rates between treatment groups.

1. **Log-rank test**:
- Example: In a clinical trial for pancreatic cancer, researchers compare the survival outcomes of patients receiving chemotherapy alone versus those undergoing surgery followed by chemotherapy. The log-rank test determines if there's a significant difference in survival rates between the two groups.

2. **Kaplan-Meier curve**:
- Example: In a study evaluating the effectiveness of a new targeted therapy for advanced melanoma, the Kaplan-Meier curve illustrates the probability of survival over time for patients receiving the experimental treatment versus those receiving standard therapy.

3. **Reverse Kaplan-Meier**:
- Example: In a long-term observational study on prostate cancer, researchers use the reverse Kaplan-Meier method to estimate the median follow-up time from the date of diagnosis to the occurrence of prostate-specific antigen (PSA) recurrence.

4. **Cox regression**:
- Example: In a clinical trial investigating the impact of smoking status on the survival of lung cancer patients treated with immunotherapy, Cox regression analysis calculates the hazard ratio (HR) to compare the risk of death between smokers and non-smokers, adjusting for age and disease stage.

5. **Binomial test of binary proportion**:
- Example: In a phase II trial evaluating the efficacy of a new drug for metastatic colorectal cancer, researchers compare the proportion of patients achieving complete tumor regression (CR) between the treatment group and the control group using a binomial test.

CHAPTER XXII

Useful SAS Techniques in Oncology Studies

Efficacy time-to-event endpoints like overall survival (OS), progression-free survival (PFS), and time to PSA (Prostate-specific Antigen) progression are commonly analyzed using survival analysis techniques. Survival analysis considers censoring observations (e.g., lost to follow-up or no event occurrence), with survival time indicating the duration from a starting point (e.g., randomization) to the event of interest (e.g., death). Here are the three main SAS procedures for survival analysis:

1. **PROC LIFETEST:**
- Produces life tables and Kaplan-Meier estimates.
- Kaplan-Meier (KM) estimate is a non-parametric estimation of the survival function, making no assumptions about the underlying hazard function or proportional hazard.

2. **PROC PHREG:**
- Cox regression assumes proportional hazards and models the effect of predictors and covariates.
- It handles both continuous-time (EXACT method) and discrete-time (DISCRETE method) data, and accommodates time-dependent covariates.

3. **PROC LIFEREG:**
- Performs parametric regressions, assuming a distribution for time-to-event variables (e.g., Weibull, exponential, or lognormal).
- Models the underlying hazard or survival function based on the specified distribution assumptions.

```
/* PROC LIFETEST */
proc lifetest data=mydata;
time survival_time*event(1);
strata treatment_group;
/* Optionally, you can specify other options like OUTSURV for survival estimates */
run;

/* PROC PHREG */
proc phreg data=mydata;
model survival_time*event(1) = treatment_group covariate1 covariate2 / ties=exact;
/* Optionally, you can specify other options like TIMEFIXED for time-dependent covariates */
run;

/* PROC LIFEREG */
proc lifereg data=mydata dist=weibull;
model survival_time*event(1) = treatment_group covariate1 covariate2;
/* Optionally, you can specify other distributions like exponential or lognormal */
run;
```

CHAPTER XXIII

Efficacy Analysis Techniques for Oncology Studies Using SAS

1. **Endpoints**:
- Objective Response Rate (ORR)
- Overall Survival (OS)
- Progression-Free Survival (PFS)
- Quality of Life (QOL)
   2. **Data Collection**:
- More detailed information in CRFs
- Includes tumor measurements and responses, and ECOG performance statuses
   3. **Adverse Event Reporting**:
- Uses National Cancer Institute (NCI) guidelines
- Graded on severity scale (1 to 5) using CTCAE
- Coded using MedDRA
- Focus on treatment-emergent adverse events (TEAEs)
   4. **Tumor Measurement and Assessment under RECIST Guidelines**:
- Utilizes RECIST criteria for tumor response assessment
- Defines categories like Complete Response (CR), Partial Response (PR), etc.
   5. **Oncology-specific SDTM Domains**:
- TU (Tumor Identification)
- TR (Tumor Results)
- RS (Response)
- Time-to-Event ADaM datasets
   6. **Censoring and Confirmation Rules**:
- Important for time-to-event endpoints like OS and PFS
- Carefully define criteria for censoring and progression confirmation

CHAPTER XXIV

Objective Response Rates Analyses

1. **Objective Response Rate Definition:**
- Objective response rate (ORR) measures the proportion of responders, where a response entails achieving complete response (CR) or partial response (PR) according to RECIST criteria.

    2. **Calculation of ORR and 95% Confidence Intervals:**
- ORR and its associated 95% confidence intervals (CI) are computed for each treatment arm to evaluate treatment efficacy.

    3. **Comparison between Treatment Arms:**
- The difference in response rates between two treatments is assessed, along with their corresponding 95% CI and statistical significance (e.g., Cochran-Mantel-Haenszel Test).

    4. **Example Mock-up Table for ORR:**
- An illustrative table is provided below to summarize objective response rates and their confidence intervals for each treatment arm.

	Drug A	Placebo	Treatment Comparison
Best Overall Response			
Complete Response (CR)	XX (XX%)	XX (XX%)	
Partial Response (PR)	XX (XX%)	XX (XX%)	
Stable Disease (SD)	XX (XX%)	XX (XX%)	
Progressive Disease (PD)	XX (XX%)	XX (XX%)	
Best Objective Response (CR or PR)	XX (XX%)	XX (XX%)	
95% CI for Objective Response Rate	XX% - XX%	XX% - XX%	
Difference in Objective Response Rate			XX%
95% CI for Difference in Objective Response Rate			(XX% - XX%)
P-value			XXX

summarize objective response rates

```
/* Best Objective Response Calculation */
data adrs;
set adrs;
if aval in (1,2) then objrespfl = 0;
else if aval ne . then objrespfl = 1;
run;
    /* Best Overall Response */
proc freq data = adrs;
by trt01pn;
tables objrespfl/out = rs0(drop=percent);
run;
    /* 95% CI for ORR based on binomial test (Clopper-Pearson CI) */
proc freq data = adrs;
```

```
by trt01pn;
table objrespfl/binomial(exact);
ods output binomialcls = rs1;
run;
    /* Difference in Response */
proc freq data = adrs;
tables trt01pn*objrespfl/riskdiff;
/* The option riskdiff computes the difference based on standard normal approximation */
ods output RiskDiffCol1 = rs2;
run;
    /* p-value based on CMH test */
proc freq data = adrs;
tables trt01pn*objrespfl/cmh;
ods output cmh=cmh (where=(AltHypothesis='Row Mean Scores Differ'));
run;
```

This SAS code performs the following tasks:

1. Calculates the best objective response and creates a flag variable (`objrespfl`).

2. Tabulates the best overall response by treatment arm.

3. Computes the 95% confidence intervals for the objective response rate using the binomial test (Clopper-Pearson CI).

4. Determines the difference in response rates between treatment arms.

5. Calculates the p-value based on the Cochran-Mantel-Haenszel (CMH) test for comparing response rates.

CHAPTER XXV

Analyses on Time to Event

Time-to-event analyses include the duration of overall survival, progression-free survival, and time to progression. Key points regarding these analyses are:

- Median durations are estimated using the 50th percentile of Kaplan-Meier (KM) estimates, along with associated confidence intervals.
- Treatment arms are compared using stratified or unstratified log-rank tests.

A p-value less than the pre-specified type I error rate (e.g., 0.05) indicates statistical significance, suggesting the drug prolongs the time to event (e.g., overall survival or time to progression).
- Hazard ratios, computed via Cox regression models, indicate the relative risk between treatment arms.

A hazard ratio less than 1 favors the experimental treatment arm.
- Careful consideration of reference groups is crucial.

For instance, setting `trt01pn = 1` for treatment and `trt01pn = 2` for placebo yields a different hazard ratio compared to the reverse setting.

Reviewing footnotes in mock-ups clarifies hazard ratio calculations.

The following code sample demonstrates setting variables and calculating hazard ratios:

```
/* Setting treatment and placebo */
data adrs;
set adrs;
if trt01pn = 1 then treatment = 1;
else if trt01pn = 2 then placebo = 1;
run;
    /* Cox regression for hazard ratio */
proc phreg data=adrs;
class treatment(ref='0');
model time*censor(1) = treatment;
strata stratum;
run;
```

	Drug A	Placebo	Treatment Comparison
Time to event			
Median (95%CI)	XX (XX,XX)	XX (XX,XX)	
P-value			XXX
Hazard Ratio (95%CI)			XX (XX,XX)

Duration of OS, duration of PFS, and time to progression

Median Survival Time and P-value:

```
    ods listing close;
ods output Quartiles=_quart(keep=trt01pn estimate lowerlimit upperlimit percent where=(percent eq 50))
HomTests=pval(keep=test probchisq where=(test='Log-Rank'));
proc lifetest data=adttee;
```

```
time aval*cnsr(1);
strata trt01pn;
run;
ods output close;
ods listing;
```

Hazard Ratio:

```
    ods listing close;
ods output parameterestimates=hzdata(keep=hazardratio hrlowercl hruppercl);
proc phreg data=adttee;
class trt01pn;
model aval*cnsr(1)=trt01pn/ties=discrete risklimit;
hazardratio trt01pn;
run;
ods output close;
```

CHAPTER XXVI

Nadir

-Nadir is defined as the minimum value of a particular biomarker, such as PSA, observed before or at the current assessment point.

In disease progression assessment, Nadir serves as a crucial reference, representing the lowest or most favorable value before the current evaluation.

- For instance, in analyzing PSA progression, Nadir denotes the minimum PSA level recorded prior to the current measurement, determined separately for each assessment point.

- PSA progression is typically identified as a PSA value exceeding the Nadir by a specified percentage, often 30%, and confirmed by a subsequent reading surpassing the Nadir threshold.

- Consequently, the event date for progression is established as the initial occurrence of confirmed PSA progression.

- When developing SAS programs for such analyses, leveraging the RETAIN statement and lag function proves effective for comparing values across multiple records.

- Below is an example SAS code demonstrating how to derive Nadir and create a dataset for time-to-event analysis.

```
    data psa;
format RANDDT mmddyy10.;
input USUBJID $ 1-3 AVISIT $ 5-12 AVISITN LBDTC $ 17-26 PSA;
retain BASE;
RANDDT='15SEP2018'd;
if avisitn=0 then base=psa;
if avisitn > 0 then postbfl=1; else postbfl=0;
datalines;
101 BASELINE 0 2018-09-21 23.31
101 WEEK 1 1 2018-09-27 44.65
101 WEEK 4 2 2018-10-09 21.78
101 WEEK 9 3 2018-11-13 13.96
101 WEEK 15 4 2018-12-27 31.34
101 WEEK 19 5 2019-01-23 26.51
;
run;
    proc sort data=psa;
by usubjid postbfl;
run;
    ** Deriving NADIR **;
data psa_nadir;
set psa;
by usubjid postbfl;
retain NADIR;
if first.usubjid then nadir=.;
lagpsa=lag(psa);
if postbfl then do;
if first.postbfl then nadir=base;
else nadir=min(nadir,lagpsa);
end;
if postbfl and psa ne . then do;
```

```
chg_nadir=psa-nadir;
if nadir ne 0 then pchg_nadir=chg_nadir/nadir*100;
end;
run;
    ** Deriving variables ge30pct_nadir and nextge30pct_nadir **;
data psa_ge30pct;
set psa_nadir;
retain nextge30pct_nadir;
by usubjid avisitn;
ge30pct_nadir=(pchg_nadir>=30);
nextge30pct_nadir=lag(ge30pct_nadir);
run;
    ** Deriving time-to-event analysis dataset **;
data adpsa;
format adt date9.;
set psa_ge30pct;
if ge30pct_nadir and nextge30pct_nadir;
ADT=input(lbdtc,yymmdd10.);
AVAL=(ADT-RANDDT+1)/30.4375;
EVNTDESC='PSA Progression';
CNSR = 0;
keep usubjid lbdtc adt randdt aval evntdesc cnsr;
run;
```

USUBJID	RANDDT	AVISIT	AVISITN	LBDTC	PSA	BASE	postbfl	NADIR	lagpsa	chg_nadir	pchg_nadir	ge30pct_nadir	nextge30pct_nadir
101	09/15/2018	BASELINE	0	2018-09-21	23.31	23.31	0					0	
101	09/15/2018	WEEK 1	1	018-09-27	44.65	23.31	1	23.31	23.31	21.34	91.549	1	0
101	09/15/2018	WEEK 4	2	018-10-09	21.78	23.31	1	23.31	44.65	-1.53	-6.564	0	1
101	09/15/2018	WEEK 9	3	018-11-13	13.96	23.31	1	21.78	21.78	-7.82	-35.904	0	0
101	09/15/2018	WEEK 15	4	018-12-27	31.34	23.31	1	13.96	13.96	17.38	124.499	1	0
101	09/15/2018	WEEK 19	5	019-01-23	26.51	23.31	1	13.96	31.34	12.55	89.900	1	1

Dataset for Demonstrating the Derivation of NADIR

USUBJID	LBDTC	ADT	RANDDT	AVAL	EVNTDESC	CNSR
101	2019-01-23	23JAN2019	09/15/2018	4.30390	PSA Progression	0

time-to-event analysis dataset

CHAPTER XXVII

Analyses on Follow-Up Time

To determine the duration of follow-up between two treatment groups, the median follow-up time can be estimated using the Reverse Kaplan-Meier method, as explained earlier.

	Drug A	Placebo
Follow-up Time Based on Reverse Kaplan-Meier Estimates		
n	XXX	XXX
25th Percentile	XXX	XXX
Median	XXX	XXX
75th Percentile	XXX	XXX

Mock-up Table for Follow-up Time

```
    /* Calculate total number */
proc means data=adeff nway noprint;
var aval;
class trt01pn;
output out=tot n=n;
run;
    proc sort data=tot;
by trt01pn;
run;
    proc transpose data=tot
out=tran_tot(drop=_label_
rename=(_name_=name _1=drug_A _2=placebo));
id trt01pn;
var n;
run;
    /* Calculate the percentile */
%macro reverse_km(num=, dsout=);
ods listing close;
ods output Lifetest.Stratum&num..TimeSummary.Quartiles = &dsout.;
proc lifetest data=adeff;
time aval*cnsr(0);
```

Reversing "events" and "censored" to estimate median follow-up time

```
strata trt01pn;
run;
ods output close;
ods listing;
proc sort data=&dsout.;
by percent;
run;
%mend;
```

```
    %reverse_km(num=1, dsout=trt1);
%reverse_km(num=2, dsout=trt2);
data percent;
    merge trt1(keep=percent estimate rename=(estimate = drug_A)) trt2(keep=percent estimate rename=(estimate
= placebo)); by percent; rename percent=col1; run;
```

CHAPTER XXVIII

Kaplan–Meier Curve

- Kaplan-Meier (KM) curves serve as effective tools for comparing survival experiences between two treatment groups, visually displaying the proportion of patients who remain event-free over time.

They are non-parametric estimators of the survival function, depicting the probability of survival beyond a certain time point.

- Alongside KM curves, a summary table of patients at-risk is typically presented, representing individuals who have not yet experienced the event of interest (e.g., disease progression) or have been censored. This table provides insight into the number of patients contributing to each time point.

- The SAS command "ATRISK" is commonly used to incorporate the number of individuals still at risk into the analysis, allowing for a comprehensive understanding of the patient population's survival status at each time point.

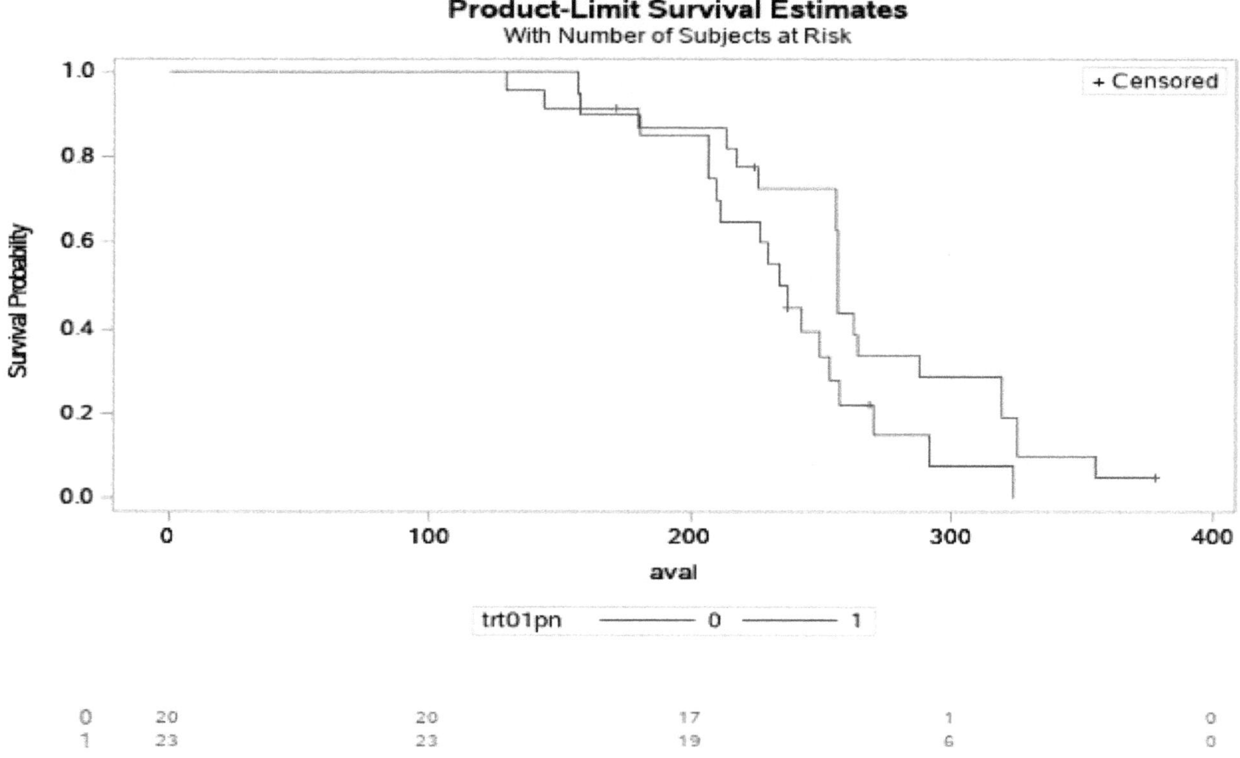


```
    ods graphics on;
ods output ProductlimitEstimates = _ple
Quartiles = _quart
CensoredSummary = _cs
Survivalplot = _splot
homtests = pval;
    proc lifetest data=adttee method=km
plots=(survival(atrisk (outside(0.15))) LS);
time aval*cnsr(1);
strata trt01pn;
```

run;

    ods output close;

ods graphics off;

    Note: It's important to carefully review the shape of KM curves and the labeling in the legend when validating KM curves. For example, if we have a hazard ratio relative to placebo that is less than 1, then the KM curve of the treatment arm would expect to be above the KM curve of the placebo arm. This is a critical aspect to keep in mind when validating the figures.

CHAPTER XXIX

Exam the Assumption of Proportional Hazards

- The Cox regression model relies on the assumption of proportional hazards, where the hazard ratio for any individual remains constant over time.
- This assumption is visually validated by observing parallel lines in the graph of -log(S(t)) versus time or log(-log(S(t))) versus log(time).
- To generate this graph in SAS, we include the option PLOTS=(LS, LLS) in the PROC LIFETEST statement, as illustrated in the provided code snippet.

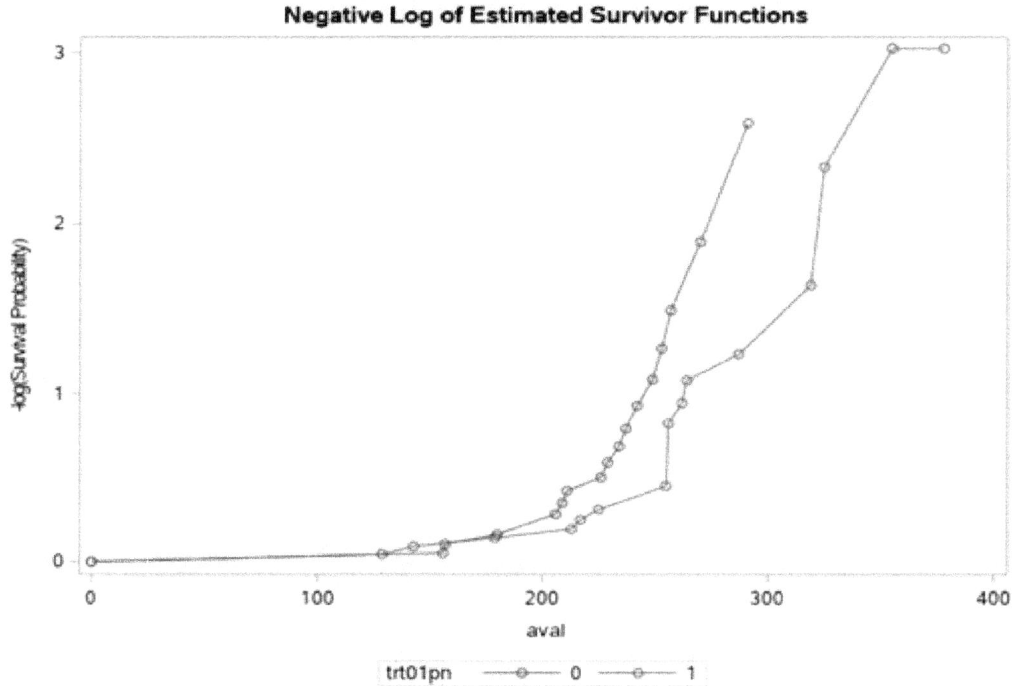

none of the curves is a straight line, which indicates the hazards are not constant, but rather, increasing with time.

CHAPTER XXX

Waterfall Plot

- Waterfall plots are common in oncology studies, aiding in visualizing changes in parameters like tumor size or PSA levels for each subject.
- Each vertical bar on the graph corresponds to an individual subject, offering a concise representation of their data.
- The x-axis of the plot ranges from the poorest to the best values, allowing for easy comparison.
- Analysis datasets used to create waterfall plots typically consist of one subject per record, organized based on the parameter of interest.
- Figure 8 exemplifies a waterfall plot illustrating the maximum percentage reduction in PSA from baseline.

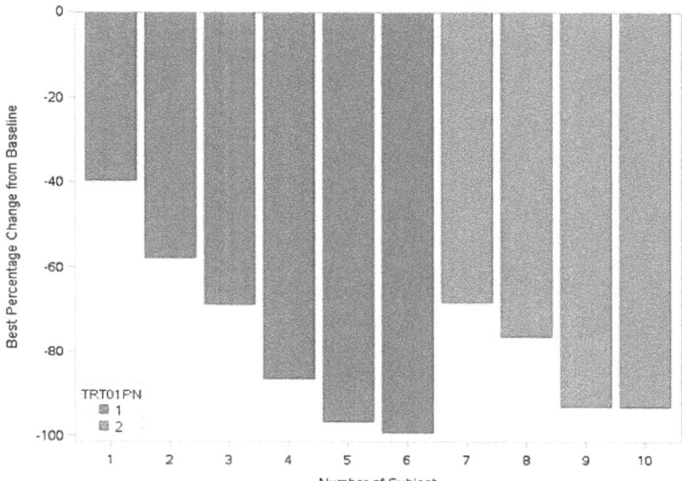

SUBJID	PCHG	TRT01PN
1001	-86.56	1
1001	-86.56	1
1001	-83.21	1
1002	-95.23	1
1002	-93.28	1
1002	-94.59	1
1002	-96.74	1
1003	-10.34	1
1003	-39.57	1
1004	-93.31	2
1004	-91.73	2
1005	-68.67	1
1006	-57.72	1
1006	-52.73	1
1007	-99.23	1
1007	-98.54	1
1007	-95.35	1
1008	-76.29	2
1009	-68.14	2
1010	-93.21	2
1010	-92.57	2

ADPSA

```
    /* Preparing dataset */
proc sort data=adpsa;
by usubjid pchg;
where PCHG ne . ;
run;
    data adpsa;
set adpsa;
by subjid pchg;
if first.usubjid;
proc sort;
by trt01pn descending pchg;
run;
    data bestpsa_;
set adpsa;
n = _n_;
run;
    /* Creating graph */
ods listing close;
```

```
ods rtf style=basic file='&path/psa_waterfall.rtf' style=styles.statistical;
ods graphics on;
    proc sgplot data=bestpsa_;
vbar n / response=pchg group=trt01pn;
xaxis label='Number of Subject' fitpolicy=thin;
yaxis label='Best Percentage Change from Baseline';
keylegend / location=inside down=2;
run;
    ods graphics off;
ods tagsets.rtf close;
ods listing;
```

CHAPTER XXXI

Bar Chart

- Bar charts provide an effective visualization method for categorical data, offering a concise summary of frequencies and percentages within each category.
- For instance, the best overall response can be effectively summarized using a bar chart, allowing for a quick comparison of response frequencies across different categories.
- Supplementary information such as objective response rate statistics can be included in the chart legend, enhancing the understanding of the data presented.
- Utilizing bar charts in data visualization enables stakeholders to grasp key insights and trends in categorical data at a glance, aiding decision-making processes.

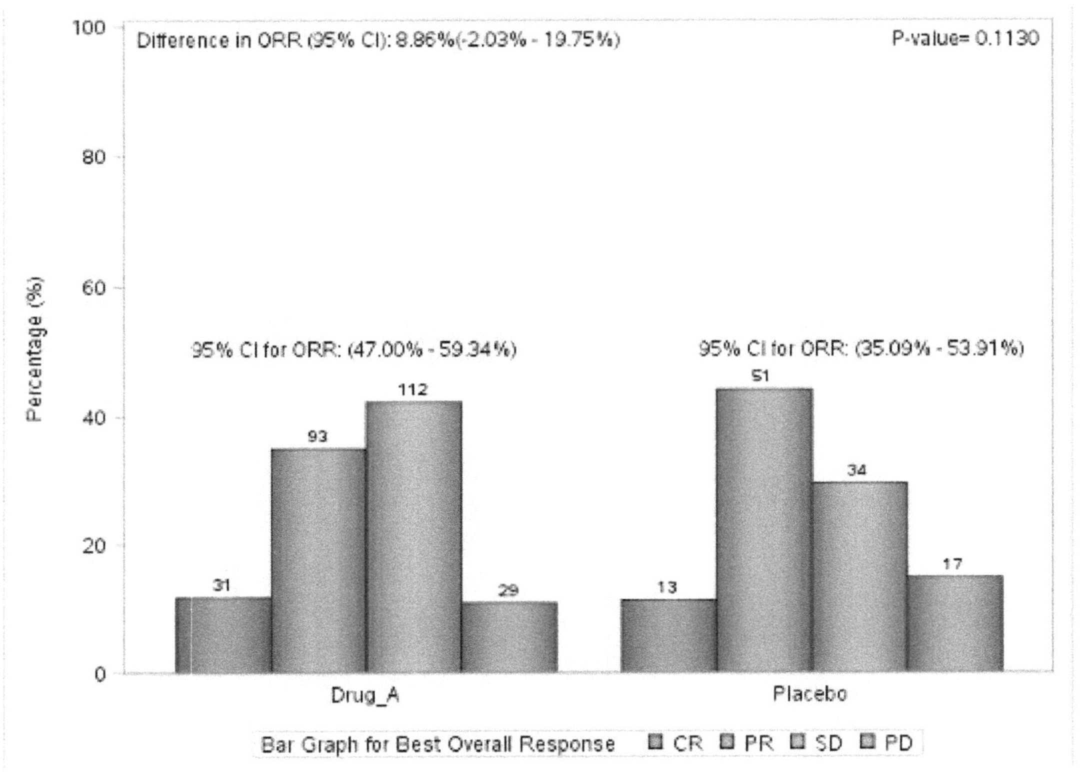

summarizing the best overall response for Drug vs. Placebo

```
    data adpsa;
input trt01p $10. aval $ count;
datalines;
Drug_A CR 31
Drug_A PR 93
Drug_A SD 112
Drug_A PD 29
Placebo CR 13
Placebo PR 51
Placebo SD 34
```

```
Placebo PD 17
;
run;
    proc sql noprint;
select sum(count) into: trt1 from adpsa where trt01p='Drug_A';
select sum(count) into: trt2 from adpsa where trt01p='Placebo';
quit;
    %let trt1=&trt1;
%let trt2=&trt2;
    %put trt1=&trt1, trt2=&trt2;
    data cat;
set adpsa;
if trt01p='Drug_A' then percent = round(count/&trt1*100, .1);
if trt01p='Placebo' then percent = round(count/&trt2*100, .1);
run;
    proc sgplot data=cat;
vbar trt01p/group=aval response=percent groupdisplay=cluster grouporder=data dataskin=pressed attrid=aval
datalabel=count;
xaxis display=(nolabel noticks);
yaxis values=(0 to 100 by 20) label='Percentage (%)';
keylegend/title='Best Overall Response' title = 'Bar Graph for Best Overall Response';
inset "P-value= &pval"/position=topright;
inset "Difference in ORR (95% CI): &df" /position=topleft;
inset " 95% CI for ORR: &ORR1 " /position=left;
inset "95% CI for ORR: &ORR2 " /position=right;
run;
```

- The dataset "adpsa" is created to store information on treatment types, response categories, and their respective counts.

- SQL queries are utilized to calculate the total counts for each treatment group, stored in macro variables "trt1" and "trt2" for "Drug_A" and "Placebo" respectively.

- The "cat" dataset is generated to calculate the percentage distribution of response categories within each treatment group.

- A bar chart is created using the "sgplot" procedure to visualize the distribution of response categories for each treatment group.

- Vertical bars represent each response category, clustered by treatment type.

- Data labels on the bars display the count of occurrences for each response category.

- The x-axis displays the treatment types, while the y-axis represents the percentage distribution of response categories.

- Key legend titles the graph as "Best Overall Response," providing clarity on the represented data.

- Statistical information such as p-value, difference in objective response rate (ORR), and their corresponding confidence intervals (95% CI) are displayed as insets in the graph for further analysis.

CHAPTER XXXII

Mean Standard Error Plot

1. **Plot Representation**: The mean change over time is often depicted with standard error bars in a graph.

2. **Axes Interpretation**: The X-axis typically represents time, while the Y-axis represents the overall mean.

3. **Data Representation**: Each point on the plot denotes the overall mean value at a particular time point, accompanied by an error bar.

4. **Error Bar Calculation**: The error bars are computed by adding one standard error above the point and subtracting one standard error below the point.

5. **Visual Insight**: Mean plots offer insights into the trend of mean values over time, while error bars provide information about the data distribution.

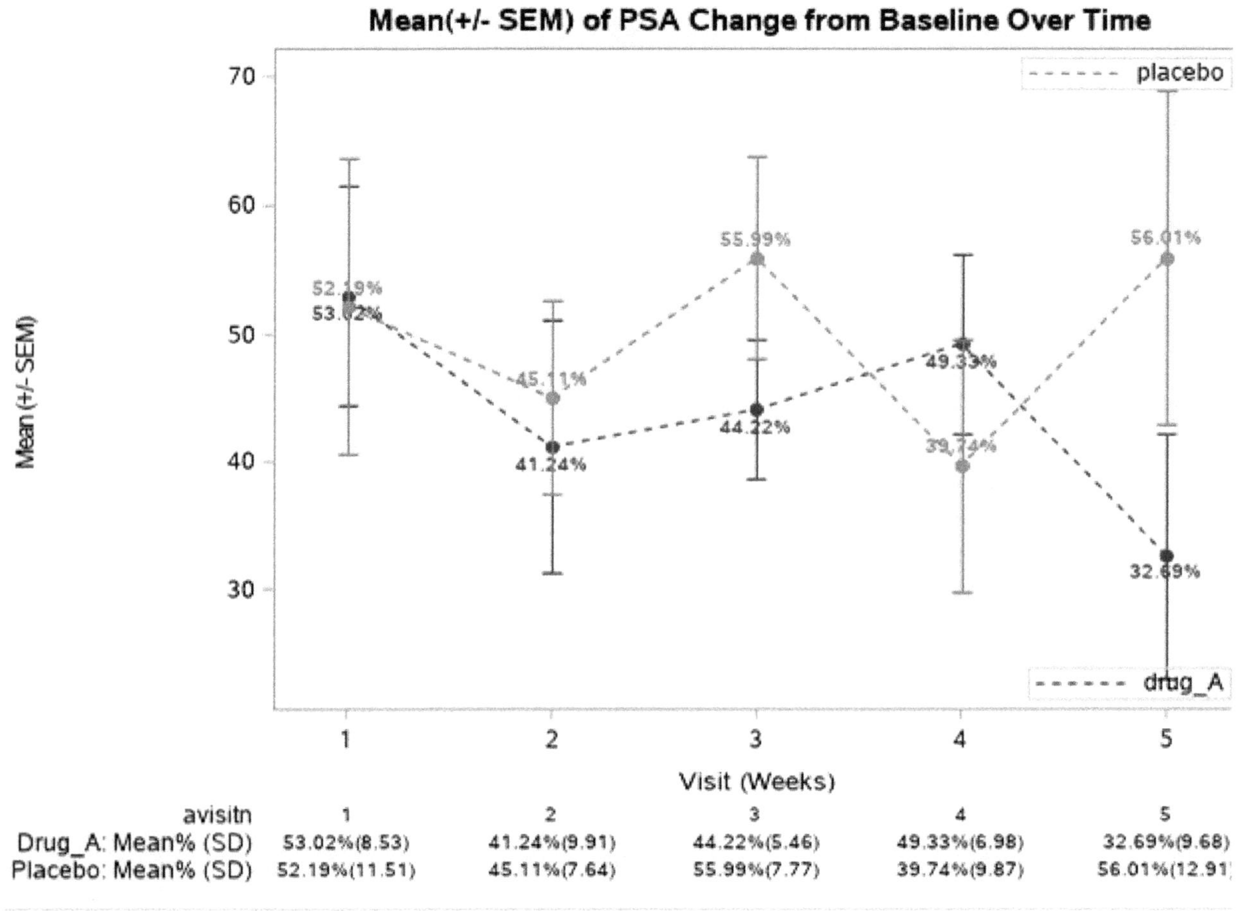

avisitn	1	2	3	4	5
Drug_A: Mean% (SD)	53.02%(8.53)	41.24%(9.91)	44.22%(5.46)	49.33%(6.98)	32.69%(9.68)
Placebo: Mean% (SD)	52.19%(11.51)	45.11%(7.64)	55.99%(7.77)	39.74%(9.87)	56.01%(12.91)

1. **Data Generation**: Sample data representing PSA change for two treatment groups, 'drug_A' and 'placebo', over multiple visits is created.

2. **Mean Calculation**: A macro named 'meanout' is defined to calculate the mean and standard error for each treatment group at each visit.

3. **Macro Execution**: The 'meanout' macro is executed twice, once for each treatment group, and the results are stored in separate datasets ('trt1' and 'trt2').

4. **Data Merging**: The mean and standard error datasets for both treatment groups are merged based on the visit

number.

5. **Data Processing**: Additional calculations are performed to format mean values and standard errors for display purposes.

6. **Graph Plotting**: Using PROC SGPLOT, a line plot with error bars is created to visualize the mean PSA change over time for both treatment groups.

7. **Data Labeling**: Data labels indicating mean values are positioned on the lines, and error bars represent the standard error of the mean.

8. **Axis Labeling**: X-axis represents visit weeks, while the Y-axis represents the mean PSA change from baseline along with standard error.

9. **Graph Customization**: Various customization options are applied, including line color, marker style, error bar appearance, and axis titles.

10. **Legend**: A legend is included to differentiate between the two treatment groups.

11. **Graph Title**: A descriptive title is added to summarize the graph's content.

CHAPTER XXXIII

Spaghetti Plot

1. **Graph Type Explanation**: A spaghetti plot resembles a tangled plate of spaghetti, illustrating individual subject trends over multiple visits.
2. **Data Representation**: Each line on the plot represents the change in a specific parameter (e.g., PSA levels) for an individual patient across various visits.
3. **Procedure Used**: The SGPLOT procedure is employed to generate the spaghetti plot using the provided dummy data.
4. **Code Example**: The following code snippet demonstrates how to create a PSA spaghetti plot.

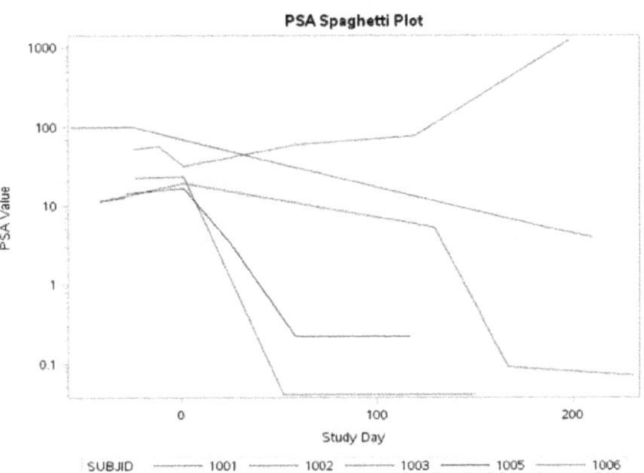


```
    /* Example code for generating a PSA spaghetti plot */
/* Dummy data */
data psa_data;
input subject_id visit psa_level;
datalines;
101 1 4.5
101 2 5.1
101 3 4.9
102 1 3.8
102 2 4.2
102 3 4.0
103 1 5.2
103 2 6.1
103 3 5.9
;
run;
    /* Generating spaghetti plot */
proc sgplot data=psa_data;
series x=visit y=psa_level / group=subject_id lineattrs=(thickness=1);
xaxis label='Visit';
yaxis label='PSA Level';
title 'PSA Spaghetti Plot';
```

run;

5. **Data Handling**: The dummy data includes columns for subject ID, visit number, and PSA level.

6. **Plot Construction**: The PROC SGPLOT procedure is utilized to construct the spaghetti plot, with each line representing a subject's PSA level changes across visits.

7. **Customization**: Axes are labeled appropriately, and a title is added to the plot for clarity.

8. **Line Attributes**: Line thickness is set to ensure clear visualization of individual subject trends.

CHAPTER XXXIV

Forest Plot

1. **Visualization Purpose**: Forest plots are commonly utilized to display statistical results for subgroup analysis within randomized controlled trials (RCTs).
2. **Structural Components**: A forest plot typically comprises three main elements:
- Subgroup labels,
- Plots representing hazard ratios with associated confidence intervals, and
- Relevant summary statistics.
3. **Statistics Panel**: Summary statistics, such as the number of patients and events for treatment versus placebo, hazard ratios with corresponding confidence intervals, and p-values, are presented in the statistics panel within the plot.
4. **Representation of Treatment Effects**: In the plot panel of a forest plot, dots symbolize treatment effects, often measured by hazard ratios. These dots or diamonds are accompanied by confidence intervals, indicating the variation in the hazard ratio estimates.
5. **Interpretation of Hazard Ratios**: The vertical line at x=1.0 represents a hazard ratio of 1, suggesting no treatment effect. If placebo serves as the reference group, a hazard ratio less than 1 favors treatment over placebo, and the dot appears on the left side of the plot panel.
6. **Validation Considerations**: When validating forest plots, it's crucial to cross-reference them with summary tables to ensure alignment between the statistics presented in the plot and those in the tables.

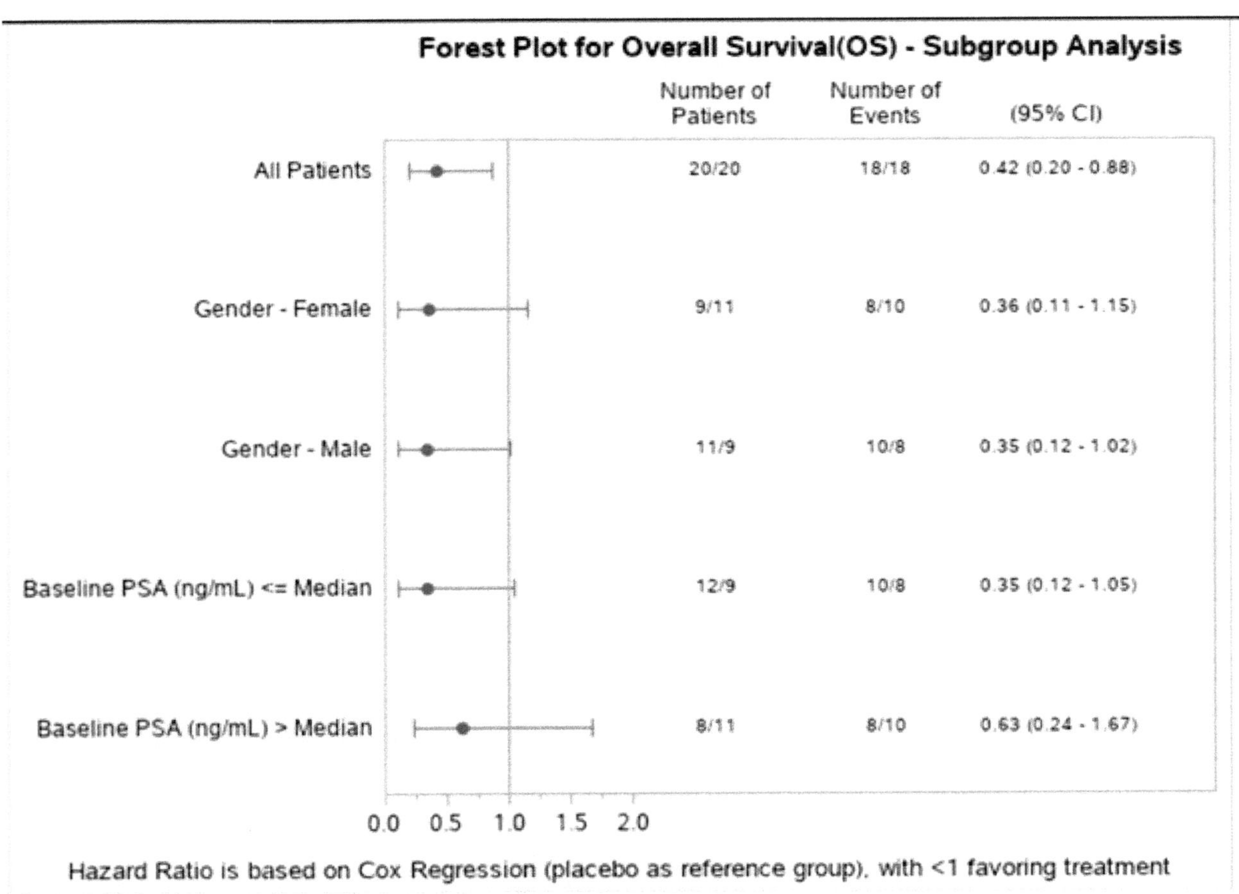

CHAPTER XXXV

What are categorical data and continuous data in statistics, and could you provide examples of each?

<u>Categorical data</u> consists of values that represent categories or groups.

These values cannot be meaningfully ordered or measured in a numerical sense.

Examples of categorical data include gender (male/female), eye color (blue, brown, green), and types of fruits (apple, banana, orange).

<u>Continuous data</u>, on the other hand, consists of numerical values that can be measured and potentially take any value within a given range. These values can be ordered and can take on any value within a range. Examples of continuous data include height, weight, temperature, and time.

In summary:

- Categorical data represents categories or groups and cannot be ordered or measured numerically.
- Continuous data consists of numerical values that can take on any value within a range and can be ordered.

CHAPTER XXXVI

Analyzing categorical data

In SAS, several procedures are commonly used for analyzing categorical data. Here are some examples:

1. **PROC FREQ**: This procedure is used to analyze the frequency distribution of categorical variables and perform chi-square tests for association between categorical variables.

Example:

```
proc freq data=mydata;
tables category_var;
run;
```

2. **PROC TABULATE**: This procedure is used to create customized tables of summary statistics for categorical variables.

Example:

```
proc tabulate data=mydata;
class category_var;
table category_var, n pctn;
run;
```

3. **PROC GENMOD**: This procedure is used for generalized linear modeling, including logistic regression for analyzing binary categorical outcomes.

Example:

```
proc genmod data=mydata;
model binary_outcome = predictor_var / dist=binomial link=logit;
run;
```

4. **PROC LOGISTIC**: This procedure is specifically designed for logistic regression analysis, which is commonly used for binary outcome variables.

Example:

```
proc logistic data=mydata;
model binary_outcome = predictor_var;
run;
```

These are just a few examples of SAS procedures commonly used for analyzing categorical data. Each procedure offers various options for customizing the analysis based on the specific research question and data characteristics.

CHAPTER XXXVII

CMH, MH, EXACT, and BINOMIAL options in the SAS PROC FREQ procedure

In the SAS `PROC FREQ` procedure, the options CMH, MH, EXACT, and BINOMIAL are used for different purposes:

1. **CMH (Cochran-Mantel-Haenszel)**: This option is used to perform the Cochran-Mantel-Haenszel test, which is a statistical test for comparing the association between two categorical variables while controlling for the effects of one or more additional categorical variables (strata).

Example:

```
proc freq data=mydata;
tables var1*var2 / cmh;
run;
```

2. **MH (Mantel-Haenszel)**: Similar to CMH, this option also performs the Mantel-Haenszel test for comparing the association between two categorical variables while controlling for the effects of one or more additional categorical variables (strata).

Example:

```
proc freq data=mydata;
tables var1*var2 / mh;
run;
```

3. **EXACT**: This option is used to request exact tests for comparing categorical variables. It calculates exact p-values instead of relying on asymptotic approximations.

Example:

```
proc freq data=mydata;
tables var1*var2 / exact;
run;
```

4. **BINOMIAL**: This option is used to compute exact confidence intervals for proportions or risk differences when performing comparisons between groups.

Example:

```
proc freq data=mydata;
tables var1*var2 / binomial;
run;
```

These options provide flexibility in conducting various statistical tests and computations in `PROC FREQ`, depending on the nature of the data and the research questions.

CHAPTER XXXVIII

What is `PROC CORR` in statistics and how is it used with an example?

`PROC CORR` is a procedure in SAS that calculates correlation coefficients and other measures of association between pairs of numeric variables. It provides several types of correlation measures, such as Pearson, Spearman, and Kendall, and also produces descriptive statistics like means and standard deviations.

Correlation measures the strength and direction of the linear relationship between two variables.

Example:

Suppose we have a dataset `exam_scores` containing the scores of students in Math and Science. We want to compute the correlation between these two subjects to understand if students who perform well in Math also perform well in Science.

```
/* Create sample data */
data exam_scores;
input StudentID MathScore ScienceScore;
datalines;
1 85 88
2 78 82
3 92 95
4 73 70
5 85 89
6 79 84
7 91 93
8 76 78
9 88 91
10 82 85
;
run;
    /* Compute correlation between MathScore and ScienceScore */
proc corr data=exam_scores;
var MathScore ScienceScore;
run;
```

Explanation:

- `data exam_scores;` creates a dataset named `exam_scores` with student IDs and their corresponding Math and Science scores.
- `input StudentID MathScore ScienceScore;` specifies the variables in the dataset.
- `datalines;` allows you to enter the data directly.
- `proc corr data=exam_scores;` invokes the `PROC CORR` procedure on the `exam_scores` dataset.
- `var MathScore ScienceScore;` specifies the variables for which the correlation is to be computed.

The output will display the Pearson correlation coefficient between MathScore and ScienceScore, along with the p-value to test the significance of the correlation. If the correlation coefficient is close to 1 or -1, it indicates a strong positive or negative linear relationship, respectively. A coefficient close to 0 indicates no linear relationship.

Understanding the Output

The output from `PROC CORR` will typically include:

- **Pearson Correlation Coefficient (r):** Measures the linear relationship between the two variables. Values range from -1 to 1.

- **P-value:** Tests the null hypothesis that the correlation coefficient is zero (no linear relationship). A small p-value (typically < 0.05) indicates strong evidence against the null hypothesis.
- **Descriptive Statistics:** Mean, standard deviation, minimum, and maximum values for each variable.

For example, if the Pearson correlation coefficient between MathScore and ScienceScore is 0.95 with a p-value of 0.0001, it indicates a very strong positive linear relationship between the scores in Math and Science, and the relationship is statistically significant.

CHAPTER XXXIX

What is `PROC REG` in statistics and how is it used with an example?

`PROC REG` is a procedure in SAS used for performing simple and multiple linear regression analyses. It estimates the parameters of the linear regression model and provides various statistics to assess the fit of the model. This procedure is used to understand the relationship between a dependent variable (response) and one or more independent variables (predictors).

Example:

Suppose we have a dataset `house_prices` containing information on the size of houses (in square feet) and their prices. We want to model the relationship between house size and price using linear regression.

```
/* Create sample data */
data house_prices;
input HouseID Size Price;
datalines;
1 1400 245000
2 1600 312000
3 1700 279000
4 1875 308000
5 1100 199000
6 1550 219000
7 2350 405000
8 2450 324000
9 1425 319000
10 1700 255000
;
run;
    /* Perform linear regression */
proc reg data=house_prices;
model Price = Size;
title "Linear Regression Analysis of House Prices";
run;
quit;
```

Explanation:

   - `data house_prices;` creates a dataset named `house_prices` with house IDs, their sizes, and prices.
- `input HouseID Size Price;` specifies the variables in the dataset.
- `datalines;` allows you to enter the data directly.
- `proc reg data=house_prices;` invokes the `PROC REG` procedure on the `house_prices` dataset.
- `model Price = Size;` specifies the regression model with `Price` as the dependent variable and `Size` as the independent variable.
- `title` adds a title to the output for clarity.
- `run;` and `quit;` execute the procedure and exit the `PROC REG` environment.

Understanding the Output

The output from `PROC REG` will typically include:

- **Parameter Estimates:** Estimates of the intercept and slope of the regression line. In this case, it will provide the coefficients for the intercept ($\beta 0$) and the slope ($\beta 1$) for the model `Price = β0 + β1*Size`.

- **R-Square:** The coefficient of determination, indicating the proportion of variance in the dependent variable explained by the independent variable(s). Values range from 0 to 1, with higher values indicating a better fit.
- **ANOVA Table:** Analysis of variance table, which includes the F-test for overall significance of the model.
- **Standard Errors:** The standard errors of the parameter estimates, which can be used to construct confidence intervals.
- **P-values:** P-values for testing the null hypothesis that each coefficient is zero. Small p-values (typically < 0.05) indicate that the corresponding predictor is significantly related to the dependent variable.

For example, if the output shows that the slope coefficient ($\beta 1$) for `Size` is 150 with a p-value of 0.0001, it indicates that for each additional square foot, the price of the house increases by \$150, and this relationship is statistically significant. The R-Square value will tell us how well the `Size` variable explains the variation in house prices.

Additional Options
`PROC REG` has many options and statements to enhance the analysis:
- **OUTPUT Statement:** To create a new dataset containing predicted values, residuals, and other diagnostics.
- **PLOT Statement:** To create diagnostic plots for checking the assumptions of the regression model.
- **SELECTION Statement:** To perform variable selection methods like stepwise regression.

Example with diagnostics and output dataset:

```
proc reg data=house_prices;
model Price = Size;
output out=reg_results p=predicted r=residuals;
plot student.*predicted.;
run;
quit;
```

This code generates predicted values and residuals, stores them in a new dataset `reg_results`, and creates a plot of studentized residuals against predicted values to check for any patterns.

CHAPTER XL

What is `PROC LOGISTIC` in statistics and how is it used with an example?

`PROC LOGISTIC` is a procedure in SAS used for performing logistic regression analysis. Logistic regression is used when the dependent variable is binary (i.e., it can take on only two possible outcomes, such as success/failure, yes/no, 1/0). This procedure models the probability of the binary outcome as a function of one or more predictor variables.

Example:

Suppose we have a dataset `patients` containing information on patients, including their age, blood pressure, cholesterol level, and whether or not they have heart disease (1 = Yes, 0 = No). We want to model the probability of having heart disease based on these predictors.

```
/* Create sample data */
data patients;
input PatientID Age BloodPressure Cholesterol HeartDisease;
datalines;
1 45 120 220 1
2 50 130 250 0
3 55 140 240 1
4 60 135 260 0
5 65 150 280 1
6 70 160 300 1
7 75 170 310 0
8 80 175 320 1
9 85 180 330 0
10 90 190 340 1
;
run;
    /* Perform logistic regression */
proc logistic data=patients;
model HeartDisease(event='1') = Age BloodPressure Cholesterol;
title "Logistic Regression Analysis of Heart Disease";
run;
quit;
```

Explanation:

- `data patients;` creates a dataset named `patients` with patient IDs, their age, blood pressure, cholesterol level, and heart disease status.
- `input PatientID Age BloodPressure Cholesterol HeartDisease;` specifies the variables in the dataset.
- `datalines;` allows you to enter the data directly.
- `proc logistic data=patients;` invokes the `PROC LOGISTIC` procedure on the `patients` dataset.
- `model HeartDisease(event='1') = Age BloodPressure Cholesterol;` specifies the logistic regression model with `HeartDisease` as the dependent variable and `Age`, `BloodPressure`, and `Cholesterol` as independent variables. The `event='1'` option specifies that we are modeling the probability of the event where `HeartDisease` equals 1 (i.e., the patient has heart disease).
- `title` adds a title to the output for clarity.
- `run;` and `quit;` execute the procedure and exit the `PROC LOGISTIC` environment.

Understanding the Output

The output from `PROC LOGISTIC` will typically include:

- **Parameter Estimates:** Estimates of the regression coefficients (β) for the model. These coefficients represent the log odds of the outcome for a one-unit change in the predictor variable.
- **Odds Ratios:** The exponentiated coefficients, which are easier to interpret. They represent the change in odds of the outcome for a one-unit change in the predictor variable.
- **Wald Chi-Square Tests:** Tests for the significance of each predictor in the model. Small p-values (typically < 0.05) indicate that the corresponding predictor is significantly related to the dependent variable.
- **Model Fit Statistics:** Measures such as -2 Log Likelihood, AIC, and SC, which help in assessing the fit of the model.
- **Classification Table:** A table that shows the observed and predicted frequencies of the outcome, which helps in evaluating the model's classification accuracy.

For example, if the output shows an odds ratio of 1.05 for `Age` with a p-value of 0.02, it indicates that each additional year of age is associated with a 5% increase in the odds of having heart disease, and this relationship is statistically significant.

Additional Options

`PROC LOGISTIC` has many options and statements to enhance the analysis:

- **CLASS Statement:** To specify categorical predictor variables.
- **OUTPUT Statement:** To create a new dataset containing predicted probabilities and other diagnostics.
- **SCORE Statement:** To apply the fitted model to a new dataset for prediction.

Example with a CLASS statement and output dataset:

```
proc logistic data=patients;
class Gender (ref='Male') / param=ref;
model HeartDisease(event='1') = Age BloodPressure Cholesterol Gender;
output out=predicted_probs p=pred;
title "Logistic Regression Analysis of Heart Disease with Gender";
run;
quit;
```

This code includes a categorical predictor `Gender`, specifies 'Male' as the reference category, and generates predicted probabilities stored in a new dataset `predicted_probs`.

CHAPTER XLI

What is `PROC NPAR1WAY` in statistics and how is it used with an example?

`PROC NPAR1WAY` is a procedure in SAS used for performing nonparametric one-way analysis of variance (ANOVA). Nonparametric tests are useful when the assumptions required for parametric tests (such as normality) are not met. `PROC NPAR1WAY` can be used to conduct tests like the Wilcoxon rank-sum test (also known as the Mann-Whitney U test), the Kruskal-Wallis test, and other rank-based tests.

Example:

Suppose we have a dataset `treatment_data` containing information on patient responses to three different treatments. We want to test if there are significant differences in responses among the three treatment groups using the Kruskal-Wallis test.

```
/* Create sample data */
data treatment_data;
input Treatment $ Response;
datalines;
A 5.2
A 3.8
A 6.1
A 4.5
B 7.2
B 5.5
B 6.8
B 7.0
C 8.1
C 9.3
C 7.6
C 8.7
;
run;
    /* Perform nonparametric one-way ANOVA using Kruskal-Wallis test */
proc npar1way data=treatment_data wilcoxon;
class Treatment;
var Response;
title "Nonparametric One-Way ANOVA Using Kruskal-Wallis Test";
run;
```

Explanation:

- `data treatment_data;` creates a dataset named `treatment_data` with variables `Treatment` and `Response`.
- `input Treatment $ Response;` specifies the variables and their types (`$` indicates a character variable).
- `datalines;` allows you to enter the data directly.
- `proc npar1way data=treatment_data wilcoxon;` invokes the `PROC NPAR1WAY` procedure on the `treatment_data` dataset and specifies the `wilcoxon` option to perform the Wilcoxon rank-sum test (which is used for the Kruskal-Wallis test when there are more than two groups).
- `class Treatment;` specifies the grouping variable.
- `var Response;` specifies the response variable.
- `title` adds a title to the output for clarity.

- `run;` executes the procedure.

Understanding the Output

The output from `PROC NPAR1WAY` typically includes:

- **Descriptive Statistics:** Basic statistics (like mean rank) for each treatment group.
- **Kruskal-Wallis Test Results:** The test statistic, degrees of freedom, and p-value. A significant p-value (typically < 0.05) indicates that there are significant differences in the median responses among the treatment groups.
- **Wilcoxon Scores (Rank Sums):** The sum of ranks for each treatment group, which is used in calculating the test statistic.

Additional Options

`PROC NPAR1WAY` has several options and statements to enhance the analysis:

- **EXACT Statement:** To request exact p-values for small sample sizes.
- **WILCOXON Statement:** To specify that the Wilcoxon rank-sum test (Mann-Whitney U test) should be performed.
- **SCORES Statement:** To specify different scoring methods (e.g., normal scores, Savage scores).
- **MULTTEST Statement:** To perform multiple comparison adjustments.

Example with the `EXACT` statement:

```
proc npar1way data=treatment_data wilcoxon;
class Treatment;
var Response;
exact;
title "Nonparametric One-Way ANOVA Using Kruskal-Wallis Test with Exact p-values";
run;
```

This code adds the `exact` statement to request exact p-values for the Kruskal-Wallis test, which is particularly useful when dealing with small sample sizes.

CHAPTER XLII

Data: Normally Distributed vs. Not Normally Distributed

Normally Distributed Data:
  1. **Definition:**
- Data that follows a normal distribution, also known as Gaussian distribution or bell curve.
- The distribution is symmetric about the mean, with most data points clustering around the mean.
  2. **Characteristics:**
- Mean, median, and mode are equal.
- The data has a bell-shaped curve.
- Approximately 68% of the data falls within one standard deviation of the mean.
- Approximately 95% of the data falls within two standard deviations of the mean.
- Approximately 99.7% of the data falls within three standard deviations of the mean.
  3. **Examples:**
- Heights of adult men.
- Scores on standardized tests (e.g., IQ scores).
- Measurement errors in scientific experiments.
  4. **Uses:**
- Many statistical tests and procedures assume normality (e.g., t-tests, ANOVA).
- Commonly used in control charts for quality control.
  Not Normally Distributed Data:
  1. **Definition:**
- Data that does not follow a normal distribution.
- The distribution can be skewed, have multiple peaks, or be uniformly distributed.
  2. **Characteristics:**
- Mean, median, and mode are not equal.
- The shape of the distribution can vary: it might be skewed left (negative skew) or skewed right (positive skew), bimodal (two peaks), or uniform (no peaks).
- The data does not fit the properties of a bell curve.
  3. **Examples:**
- Income distribution in most countries (typically right-skewed).
- Age at retirement (often skewed depending on the population).
- Number of goals scored in a soccer season (often right-skewed with many low values and few high values).
  4. **Uses:**
- Non-parametric statistical tests are used for analysis (e.g., Mann-Whitney U test, Kruskal-Wallis test).
- Transformation methods can be applied to normalize data for certain analyses (e.g., log transformation, square root transformation).
  ### Key Points to Remember:
  - **Normal Distribution:**
- Symmetric bell curve.
- Equally distributed around the mean.
- Suitable for parametric tests.
  - **Not Normal Distribution:**
- Asymmetric, may have skewness or multiple modes.
- Mean, median, and mode are not equal.
- Suitable for non-parametric tests or transformation techniques to achieve normality.

CHAPTER XLIII

PROC TTEST

The `PROC TTEST` procedure in SAS is used to perform t-tests, which are statistical tests used to compare the means of two groups. This procedure can be used for various types of t-tests, including:

- **One-sample t-test:** Tests whether the mean of a single sample differs from a known or hypothesized population mean.
- **Two-sample t-test (independent):** Tests whether the means of two independent samples are different.
- **Paired t-test:** Tests whether the means of two related groups (e.g., pre-test and post-test scores) are different.

Examples

One-Sample T-Test

This example tests whether the mean of a sample differs from a hypothesized value (e.g., 50).

```
data one_sample;
input score;
datalines;
49
52
48
51
47
50
52
46
50
;
run;
    proc ttest data=one_sample h0=50;
var score;
run;
```

Two-Sample T-Test (Independent)

This example compares the means of two independent groups (e.g., Treatment A and Treatment B).

```
data two_sample;
input group $ score;
datalines;
A 55
A 58
A 60
A 54
A 59
B 62
B 64
B 61
B 63
B 65
```

```
;
run;
    proc ttest data=two_sample;
class group;
var score;
run;
```

Paired T-Test

This example compares the means of two related groups (e.g., scores before and after treatment).

```
data paired_sample;
input pre_treatment post_treatment;
datalines;
56 60
57 62
58 61
59 64
55 63
;
run;
    proc ttest data=paired_sample;
paired pre_treatment*post_treatment;
run;
```

Key Points

1. **One-Sample T-Test:**
- Compares the sample mean to a known value.
- Syntax: `proc ttest data=dataset h0=value; var variable; run;`
    2. **Two-Sample T-Test (Independent):**
- Compares the means of two independent groups.
- Syntax: `proc ttest data=dataset; class group_variable; var variable; run;`
    3. **Paired T-Test:**
- Compares the means of two related groups.
- Syntax: `proc ttest data=dataset; paired variable1*variable2; run;`
    4. **Interpretation:**
- **p-value:** Indicates whether there is a statistically significant difference between the means.
- **Confidence Interval:** Provides a range of values within which the true mean difference is likely to fall.

Using `PROC TTEST`, you can perform these tests efficiently and interpret the results to understand whether the means of your groups are statistically different.

CHAPTER XLIV

PROC MIXED

The `PROC MIXED` procedure in SAS is used for fitting mixed linear models, which are models that contain both fixed and random effects. These models are particularly useful for handling data where observations are not independent, such as repeated measures, clustered data, or hierarchical data.

Key Features of `PROC MIXED`

1. **Fixed Effects:** These are the effects of interest that are consistent across the population (e.g., treatment effects).

2. **Random Effects:** These are the effects that vary randomly across the population (e.g., random intercepts for different subjects).

3. **Repeated Measures:** `PROC MIXED` can handle data where multiple measurements are taken from the same subject over time.

Examples

Example 1: Random Intercept Model

This example demonstrates how to fit a random intercept model, where each subject has a different intercept.

```sas
data example1;
input subject treatment $ y;
datalines;
1 A 10.5
1 A 12.3
1 A 11.8
2 B 13.2
2 B 14.0
2 B 13.5
3 A 9.8
3 A 10.5
3 A 11.2
;
run;

proc mixed data=example1 method=ml;
class subject treatment;
model y = treatment;
random intercept / subject=subject;
run;
```

Example 2: Repeated Measures Model

This example demonstrates how to fit a model for repeated measures data, where measurements are taken at multiple time points for each subject.

```sas
data example2;
input subject time y;
datalines;
1 1 10.5
1 2 12.3
```

```
1 3 11.8
2 1 13.2
2 2 14.0
2 3 13.5
3 1 9.8
3 2 10.5
3 3 11.2
;
run;
    proc mixed data=example2 method=ml;
class subject time;
model y = time;
repeated time / subject=subject type=cs;
run;
```

Key Points
1. **Model Statement:**
- Specifies the fixed effects in the model.
- Syntax: `model dependent_variable = fixed_effects;`
    2. **Random Statement:**
- Specifies the random effects in the model.
- Syntax: `random intercept / subject=subject_variable;`
    3. **Repeated Statement:**
- Specifies the structure of the repeated measures.
- Syntax: `repeated time_variable / subject=subject_variable type=covariance_structure;`
    4. **Covariance Structures:**
- Different covariance structures can be specified (e.g., compound symmetry (CS), autoregressive (AR(1))).
- Useful for modeling the correlation between repeated measures.
    5. **Method=ML or REML:**
- Specifies the estimation method. `ML` is Maximum Likelihood, and `REML` is Restricted Maximum Likelihood.
- `REML` is often preferred for variance component estimation.

Practical Tips
    - **Choosing Covariance Structures:** Start with simple structures like compound symmetry (CS) and move to more complex ones like autoregressive (AR(1)) if needed.
- **Model Comparison:** Use information criteria like AIC (Akaike Information Criterion) to compare models with different covariance structures.
- **Diagnostics:** Check residual plots to assess model fit and assumptions.

Using `PROC MIXED`, you can effectively analyze data with complex correlation structures and random effects, making it a powerful tool for mixed models.

CHAPTER XLV

PROC ANOVA

`PROC ANOVA` in SAS is used to perform analysis of variance (ANOVA), which helps to determine if there are statistically significant differences between the means of three or more independent groups. It is particularly useful for comparing the means of different levels of a categorical variable.

Key Features of `PROC ANOVA`

1. **One-Way ANOVA:** Compare means across different levels of a single factor.
2. **Two-Way ANOVA:** Compare means across two factors and their interaction.
3. **Factorial ANOVA:** More complex designs involving multiple factors.
4. **Post-Hoc Tests:** Conduct multiple comparisons to understand differences between group means.

Examples

Example 1: One-Way ANOVA

This example demonstrates a one-way ANOVA, comparing the means of a response variable across different groups.

```
data example1;
input group $ value;
datalines;
A 23
A 25
A 22
B 27
B 30
B 28
C 19
C 18
C 20
;
run;

proc anova data=example1;
class group;
model value = group;
means group / tukey;
run;
```

In this example:
- The `class` statement specifies the grouping variable.
- The `model` statement specifies the dependent variable and the independent variable (group).
- The `means` statement with `tukey` performs post-hoc Tukey's test to compare group means.

Example 2: Two-Way ANOVA

This example demonstrates a two-way ANOVA with interaction, comparing the means across two factors and their interaction.

```
data example2;
input factor1 $ factor2 $ value;
datalines;
A X 23
```

```
A X 25
A X 22
A Y 27
A Y 30
A Y 28
B X 19
B X 18
B X 20
B Y 21
B Y 23
B Y 22
;
run;
    proc anova data=example2;
class factor1 factor2;
model value = factor1 factor2 factor1*factor2;
means factor1 factor2 / tukey;
run;
```

In this example:
- The `class` statement specifies the grouping variables (`factor1` and `factor2`).
- The `model` statement specifies the dependent variable and the independent variables, including their interaction (`factor1*factor2`).
- The `means` statement performs post-hoc tests for both factors.

Key Points

1. **Model Statement:**
- Specifies the response variable and the factors.
- Syntax: `model dependent_variable = independent_variables;`

2. **Class Statement:**
- Specifies the categorical variables.
- Syntax: `class categorical_variable;`

3. **Means Statement:**
- Used for multiple comparison tests (e.g., Tukey, Bonferroni).
- Syntax: `means variable / option;`

4. **Post-Hoc Tests:**
- Conducted to determine which specific means are significantly different.
- Common options include `tukey`, `bonferroni`, and `scheffe`.

5. **Interaction Terms:**
- Important for understanding the combined effect of two or more factors.
- Specified in the model statement as `factor1*factor2`.

Practical Tips

- **Checking Assumptions:** Ensure that ANOVA assumptions (normality, homogeneity of variance) are met. Use diagnostic plots and tests to check these assumptions.
- **Post-Hoc Analysis:** Use post-hoc tests to understand where differences lie if the overall ANOVA is significant.
- **Model Fit:** Examine residual plots and other diagnostic measures to assess the fit of the model.
- **Interpreting Interactions:** Interaction terms can be complex to interpret. Plot interactions to better understand the effects.

`PROC ANOVA` is a powerful tool for comparing group means and understanding the effects of different factors on a response variable, making it essential for many statistical analyses in various fields.

CHAPTER XLVI

95% Confidence Interval (CI)

The 95% Confidence Interval (CI) is a range of values calculated from sample data that is believed to contain the true population parameter with a 95% probability. In other words, it provides a **range** within which we are reasonably confident that the true parameter lies.

Calculation of 95% CI

1. **Sample Mean and Standard Error:** Calculate the sample mean (X) and the standard error (SE) of the sample mean.

- Sample Mean (X): Average value of the sample data.
- Standard Error (SE): Measure of the variability of the sample mean. It is calculated as the sample standard deviation divided by the square root of the sample size.

SE = s\sqrt{n}}

2. **Critical Value (z-score or t-score):** Determine the critical value from the standard normal distribution (z-distribution) or the t-distribution based on the desired confidence level (95% CI).

3. **Confidence Interval Calculation:** Calculate the lower and upper bounds of the confidence interval using the formula:

Lower Bound = X - (Critical Value} \{SE})]
Upper Bound}= X + (Critical Value} \{SE})]

Example

Suppose we have a sample of 100 individuals and we want to estimate the mean height of the population with a 95% confidence interval. If the sample mean height is 170 cm and the sample standard deviation is 5 cm, the calculation would be as follows:

- Sample Mean (X) = 170 cm
- Standard Error (SE) = $\left(\frac{5}{\sqrt{100}} = 0.5 \right)$ cm (assuming the population standard deviation is unknown)
- Critical Value (z-score) for 95% CI ≈ 1.96 (from standard normal distribution)

Using the formula:

Lower Bound= 170 - (1.96 \times 0.5)
Upper Bound = 170 + (1.96 \times 0.5)

We can calculate the 95% CI for the mean height to be approximately (169.02 cm, 170.98 cm).

Interpretation

We are 95% confident that the true population mean height lies within the interval (169.02 cm, 170.98 cm). This means that if we were to repeat the sampling process and construct 95% confidence intervals for the population mean height, approximately 95 out of 100 intervals would contain the true population mean height.

CHAPTER XLVII

Null Hypothesis-Rejecting the Null Hypothesis

- **Null Hypothesis Definition**: It states that there is no difference between groups or no relationship between variables.
- **Denotation**: Often represented as H0 or HA in statistical analysis.
- **Alternative Hypothesis**: Denoted as HA, it asserts the existence of an effect or relationship.
- **Assumption**: Researchers initially assume the null hypothesis to be true until evidence suggests otherwise.
- **Rejecting the Null Hypothesis**: Requires sufficient evidence from the sample to conclude that the effect is statistically significant.
- **Analysts' Perspective**: Analysts typically aim to reject the null hypothesis as it leads to more significant findings about effects or relationships.
- **Analogy**: Similar to the presumption of innocence in a trial, where guilt must be proven beyond a reasonable doubt.
- **Evidence Collection**: Researchers must collect substantial evidence to overturn the presumption of no effect.
- **Null Hypothesis Examples**: Research questions are rephrased as statements indicating no effect or relationship.

	Null hypothesis is TRUE	Null hypothesis is FALSE
Reject null hypothesis	Type I Error (False positive)	Correct outcome! (True positive)
Fail to reject null hypothesis	Correct outcome! (True negative)	Type II Error (False negative)

- **Statistics and Hypothesis Testing**: Following data collection, statistical analysis and hypothesis testing are employed to assess the consistency of the sample data with the null hypothesis.
- **Significance Level and p-value**: The p-value, a crucial component of statistical results, measures the strength of evidence against the null hypothesis by comparing it to the significance level.
- **Rejecting the Null Hypothesis**: If the sample data provide significant evidence, the null hypothesis can be rejected based on hypothesis testing, typically by comparing the p-value to the significance level.

odds ratio

The **odds ratio** is a statistical measure used to quantify the strength and direction of the association between two categorical variables. It represents the ratio of the odds of an event occurring in one group to the odds of the same event occurring in another group.

- **Interpretation**: An odds ratio greater than 1 indicates that the event is more likely to occur in the first group compared to the second group. Conversely, an odds ratio less than 1 suggests that the event is less likely to occur in the first group compared to the second group.
- **Calculation**: The odds ratio is calculated as the ratio of the odds of the event (success) in one group to the odds of the event in the other group. It can be computed from a 2x2 contingency table.
- **Application**: The odds ratio is commonly used in medical research, epidemiology, and social sciences to assess the association between exposure and outcome variables, particularly in case-control studies and logistic regression analysis.
- **Example**: In a study comparing the odds of developing a disease between smokers and non-smokers, an odds ratio of 2 would indicate that smokers are twice as likely to develop the disease compared to non-smokers.

compute the odds ratio using SAS:

```
/* Example dataset */
data disease;
input group $ outcome $ count;
datalines;
Control Disease 100
Control NoDisease 300
Treatment Disease 150
Treatment NoDisease 250
;
run;
    /* Compute odds ratio using PROC FREQ */
proc freq data=disease;
tables group * outcome / chisq;
exact chisq; /* Exact test for small sample sizes */
run;
```

In this example, the dataset `disease` contains information about the occurrence of a disease in two groups (Control and Treatment). The variable `outcome` indicates whether the individual has the disease or not. We then use PROC FREQ to create a contingency table of the variables `group` and `outcome` and calculate the odds ratio using a chi-square test. The `exact chisq` option performs an exact test when the sample size is small.

CHAPTER XLIX

ODS (Output Delivery System)

ODS (Output Delivery System) tracing in SAS is a feature that allows you to trace the creation and modification of ODS objects. ODS objects are the elements generated by SAS procedures that are used to produce output in various formats such as HTML, PDF, RTF, and others.

Here's what ODS tracing enables you to do:

1. **Debugging**: ODS tracing helps you debug your SAS programs by providing detailed information about the creation and modification of ODS objects. If you encounter issues with your output, ODS tracing can help you identify where the problem lies.

2. **Understanding Output Generation**: It helps you understand how SAS generates output in different formats. By tracing the creation of ODS objects, you can see the sequence of steps involved in producing the output, which can be useful for troubleshooting or optimizing your code.

3. **Optimization**: ODS tracing can also be used for optimizing the performance of your SAS programs. By analyzing the output generation process, you can identify areas where improvements can be made to make the code more efficient.

In summary, ODS tracing is a useful tool for debugging, understanding, and optimizing SAS programs that generate output using ODS. It provides insight into the internal workings of SAS procedures and helps you diagnose and fix issues with your output.

Here's an example of how you can use ODS tracing in SAS:

```
/* Turn on ODS tracing */
ods trace on;
    /* Your SAS code generating output */
proc freq data=sashelp.class;
tables sex;
run;
    /* Turn off ODS tracing */
ods trace off;
```

In this example:

- `ods trace on;` activates the ODS tracing feature.

- The SAS code between `ods trace on;` and `ods trace off;` generates output using the `proc freq` procedure, which produces frequency tables for the `sex` variable in the `sashelp.class` dataset.

- `ods trace off;` deactivates the ODS tracing feature after the code generating output is complete.

When ODS tracing is enabled, SAS will provide detailed information about the creation and modification of ODS objects during the execution of the code between `ods trace on;` and `ods trace off;`. This information can help you understand how the output is generated and diagnose any issues that may arise.

CHAPTER L

What statistical methods are proposed for analyzing the primary efficacy variable, SPI24, in the study?

1. Primary Efficacy Variable: SPI24 (Summed Pain Intensity over 24 hours) based on the NPRS (Numeric Pain Rating Scale).
2. Analysis Method: ANCOVA (Analysis of Covariance).
3. Main Effects: Treatment and BMI (Body Mass Index).
4. Summary Statistics: Including sample size, mean, standard deviation, median, minimum, maximum, and percentiles.
5. ANCOVA Results: LS (Least Squares) means, standard error (SE), 95% confidence intervals, difference in LS means, and p-values.
6. Combining Multiple Imputation Replications: Utilizing SAS Proc MI ANALYZE for robust analysis.

The primary efficacy variable, SPI24 (Summed Pain Intensity over 24 hours), assessed using the NPRS (Numeric Pain Rating Scale), will be the focus of analysis. Here's how the analysis plan will proceed:

1. **ANCOVA Model:**
- The primary analysis will employ an ANCOVA model.
- Treatment will serve as the main effect, while BMI will be included as a covariate.

2. **Summary Statistics:**
- Summary statistics for SPI24 will include sample size, mean, standard deviation (SD), median, minimum, maximum, and 25th and 75th percentiles.

3. **ANCOVA Results:**
- Results from the ANCOVA model will feature least-square (LS) means, standard error (SE), 95% confidence intervals, difference in LS means, and p-values.

4. **Multiple Imputation:**
- Multiple imputation will be employed to address missing data.
- Twenty replications of imputation will be performed.
- SAS Proc MI ANALYZE will be utilized to combine results from the imputation replications for robust analysis.

By following this analysis plan, we aim to comprehensively evaluate the efficacy of treatment on SPI24 while considering the potential influence of BMI as a covariate. The inclusion of summary statistics and robust handling of missing data through multiple imputation enhances the reliability and validity of our findings.

CHAPTER LI

Proc MI ANALYZE

Proc MI ANALYZE is a SAS procedure used for analyzing results obtained from multiple imputation (MI) procedures. When missing data are present in a dataset, multiple imputation techniques are employed to estimate plausible values for the missing observations. After imputation, MI ANALYZE is used to combine the results from multiple imputed datasets into a single set of inferential statistics.

<u>Key features and uses of Proc MI ANALYZE include:</u>

1. **Combining Results**: It combines parameter estimates, standard errors, confidence intervals, and hypothesis tests obtained from each imputed dataset.

2. **Robust Analysis**: Provides robust estimates by accounting for uncertainty due to missing data.

3. **Statistical Inference**: Performs statistical tests and hypothesis testing based on the combined results.

4. **Compatibility**: Works seamlessly with other SAS procedures for analysis and reporting.

5. **Flexibility**: Allows customization of analysis settings and output options to suit specific research needs.

In summary, Proc MI ANALYZE is a powerful tool for analyzing multiply imputed data, providing valid and reliable statistical inference in the presence of missing data.

```
/* Assume that you have imputed multiple datasets named imp1, imp2, imp3, etc. */
    /* Combine the imputed datasets */
proc mianalyze data=imp1 imp2 imp3;
modeleffects Intercept Age BMI;
estimate 'Mean SPI24' SPI24 /print=mi;
estimate 'Difference in LS Means' Intercept 1 - Intercept 2 /print=mi;
estimate 'Effect of BMI' BMI /print=mi;
run;
```

In this example:

- `proc mianalyze` is used to specify the imputed datasets (`imp1`, `imp2`, `imp3`, etc.).

- `modeleffects` specifies the variables to include in the model (e.g., Intercept, Age, BMI).

- `estimate` statements are used to calculate estimates for specific effects (e.g., Mean SPI24, Difference in LS Means, Effect of BMI).

- The `/print=mi` option is used to display results for each imputed dataset.

This code will produce combined estimates and standard errors for the specified effects, accounting for the uncertainty introduced by missing data through multiple imputation.

CHAPTER LII

Implementing Laboratory Toxicity Grading for CTCAE Version 5

Introduction
- **Since 1999:** Laboratory toxicity grading is crucial for safety reporting, aligned with the FDA's acceptance of electronic data.
- **CTCAE Updates:** Staying current with various CTCAE versions is challenging.
- **CTCAE Version 5.0:** Introduces complexity with grading criteria based on baseline measurements.
- **Objective:** Present a practical method to:
- Derive toxicity grades in the SDTM LB domain using CTCAE v5.0.
- Report toxicity events in an OCCDS dataset, derived separately from the BDS dataset with laboratory findings.
    ### Evolution in Complexity
    - **Lab Parameter Example:** Alkaline Phosphatase (LBTESTCD = "ALP") in the SDTM LB domain.
- **Adverse Event:** Abnormally high ALP values result in "Alkaline phosphatase increased."
    CTCAE v4.03 Toxicity Grading
- **Table 1:** Ranges related to the upper limit of normal (ULN).
- Grade 1: > ULN to 2.5 x ULN
- Grade 2: > 2.5 x ULN to 5.0 x ULN
- Grade 3: > 5.0 x ULN to 20.0 x ULN
- Grade 4: > 20.0 x ULN
- Grade 5: Excluded, applies only when event results in death
    - **Implementation:** Simple comparison of LBSTRESN (result) with LBSTNRHI (ULN).
    CTCAE v5.0 Toxicity Grading
- **Table 2:** Adds complexity by considering baseline measurements.
- Grade 1:
- Normal baseline: > ULN to 2.5 x ULN
- Abnormal baseline: 1.5 x baseline to 2.5 x baseline
- Grade 2:
- Normal baseline: > 2.5 x ULN to 5.0 x ULN
- Abnormal baseline: > 2.5 x baseline to 5.0 x baseline
- Grade 3:
- Normal baseline: > 5.0 x ULN to 20.0 x ULN
- Abnormal baseline: > 5.0 x baseline to 20.0 x baseline
- Grade 4:
- Normal baseline: > 20.0 x ULN
- Abnormal baseline: > 20.0 x baseline
    - **Implementation:**
- Requires LBSTRESN (current result), LBSTNRHI (ULN), and baseline LBSTRESN.
- Determine if baseline LBSTRESN is > ULN:
- If ≤ ULN, derive grade based on ULN.
- If > ULN, derive grade by comparing current LBSTRESN to baseline LBSTRESN.
    - **Note:** Baseline records are graded according to ULN, as an abnormal baseline cannot be compared to itself.

Grade 1	Grade 2	Grade 3	Grade 4
>ULN - 2.5 x ULN	>2.5 - 5.0 x ULN	>5.0 - 20.0 x ULN	>20.0 x ULN

Alkaline Phosphatase Increased" grading criteria from CTCAE version 4.03

Grade 1	Grade 2	Grade 3	Grade 4
>ULN - 2.5 x ULN if baseline was normal; 2.0 - 2.5 x baseline if baseline was abnormal	>2.5 - 5.0 x ULN if baseline was normal; >2.5 - 5.0 x baseline if baseline was abnormal	>5.0 - 20.0 x ULN if baseline was normal; >5.0 - 20.0 x baseline if baseline was abnormal	>20.0 x ULN if baseline was normal; >20.0 x baseline if baseline was abnormal

Table 2: "Alkaline Phosphatase Increased" grading criteria from CTCAE version 5.0

Deriving the Toxicity Grades

- **Process Overview:**
- Utilize an Excel spreadsheet for complex grade criteria.
- Call these criteria programmatically using a SAS macro.
- Spreadsheet specifies macro variables applied via Call Execute routine.
  Macro Variables:
- `&R`: Result from the record being graded (LBSTRESN).
- `&ULN`: Upper limit of normal (LBSTNRHI).
- `&VISN`: Visit number of the record being graded (VISITNUM).
- `&B`: Baseline result (LBSTRESN of the baseline record).
- `&BVISN`: Baseline visit number (VISITNUM of the baseline record).
  - **Directionality:**
- For ALP, grading direction is met if the result is greater than the ULN or baseline.
- *Necessary for both increase and decrease-based lab tests.*
  SAS Macro Implementation:
- Define dataset name, CTCAE version, and macro parameters:
- `ds`: SDTM domain name (e.g., "LB").
- Default CTCAE version set to 5.0, can be manually set.
- `LLN`: Lower limit of normal (LBSTNRLO), needed for tests like "Hypocalcemia".
  Steps:
1. **Determine Baseline Values:**
- Baseline: Last populated record before initial treatment.
- Use `LBLOXFL` (last observation before treatment flag).
  2. **Import Grading Criteria:**
- Read associated CTCAE grading criteria Excel file using `proc import`.
- Store version 5.0 criteria in a SAS dataset named `ctcaev5`.
- Store version 4.03 criteria in a SAS dataset named `ctcaev4`.
- Select version based on macro call.

3. **Transpose Grading Criteria:**

- Transpose table for downstream use.
- Example for CTCAE version 5.0 "Alkaline phosphatase increased" event.
  Table 3: ALP Increased Criteria in Spreadsheet for CTCAE v5.0
- The criteria defined for ALP (from CTCAE v5.0) to be programmatically applied.
  Table 4: Transposed CTCAE v5.0 Grading Criteria for ALP
- Example of how the criteria appear once transposed in the SAS dataset.
  Note: The appendix contains the specific SAS macro code for performing these derivations.

TESTCD	TOX	DIR	G1	G2
ALP	Alkaline phosphatase increased	(&R > &ULN OR &R > &B)	((&BVISN = &VISN OR &B <= &ULN) AND &ULN < &R <= 2.5*&ULN) OR (&B > &ULN AND 2*&B <= &R <= 2.5*&B)	((&BVISN = &VISN OR &B <= &ULN) AND 2.5*&ULN < &R <= 5*&ULN) OR (&B > &ULN AND 2.5*&B < &R <= 5*&B)

Table 3: "Alkaline Phosphatase Increased" grading criteria from CTCAE version 5.0 written in SAS macro variables. (Note that Grades 3 and 4 are excluded from this display.)

TESTCD	TOX	DIR	GRADE	CODE
ALP	Alkaline phosphatase increased	(&R > &ULN OR &R > &B)	G1	((&BVISN = &VISN OR &B <= &ULN) AND &ULN < &R <= 2.5*&ULN) OR (&B > &ULN AND 2*&B <= &R <= 2.5*&B)
ALP	Alkaline phosphatase increased	(&R > &ULN OR &R > &B)	G2	((&BVISN = &VISN OR &B <= &ULN) AND &ULN < &R <= 2.5*&ULN) OR (&B > &ULN AND 2*&B <= &R <= 2.5*&B)
ALP	Alkaline phosphatase increased	(&R > &ULN OR &R > &B)	G3	((&BVISN = &VISN OR &B <= &ULN) AND 5*&ULN < &R <= 20*&ULN) OR (&B > &ULN AND 5*&B < &R <= 20*&B)
ALP	Alkaline phosphatase increased	(&R > &ULN OR &R > &B)	G4	((&BVISN = &VISN OR &B <= &ULN) AND &R > 20*&ULN) OR (&B > &ULN AND &R > 20*&B)

Table 4: SAS dataset containing transposed grating criteria for the "Alkaline phosphatase increased" event

Creatinine Toxicity Grading

Lab Parameter Example: Creatinine (LBTESTCD = "CREAT")

Adverse Event: "Creatinine increased"

CTCAE v4.03 Criteria (Table 9):

- Grade 1: > baseline value but not > ULN
- Grade 2: > 1.5 x ULN
- Grade 3: > 3.0 x ULN
- Grade 4: > 6.0 x ULN

CTCAE v5.0 Criteria (Table 10):

- Grade 1: > 1.5 x baseline

- Grade 2: > 1.5 x ULN
- Grade 3: > 3.0 x ULN
- Grade 4: > 6.0 x ULN
    Key Differences:
- **Grade 1:**
- **CTCAE v4.03:** Given if result > baseline but ≤ ULN.
- **CTCAE v5.0:** Given only if result > 1.5 x baseline.
    Example of Subtle Change Impact:
- **Subject 001:**
- **Baseline Measurement:** 0.6
- **Post-baseline Measurement:** 0.84
- **ULN:** 1.1
    Using CTCAE v4.03 (Table 11):
- Post-baseline measurement (0.84) > baseline (0.6) but ≤ ULN (1.1).
- **Result:** Grade 1
    Using CTCAE v5.0 (Table 12):
- Post-baseline measurement (0.84) < 1.5 x baseline (0.6 * 1.5 = 0.9).
- **Result:** No grade
    Conclusion:
- Transitioning from CTCAE v4.03 to v5.0 requires careful attention to changes in grading criteria.
- Subtle differences can lead to discrepancies in toxicity event reporting.
- In this example, a measurement graded as 1 in v4.03 is not graded in v5.0, avoiding unnecessary toxicity events.

TESTCD	TOX	DIR	G1	G2	G3	G4
CREAT	Creatinine increased	(&R > &ULN OR &R > &B)	(&ULN < &R <= 1.5*&ULN) OR (&B < &R <= 1.5*&B)	(1.5*&ULN < &R <= 3*&ULN) OR (1.5*&B < &R <= 3*&B)	(3*&ULN < &R <= 6*&ULN) OR (&R > 3*&B)	&R > 6*&ULN

Table 9: CTCAE Version 4.03 toxicity grading criteria for "Creatinine increased" written in terms of SAS macro variables

TESTCD	TOX	DIR	G1	G2	G3	G4
CREAT	Creatinine increased	(&R > &ULN OR &R > &B)	&ULN < &R <= 1.5*&ULN	(1.5*&ULN < &R <= 3*&ULN) OR (1.5*&B < &R <= 3*&B)	(3*&ULN < &R <= 6*&ULN) OR (&R > 3*&B)	&R > 6*&ULN

Table 10: CTCAE Version 5.0 toxicity grading criteria for "Creatinine increased" written in terms of SAS macro variables

USUBJID	LBTESTCD	LBSTRESN	LBSTNRHI	LBLOBXFL	VISITNUM	VISIT	LBTOX	LBTOXGR
001	CREAT	0.6	1.1	Y	2	Day 1		
001	CREAT	0.84	1.1		3	Day 2	Creatinine increased	1

Table 11: Sample "Creatinine increased" derived using CTCAE version 4.03 criteria

USUBJID	LBTESTCD	LBSTRESN	LBSTNRHI	LBLOBXFL	VISITNUM	VISIT	LBTOX	LBTOXGR
001	CREAT	0.6	1.1	Y	2	Day 1		
001	CREAT	0.84	1.1		3	Day 2		

Table 12: Sample "Creatinine increased" derived using CTCAE version 5.0 criteria

CHAPTER LIII

Bi-directional Toxicity Grade Shift Tables

Creating a lab shift table that handles **bi-directional grading involves** comparing lab results at baseline and post-baseline to determine shifts in toxicity grades.

Toxicity Grade Variables for Calcium, Albumin, and Alanine Aminotransferase

Case 1: Bi-directional Toxicity Grade

Row	PARAMCD	WAYSHIFT	AVISIT	SDTM LB LBTOX	SDTM LB LBTOXGR	ATOXDIR	ATOXGR	ATOXGRL	ATOXGRH
1	CA	HIGHLOW	Visit 1	NORMAL	0		Grade 0	Grade 0	Grade 0
2	CA	HIGHLOW	Visit 2	HIGH 1	1	H	Grade 1	Grade 0	Grade 1
3	CA	HIGHLOW	Visit 3	LOW 1	1	L	Grade 1	Grade 1	Grade 0
4	CA	HIGHLOW	Unsch	NORMAL	0		Grade 0	Grade 0	Grade 0
5	CA	HIGHLOW	Unsch	NORMAL	0		Grade 0	Grade 0	Grade 0
6	CA	HIGHLOW	Visit 4	NORMAL	0		Grade 0	Grade 0	Grade 0
7	CA	HIGHLOW	Visit 5	LOW 2	2	L	Grade 2	Grade 2	Grade 0
8	CA	HIGHLOW	Visit 6	LOW 2	2	L	Grade 2	Grade 2	Grade 0
9	CA	HIGHLOW	Visit 7	LOW 3	3	L	Grade 3	Grade 3	Grade 0

1. **Calcium Toxicity Test**: The passage discusses a test related to calcium toxicity, implying it's used to assess levels of calcium in a system.

2. **Bi-Directional Scale**: The test utilizes a scale that measures calcium levels in both high and low directions, denoted by the term "HIGHLOW".

3. **Grade Adjustments**: It mentions adjustments in toxicity grades based on the direction and magnitude of changes in calcium levels. For instance, when calcium levels increase, the grade may go up, and when they decrease, the grade may decrease.

4. **Specific Records**: The passage highlights specific rows where changes in calcium levels and corresponding toxicity grades occur, providing details about the direction of change (high or low) and the resulting adjustments in toxicity grades.

By focusing on these points, you can effectively convey the main information about the calcium toxicity test and its grading system.

Case 2: Uni-directional Toxicity Grade Low

Row	PARAMCD	WAYSHIFT	AVISIT	SDTM LB LBTOX	SDTM LB LBTOXGR	ATOXDIR	ATOXGR	ATOXGRL	ATOXGRH
1	ALB	ONLYLOW	Visit 1	NORMAL	0		Grade 0	Grade 0	
2	ALB	ONLYLOW	Visit 2	LOW 1	1	L	Grade 1	Grade 1	
3	ALB	ONLYLOW	Visit 3	LOW 1	1	L	Grade 1	Grade 1	
4	ALB	ONLYLOW	Unsch	NORMAL	0		Grade 0	Grade 0	
5	ALB	ONLYLOW	Unsch	NORMAL	0		Grade 0	Grade 0	
6	ALB	ONLYLOW	Visit 4	LOW 1	1	L	Grade 1	Grade 1	
7	ALB	ONLYLOW	Visit 5	LOW 1	1	L	Grade 1	Grade 1	
8	ALB	ONLYLOW	Visit 6	LOW 2	2	L	Grade 2	Grade 2	
9	ALB	ONLYLOW	Visit 7	LOW 2	2	L	Grade 2	Grade 2	

Albumin, unlike calcium, operates on a uni-directional toxicity scale, marked by WAYSHIFT="ONLYLOW". This means it's solely graded in the low direction.

In rows 2, 3, and 6 through 9, there's a noticeable decrease in values, resulting in toxicity grades of "Grade 1" or "Grade 2", with ATOXDIR indicating a low direction ("L"). Interestingly, the ATOXGRH value is null for all these rows, suggesting a unique aspect of the grading system for albumin.

Case 3: Uni-directional Toxicity Grade High

Row	PARAMCD	WAYSHIFT	AVISIT	SDTM LB LBTOX	SDTM LB LBTOXGR	ATOXDIR	ATOXGR	ATOXGRL	ATOXGRH
1	ALT	ONLYHIGH	Visit 1	NORMAL	0		Grade 0		Grade 0
2	ALT	ONLYHIGH	Visit 2	NORMAL	0		Grade 0		Grade 0
3	ALT	ONLYHIGH	Visit 3	NORMAL	0		Grade 0		Grade 0
4	ALT	ONLYHIGH	Unsch	NORMAL	0		Grade 0		Grade 0
5	ALT	ONLYHIGH	Unsch	NORMAL	0		Grade 0		Grade 0
6	ALT	ONLYHIGH	Visit 4	NORMAL	0		Grade 0		Grade 0
7	ALT	ONLYHIGH	Visit 5	NORMAL	0		Grade 0		Grade 0
8	ALT	ONLYHIGH	Visit 6	NORMAL	0		Grade 0		Grade 0
9	ALT	ONLYHIGH	Visit 7	HIGH 1	1	H	Grade 1		Grade 1

Alanine Aminotransferase (ALT) follows a uni-directional toxicity grading system, denoted by WAYSHIFT="ONLYHIGH", which means it's exclusively graded in the high direction. Specifically, in row 9, there's an elevation in value, resulting in a toxicity direction (ATOXDIR) marked as 'H'. Interestingly, for all rows, the ATOXGRL value is set to null, indicating a specific characteristic of the grading system for ALT.

Example 2: Variables of Baseline Toxicity Grade

Example 2 data indicates that Row 3 record is the baseline record with ABLFL=Y. The values of ATOXDIR, ATOXGR, ATOXGRL, and ATOXGRH from Row 3 are populated for BTOXGR, BTOXGRL, and BTOXGRH in Row 1 - Row 9.

Row	PARAMCD	WAYSHIFT	AVISIT	ATOXDIR	ATOXGR	ATOXGRL	ATOXGRH	ABLFL	BTOXGR	BTOXGRL	BTOXGRH
1	CA	HIGHLOW	Visit 1		Grade 0	Grade 0	Grade 0		Grade 1	Grade 1	Grade 0
2	CA	HIGHLOW	Visit 2	H	Grade 1	Grade 0	Grade 1		Grade 1	Grade 1	Grade 0
3	CA	HIGHLOW	Visit 3	L	Grade 1	Grade 1	Grade 0	Y	Grade 1	Grade 1	Grade 0
4	CA	HIGHLOW	Unsch		Grade 0	Grade 0	Grade 0		Grade 1	Grade 1	Grade 0
5	CA	HIGHLOW	Unsch		Grade 0	Grade 0	Grade 0		Grade 1	Grade 1	Grade 0
6	CA	HIGHLOW	Visit 4		Grade 0	Grade 0	Grade 0		Grade 1	Grade 1	Grade 0
7	CA	HIGHLOW	Visit 5	L	Grade 2	Grade 2	Grade 0		Grade 1	Grade 1	Grade 0
8	CA	HIGHLOW	Visit 6	L	Grade 2	Grade 2	Grade 0		Grade 1	Grade 1	Grade 0
9	CA	HIGHLOW	Visit 7	L	Grade 3	Grade 3	Grade 0		Grade 1	Grade 1	Grade 0

the **Baseline Toxicity Grade** variables are crucial. They reveal that in Row 3, we find the baseline record, identified by ABLFL=Y. Notably, the values of ATOXDIR, ATOXGR, ATOXGRL, and ATOXGRH from Row 3 serve as the basis for populating BTOXGR, BTOXGRL, and BTOXGRH in Rows 1 through 9. This indicates a clear transfer of information from the baseline record to subsequent rows, ensuring consistency and reference across the dataset.

Variables of Analysis Multi-response Criterion

In Example 3, the value of MCRIT1 is populated for all rows within the same parameter. The value of MCRIT1ML and MCRIT1MN are derived for each post-baseline record in Row 6-Row 9.

Row	PARAMCD	WAYSHIFT	AVISIT	ABLFL	POSTFL	ATOXGRL	BTOXGRL	ATOXGRH	BTOXGRH	MCRIT1	MCRIT1ML
1	CA	HIGHLOW	Visit 1			Grade 0	Grade 1	Grade 0	Grade 0	[a]	
2	CA	HIGHLOW	Visit 2			Grade 0	Grade 1	Grade 1	Grade 0	[a]	
3	CA	HIGHLOW	Visit 3	Y		Grade 1	Grade 1	Grade 0	Grade 0	[a]	
4	CA	HIGHLOW	Unsch			Grade 0	Grade 1	Grade 0	Grade 0	[a]	
5	CA	HIGHLOW	Unsch			Grade 0	Grade 1	Grade 0	Grade 0	[a]	
6	CA	HIGHLOW	Visit 4		Y	Grade 0	Grade 1	Grade 0	Grade 0	[a]	Toxicity Grade Not Worse
7	CA	HIGHLOW	Visit 5		Y	Grade 2	Grade 1	Grade 0	Grade 0	[a]	Worse Toxicity Grade, Low
8	CA	HIGHLOW	Visit 6		Y	Grade 2	Grade 1	Grade 0	Grade 0	[a]	Worse Toxicity Grade, Low
9	CA	HIGHLOW	Visit 7		Y	Grade 3	Grade 1	Grade 0	Grade 0	[a]	Worse Toxicity Grade, Low

[a] "Worse-than-baseline Tox Gr by Abn Dir"

1. **Comparison Context**: The passage discusses comparisons between toxicity grades in different rows, focusing on ATOXGRL and BTOXGRL, as well as ATOXGRH and BTOXGRH.

2. **Row 6 Evaluation**: In Row 6, it's observed that ATOXGRL being "Grade 0" is not worse than BTOXGRL being "Grade 1". Similarly, ATOXGRH as "Grade 0" is not worse than BTOXGRH as "Grade 0", leading to the classification of MCRIT1ML as "Toxicity Grade Not Worse".

3. **Row 9 Evaluation**: Contrarily, in Row 9, ATOXGRL as "Grade 3" is worse than BTOXGRL as "Grade 1", while ATOXGRH as "Grade 0" is not worse than BTOXGRH as "Grade 0". Consequently, the classification of MCRIT1ML for Row 9 is "Worse Toxicity Grade Low".

By focusing on these points, you can effectively convey the comparison process and resulting classifications in the dataset.

Variables of Analysis Flag ANL01FL and ANL02FL for Maximum Postbaseline Toxicity Grade

Row	PARAMCD	WAYSHIFT	AVISIT	ABLFL	POSTFL	ATOXGRL	ANL01FL	ATOXGRH	ANL02FL
1	CA	HIGHLOW	Visit 1			Grade 0		Grade 0	
2	CA	HIGHLOW	Visit 2			Grade 0		Grade 1	
3	CA	HIGHLOW	Visit 3	Y		Grade 1		Grade 0	
4	CA	HIGHLOW	Unsch			Grade 0		Grade 0	
5	CA	HIGHLOW	Unsch			Grade 0		Grade 0	
6	CA	HIGHLOW	Visit 4		Y	Grade 0		Grade 0	Y
7	CA	HIGHLOW	Visit 5		Y	Grade 2		Grade 0	Y
8	CA	HIGHLOW	Visit 6		Y	Grade 2		Grade 0	Y
9	CA	HIGHLOW	Visit 7		Y	Grade 3	Y	Grade 0	Y

ANL01FL is flagged as "Y" in Row 9 because ATOXGRL as "Grade 3" in Row 9 is the worst post-baseline toxicity grade low. Row 4 - Row 9 have ANL02FL as "Y" because ATOXGRH as "Grade 0" is the worst post-baseline toxicity grade high.

Shift Variables

Row	WAYSHIFT	AVISIT	ABLFL	POSTFL	BTOXGRL	ATOXGRL	SHIFT1	SHIFT1N	BTOXGRH	ATOXGRH	SHIFT2	SHIFT2N
1	HIGHLOW	Visit 1			Grade 1	Grade 0			Grade 0	Grade 0		
2	HIGHLOW	Visit 2			Grade 1	Grade 0			Grade 0	Grade 1		
3	HIGHLOW	Visit 3	Y		Grade 1	Grade 1			Grade 0	Grade 0		
4	HIGHLOW	Unsch			Grade 1	Grade 0			Grade 0	Grade 0		
5	HIGHLOW	Unsch			Grade 1	Grade 0			Grade 0	Grade 0		
6	HIGHLOW	Visit 4		Y	Grade 1	Grade 0	Grade 1 to Grade 0	14	Grade 0	Grade 0	Grade 0 to Grade 0	8
7	HIGHLOW	Visit 5		Y	Grade 1	Grade 2	Grade 1 to Grade 2	16	Grade 0	Grade 0	Grade 0 to Grade 0	8
8	HIGHLOW	Visit 6		Y	Grade 1	Grade 2	Grade 1 to Grade 2	16	Grade 0	Grade 0	Grade 0 to Grade 0	8
9	HIGHLOW	Visit 7		Y	Grade 1	Grade 3	Grade 1 to Grade 3	17	Grade 0	Grade 0	Grade 0 to Grade 0	8

The value of SHIFT1 is the concatenation of BTOXGRL and ATOXGRL and the value of SHIFT2 uses BTOXGRH and ATOXGRH in each post-baseline row and SHIFT1N and SHIFT2N are the numeric codes for SHIFT1 and SHIFT2.

CHAPTER LIV

How is censoring typically handled in oncology studies when analyzing overall survival?

Censoring in overall survival analysis in oncology studies is managed to accommodate patients who have not experienced the event of interest, such as death, by the end of the study or have been lost to follow-up. This approach ensures unbiased inclusion of patients in the analysis until the point where data is available. Here's how it's typically done:

1. **<u>Definition of Time-to-Event Data</u>**: In overall survival analysis, researchers track the time from a defined starting point, like cancer diagnosis or treatment initiation, to the occurrence of a specific event, usually death.

2. **<u>Censoring Mechanism</u>**: Censoring occurs when patients are still alive at the study's conclusion or are lost to follow-up before experiencing the event of interest. This implies that their exact event time is unknown but is known to have happened after a certain time point.

3. **<u>Types of Censoring</u>**:
- **Right Censoring**: This is the most common type in oncology studies, where patients remain alive at the study's end. Their survival time is known only up to the last follow-up.
- **Administrative Censoring**: This happens when the study ends before all patients experience the event of interest, with survival times known only up to the study's conclusion.

4. **<u>Survival Analysis Techniques</u>**: Statistical methods such as Kaplan-Meier estimator and Cox proportional hazards model are often used. These techniques properly handle censoring and provide estimates of survival probabilities over time, as well as comparisons between different patient groups or treatment arms.

5. **<u>Reporting</u>**: It's customary to report the proportion of censored observations and the reasons for censoring in oncology research. This transparency aids in understanding the impact of censoring on the study findings.

Overall, handling censoring in oncology studies ensures valid inferences about patient outcomes while accounting for those who haven't experienced the event of interest during the study period.

CHAPTER LV

What are the differences between solid tumor oncology and hematology oncology?

Solid tumor oncology and hematology oncology represent distinct branches within oncology, focusing on different types of cancers and treatment approaches. Here's how they differ:

1. **Nature of Cancer**:
- **Solid Tumor Oncology**: This branch deals with cancers that originate in solid tissues or organs of the body, such as the lungs, breast, colon, and prostate.
- **Hematology Oncology**: Hematology oncology primarily focuses on cancers that affect the blood, bone marrow, and lymphatic system, including leukemias, lymphomas, and myelomas.

2. **Treatment Modalities**:
- **Solid Tumor Oncology**: Treatment modalities for solid tumors often include surgery, radiation therapy, chemotherapy, targeted therapy, and immunotherapy, depending on factors such as tumor type, stage, and patient's health status.
- **Hematology Oncology**: Treatment for hematologic cancers may involve chemotherapy, radiation therapy, immunotherapy, targeted therapy, stem cell transplantation, and hematopoietic growth factors. Additionally, management of hematologic cancers often requires specialized approaches such as blood transfusions and bone marrow biopsies.

3. **Diagnostic Techniques**:
- **Solid Tumor Oncology**: Diagnosis of solid tumors typically involves imaging techniques like X-rays, CT scans, MRI scans, and PET scans, along with tissue biopsy for histological examination.
- **Hematology Oncology**: Hematologic cancers are diagnosed through blood tests, bone marrow biopsy, lymph node biopsy, and imaging studies. Analysis of blood cell counts, blood smears, and specific biomarkers is crucial for diagnosis and monitoring in hematology oncology.

4. **Multidisciplinary Approach**:
- **Solid Tumor Oncology**: Managing solid tumors often requires a multidisciplinary team approach involving surgeons, medical oncologists, radiation oncologists, radiologists, pathologists, and other specialists.
- **Hematology Oncology**: Similarly, hematologic cancers are managed through collaboration among hematologists, medical oncologists, radiation oncologists, hematopathologists, and sometimes bone marrow transplant specialists.

5. **Prognosis and Outcomes**:
- **Solid Tumor Oncology**: Prognosis and outcomes in solid tumor oncology vary widely depending on factors such as tumor type, stage at diagnosis, treatment response, and patient's overall health.
- **Hematology Oncology**: Hematologic cancers also exhibit diverse prognoses, influenced by factors like the specific type of cancer, genetic mutations, response to treatment, and availability of novel therapies.

In summary, while both solid tumor oncology and hematology oncology are integral parts of oncology, they differ in the types of cancers they focus on, diagnostic and treatment modalities employed, and multidisciplinary approaches to patient care.

CHAPTER LVI

Classification of oncology drugs

classification of oncology drugs along with some common examples and their mechanisms of action:
   1. **Chemotherapy Agents**:
- *Mechanism of Action*: Chemotherapy drugs target rapidly dividing cells, including cancer cells, by disrupting their DNA synthesis, cell division, or protein synthesis.
- *Examples*:
- *Alkylating Agents*: Cyclophosphamide, cisplatin.
- *Antimetabolites*: Methotrexate, 5-fluorouracil.
- *Topoisomerase Inhibitors*: Etoposide, doxorubicin.
- *Mitotic Inhibitors*: Paclitaxel, vinblastine.
   2. **Targeted Therapy**:
- *Mechanism of Action*: Targeted therapies specifically inhibit proteins or pathways involved in cancer growth and progression, often with fewer side effects compared to chemotherapy.
- *Examples*:
- *Tyrosine Kinase Inhibitors (TKIs)*: Imatinib (targets BCR-ABL in chronic myeloid leukemia).
- *Monoclonal Antibodies*: Trastuzumab (targets HER2 in breast cancer), Rituximab (targets CD20 in B-cell lymphoma).
- *PARP Inhibitors*: Olaparib (targets DNA repair in BRCA-mutated cancers).
   3. **Immunotherapy**:
- *Mechanism of Action*: Immunotherapy drugs enhance the body's immune response against cancer cells by targeting immune checkpoints or stimulating immune cells.
- *Examples*:
- *Checkpoint Inhibitors*: Pembrolizumab, nivolumab (target PD-1/PD-L1 axis).
- *CAR-T Cell Therapy*: Tisagenlecleucel, axicabtagene ciloleucel (engineered T cells target specific antigens on cancer cells).
- *Cytokine Therapy*: Interferon-alpha, interleukin-2 (stimulate immune cells).
   4. **Hormonal Therapy**:
- *Mechanism of Action*: Hormonal therapies interfere with hormone signaling pathways to inhibit hormone-sensitive cancers' growth.
- *Examples*:
- *Selective Estrogen Receptor Modulators (SERMs)*: Tamoxifen (blocks estrogen receptors in breast cancer).
- *Aromatase Inhibitors*: Anastrozole, letrozole (inhibit estrogen synthesis).
- *Androgen Receptor Antagonists*: Bicalutamide (blocks androgen receptors in prostate cancer).
   5. **Radiation Therapy**:
- *Mechanism of Action*: Radiation therapy uses high-energy radiation to destroy cancer cells by damaging their DNA, leading to cell death or impairing their ability to divide and grow.
- *Examples*: External beam radiation, brachytherapy.

   These are broad categories, and many drugs may have multiple mechanisms of action or may belong to more than one category. Additionally, new classes of oncology drugs continue to emerge as research advances, leading to innovative treatment options for cancer patients.

CHAPTER LVII

Different type of Oncology studies

In the field of oncology, various statistical methods are employed to analyze and interpret data related to cancer research and patient outcomes. Here are a few examples of statistical methods commonly used in oncology:

Observational Studies:

Definition: Observational studies involve observing and collecting data on individuals without intervening or manipulating any variables.

Purpose: These studies help identify associations between certain factors (e.g., risk factors, exposures) and cancer outcomes.

Example: A cohort study following a group of individuals over time to investigate the relationship between smoking habits and lung cancer incidence.

Case-Control Studies:

Definition: Case-control studies compare individuals with a specific outcome (cases) to a group without that outcome (controls) and retrospectively analyze their exposure history.

Purpose: These studies help assess the potential risk factors associated with developing cancer.

Example: Comparing the past exposure to a suspected carcinogen in lung cancer patients (cases) to individuals without lung cancer (controls) to determine its association with the disease.

Clinical Trials:

Definition: Clinical trials evaluate the safety and effectiveness of new treatments or interventions in human subjects.

Purpose: These studies assess the efficacy of novel cancer therapies and compare them to standard treatments.

Example: A randomized controlled trial comparing the outcomes of a new immunotherapy drug with chemotherapy for metastatic breast cancer patients.

Survival Analysis:

Definition: Survival analysis is a statistical method used to analyze the time until a specific event (e.g., death, disease recurrence) occurs.

Purpose: It helps estimate survival probabilities and compare survival outcomes between different groups.

Example: Analyzing the overall survival rates of lung cancer patients who underwent surgery compared to those who received chemotherapy alone.

Meta-analysis:

Definition: Meta-analysis is a statistical technique that combines results from multiple independent studies to generate a more precise estimate of the treatment effect.

Purpose: It allows for a comprehensive analysis of existing research and provides a more robust conclusion.

Example: Combining data from multiple clinical trials to determine the overall efficacy of a specific type of targeted therapy in colorectal cancer patients.

Statistical Modeling:

Definition: Statistical modeling involves using mathematical equations and statistical methods to create models that predict cancer outcomes or evaluate the impact of certain variables.

Purpose: It helps in understanding the relationships between different factors and making predictions about cancer prognosis or treatment response.

Example: Developing a predictive model using patient characteristics and genetic markers to estimate the probability of disease recurrence in breast cancer patients.

These are just a few examples of statistical methods used in oncology research. Each method serves a specific purpose in analyzing and interpreting data to advance our understanding of cancer and improve patient care.

Multivariate Analysis:

Definition: Multivariate analysis involves examining the relationships between multiple variables simultaneously to understand their combined effects on cancer outcomes.

Purpose: It helps identify independent predictors and control for confounding factors.

Example: Assessing the impact of age, tumor stage, and treatment modality on overall survival in pancreatic cancer patients using multivariate Cox regression analysis.

Propensity Score Analysis:

Definition: Propensity score analysis is used to adjust for potential confounding variables in non-randomized studies, aiming to mimic a randomized controlled trial design.

Purpose: It helps estimate treatment effects by matching or stratifying individuals based on their propensity scores.

Example: Evaluating the effectiveness of a new surgical technique for prostate cancer by matching patients who underwent the new procedure with those who had traditional surgery based on their propensity scores.

Decision Analysis:

Definition: Decision analysis combines statistical methods with decision-making models to evaluate the potential outcomes and benefits of different treatment options.

Purpose: It assists in determining the most favorable treatment strategy based on the available evidence and patient preferences.

Example: Using decision analysis to compare the cost-effectiveness and quality-adjusted life years gained from different treatment approaches for advanced lung cancer.

Risk Assessment:

Definition: Risk assessment involves estimating the probability of developing cancer or experiencing adverse events based on various factors such as genetic markers, lifestyle, and environmental exposures.

Purpose: It helps identify high-risk individuals and guide personalized prevention or screening strategies.

Example: Assessing the risk of developing breast cancer in a population based on genetic mutations (e.g., BRCA1/2) and other risk factors such as family history and reproductive factors.

Spatial Analysis:

Definition: Spatial analysis examines the geographic distribution of cancer cases to identify patterns, clusters, or potential environmental risk factors.

Purpose: It helps understand the spatial variation of cancer incidence and provides insights for targeted interventions.

Example: Mapping the distribution of lung cancer cases in a particular region to identify areas with higher incidence rates and investigate potential environmental exposures.

These additional statistical methods contribute to the comprehensive analysis of cancer data, facilitating a deeper understanding of the disease, its risk factors, treatment options, and outcomes. Researchers employ these methods to generate evidence-based insights that can inform clinical practice and public health interventions.

CHAPTER LVIII

Analyzing Efficacy with Imputations: Approaches and Considerations

1. **Purpose:** Efficacy analysis evaluates treatment effectiveness in clinical trials.

Objective: Enhancing precision and reliability of efficacy analyses in clinical trials by addressing missing data through imputation methods.

Methods Covered: Various imputation techniques explored, including mean imputation to advanced regression methods, tailored to diverse trial settings.

- **Imputation in Clinical Trials**: Addresses missing data challenges, preserving data integrity and statistical power.

- **Methods**: Various techniques from mean to complex regression models are employed based on data nature and missingness assumptions.

- **Benefits**: Maintains sample sizes, reduces bias, and enhances analysis precision.

- **Considerations**: Assumptions underlying imputation and sensitivity analyses for result validation are crucial.

- **Imputation Methods**: Mean, mode, median, LOCF, regression, stochastic regression, multiple imputation, among others, cater to different scenarios.

- **Single vs. Multiple Imputation**: Single underestimates variability, while multiple offers robust estimates by generating several datasets and combining results.

CHAPTER LIX

IMPUTATION METHODS

In addressing missing data, various imputation methods are commonly employed. Here are some examples:

1. **Mean Imputation**: If we have a dataset with missing values for a continuous variable like age, we can calculate the mean age of the observed data and replace the missing values with this average. For example, if we have ages of 25, 30, and a missing value, the mean of 25 and 30 (which is 27.5) would replace the missing value.

2. **Mode Imputation**: In a categorical variable such as blood type, where 'A' is the most frequent category, we can replace missing values with 'A', assuming it's the most likely option.

3. **Median Imputation**: Consider a dataset with incomes as a continuous variable. If we have incomes of $40,000, $50,000, and a missing value, the median of $40,000 and $50,000 (which is $45,000) would replace the missing value.

4. **Last Observation Carried Forward (LOCF)**: Let's say we're tracking patient blood pressure over time, and a patient's last recorded blood pressure was 120/80. If the subsequent reading is missing, we assume it remains at 120/80.

5. **Regression Imputation**: Using observed variables like age, gender, and BMI, we predict missing values such as cholesterol levels through regression analysis.

6. **Stochastic Regression Imputation**: Similar to regression imputation, but with added random noise to account for uncertainty in prediction.

7. **Multiple Imputation**: Instead of imputing a single value, multiple datasets are generated with different plausible imputed values. These datasets are analyzed separately, and the results are combined for more accurate estimates.

8. **Hot Deck Imputation**: Missing values are replaced with values from similar cases within the dataset.

9. **Probabilistic Principal Component Analysis (PPCA)**: A statistical method that can impute missing values based on the relationships between variables.

10. **Random Imputation**: Missing values are randomly replaced with values from the observed data.

11. **Extrapolation Imputation**: Imputes missing values based on trends observed in the data.

12. **Blocf (Baseline Observation Carried Forward)**: Similar to LOCF, but based on the initial or baseline observation.

13. **WOC (Worst Observation Carried Forward)**: Imputes missing values with the worst-case scenario from previous observations.

These methods offer diverse strategies for handling missing data, each with its own strengths and limitations.

CHAPTER LX

What is Hy's Law, and what does it indicate?

Hy's Law is a guideline proposed by Hy Zimmerman, **indicating the risk of fatal drug-induced liver injury**.
- It suggests that a patient is at high risk if a medication causes hepatocellular injury with jaundice, not hepatobiliary injury.
   three components of Hy's Law?**

1. The drug causes hepatocellular injury, with ALT or AST levels typically elevated by 3-fold or more above the upper limit of normal.
2. Patients exhibit elevated serum total bilirubin levels, exceeding 2 times the upper limit of normal, without signs of cholestasis.
3. No other identifiable reasons explain the elevation in aminotransferases and serum total bilirubin levels.
   How can we implement Hy's Law in data analysis using SAS?**
   We can use SAS to analyze liver function tests and identify patients meeting Hy's Law criteria.
- For example, we can calculate ALT and AST levels using PROC MEANS or PROC SUMMARY and compare them against the upper limit of normal.
- Similarly, we can calculate serum total bilirubin levels and assess for elevations exceeding 2 times the upper limit of normal using SAS functions.
- By examining patient data for these criteria, we can identify cases meeting Hy's Law guidelines.
   Question: Can you provide an example SAS code to calculate ALT and AST levels?
   /* Example SAS code to calculate ALT and AST levels */

```
data liver_tests;
input patient_id ALT AST;
datalines;
1 50 60
2 80 90
3 120 150
4 40 55
5 100 130
;
run;
    proc means data=liver_tests mean;
var ALT AST;
run;
```

   **** How can we assess serum total bilirubin levels in SAS?****
   We can calculate serum total bilirubin levels using SAS functions like MEAN, MEDIAN, or PROC UNIVARIATE.
- We compare the calculated values against the upper limit of normal (ULN) to identify elevations.
- For instance, we can use PROC UNIVARIATE to compute summary statistics and examine bilirubin levels exceeding 2 times the ULN.
   Question: Can you provide an example SAS code to calculate serum total bilirubin levels?

```
/* Example SAS code to calculate serum total bilirubin levels */
data bilirubin;
input patient_id total_bilirubin;
datalines;
```

```
1 1.2
2 2.5
3 3.0
4 1.8
5 2.2
;
run;
    proc univariate data=bilirubin;
var total_bilirubin;
histogram / normal;
run;
```

Question: How can SAS help identify patients meeting Hy's Law criteria?

- SAS can analyze patient data, calculate liver function test results, and identify cases meeting Hy's Law criteria.

- By comparing ALT, AST, and total bilirubin levels against established thresholds, SAS can flag patients at high risk of drug-induced liver injury.

- Additionally, SAS can generate summary reports or visualizations to facilitate interpretation and decision-making based on Hy's Law guidelines.

CHAPTER LXI

EFFICACY ENDPOINTS IN THE ONCOLOGY CLINICAL TRIALS

1. **Purpose of Clinical Trials**:
- To confirm or reject the effectiveness of a therapy.
    2. **Clinical Endpoints**:
- Objective measures to gauge the benefit of a medical intervention.
- Assess patient's feeling, function, and survival.
    3. **Importance in Trials**:
- Crucial for assessing study validity and generalizability.
- Essential for both clinicians and patients.
    4. **Classification of Endpoints in Oncologic Trials**:
- **Patient-centered Clinical Endpoints**:
- Include Overall Survival (OS) and Quality of Life (QoL).
- **Tumor-centered Clinical Endpoints**:
- Include Disease-Free Survival (DFS) and Progression-Free Survival (PFS).
    Patient-Centered Clinical Endpoints:
- Reflect a patient's well-being or survival.
- Assess the direct benefit of therapeutic interventions.
- Examples include Overall Survival (OS) and Health-Related Quality of Life (HRQoL).
    Overall Survival (OS):
- Time from randomization to death.
- Considered the gold standard endpoint in oncology trials.
- Objective and minimizes researcher bias.
- Requires long-term follow-up, larger patient populations, and financial support.
- Limitations in slowly progressing diseases and non-cancer deaths influence.
    Health-Related Quality of Life (HRQoL):
- Reflects direct clinical benefit for the patient.
- Includes overall health, physical health, mental health, and daily activities.
- Subjective nature and lack of standardization pose challenges.
- Used as a secondary or co-primary endpoint alongside OS.
    Tumor-Centered Endpoints:
- Composite endpoints based on tumor assessment.
- Combines events like progression, recurrence, and death.
- Used as substitutes for patient-centered endpoints.
- Examples include tumor response (RECIST), Disease-Free Survival (DFS), and Progression-Free Survival (PFS).
    Surrogate Endpoints for Adjuvant and Neoadjuvant Therapies:
- Alternative measures of treatment benefit.
- Easier or quicker to measure than ultimate clinical outcomes.
- Aim to predict long-term outcomes without waiting for them to occur.
- Commonly used in adjuvant and neoadjuvant trials.
    Here are the additional endpoints specific to **adjuvant clinical trials:**
    Relapse-Free Survival (RFS):
- Time to any event except for second primary cancers.
- Events include recurrence of the same cancer and treatment-related deaths.
- Second primary and other primary cancers are ignored, loss to follow-up is censored.

Time to Recurrence (TTR):
- Time to any event related to the same cancer.
- Events include same cancer recurrences and deaths from the same cancer.
- Second primary and other primary cancers are ignored, non-cancer-related deaths are censored.

Time to Treatment Failure (TTF):
- Time to any event except non-cancer-related death.
- Events include recurrences, treatment-related deaths, and second same or other primary cancers.
- Non-cancer-related deaths are censored.

Cancer-Specific Survival (CSS):
- Time to death caused by the same cancer.
- Events include death from the same cancer, regardless of whether it's the primary tumor or a second primary same cancer.
- Second primary and other primary cancers are ignored, non-cancer-related deaths are censored.

Here's a summary of additional efficacy endpoints specific to **neoadjuvant trials** and challenges in selecting and validating surrogate endpoints:

Efficacy Endpoints in Neoadjuvant Trials:
- **Pathological Complete Response (pCR):**
- Defined as the absence of viable cancer cells in tumors after treatment.
- **Major Pathological Response (MPR):**
- Defined as less than 10% residual viable tumor after neoadjuvant therapy.
- **Downstaging (DS):**
- Proportion of participants showing reduction in tumor size, extent, or characteristics after neoadjuvant therapy.

Challenges in Surrogate Endpoints Selection and Validation:
- **Statistical Validation:**
- Difficult but necessary process.
- **Endpoint Selection:**
- Crucial for trial success but challenging to identify clinically meaningful and measurable endpoints.
- **Interpretation and Implementation:**
- Poor selection hampers interpretation, implementation, and evidence synthesis.
- **Specificity and Precision:**
- Surrogate endpoints need validation specific to therapeutic class, disease, and stage.
- **Endpoint Definitions:**
- Lack of international consensus leads to variable interpretation across studies.
- **Direct Clinical Benefit:**
- Surrogate endpoints may not directly benefit patients.
- **Lack of Consistency:**
- Definitions lack consistency and systematic validation for overall survival (OS) surrogate status.

This information emphasizes the importance of precise endpoint selection and clarity in definitions to ensure meaningful interpretation and application of trial findings.

CHAPTER LXII

Multi–Phase Oncology Clinical Trial Key Challenges and Solutions

When preparing for an interview for a SAS Clinical Oncology Statistical Programmer position, it's important to be ready to discuss complex projects you've worked on. Here's an example of a complex project and how you might discuss it:

Example Project: Multi-Phase Oncology Clinical Trial

Project Overview:

I worked on a multi-phase clinical trial aimed at evaluating the efficacy and safety of a new oncology drug intended for the treatment of metastatic breast cancer. This project was particularly complex due to the extensive data collected across different phases of the trial, including Phase II and Phase III, and the need for sophisticated statistical analysis methods.

Key Challenges and Solutions:

1. **Data Integration from Multiple Phases:**
- *Challenge:* Integrating and harmonizing data collected from different phases of the trial, each with its own data structure and variables.
- *Solution:* I developed detailed data mapping and transformation plans. Using SAS, I created scripts to standardize variable names and formats across datasets. I employed PROC SQL for merging datasets and ensuring the integrity of combined data. Regular data audits and validation checks were conducted to confirm consistency.

2. **Handling Missing Data:**
- *Challenge:* Missing data points were inevitable due to patient dropouts, incomplete records, and varying follow-up times.
- *Solution:* I utilized multiple imputation techniques available in SAS (PROC MI and PROC MIANALYZE) to handle missing data. This approach allowed us to create several imputed datasets, perform analyses on each, and combine the results to obtain robust estimates and confidence intervals.

3. **Survival Analysis:**
- *Challenge:* Analyzing time-to-event data, which is crucial in oncology studies for endpoints such as Overall Survival (OS) and Progression-Free Survival (PFS).
- *Solution:* I conducted Kaplan-Meier survival analyses using PROC LIFETEST to estimate survival functions and compared survival curves using the log-rank test. Additionally, I employed Cox proportional hazards models (PROC PHREG) to identify significant prognostic factors. Assumptions of the Cox model were thoroughly checked, and appropriate adjustments were made.

4. **Adverse Event Analysis:**
- *Challenge:* Comprehensive analysis of adverse event (AE) data to assess the safety profile of the new drug.
- *Solution:* I created detailed summary tables and listings of AEs using PROC FREQ and PROC REPORT. Subgroup analyses were performed to identify patterns related to age, gender, and other demographic factors. I also used PROC LOGISTIC to evaluate the relationship between treatment and the occurrence of severe AEs, adjusting for potential confounders.

5. **Regulatory Submission and Reporting:**
- *Challenge:* Preparing data and results for regulatory submission to agencies such as the FDA.
- *Solution:* I ensured that all analyses and outputs adhered to CDISC standards, specifically SDTM and ADaM datasets. I wrote detailed SAS macros to automate the creation of these datasets and ensure compliance. I also prepared the Clinical Study Report (CSR), including statistical sections and appendices, with clear documentation of methods and results.

Key Achievements:

- Successfully integrated and analyzed data from multiple trial phases, ensuring high data quality and reliability.

- Developed robust statistical models that provided insightful results on the efficacy and safety of the drug.
- Contributed to the successful submission of trial data to regulatory authorities, supporting the approval process of the new oncology treatment.

Discussion in Interview:

When discussing this project in an interview, emphasize the following points:
- Your role and specific contributions to the project.
- The challenges you faced and the technical solutions you implemented.
- How your work impacted the overall study and its outcomes.
- Any collaboration with other team members or departments (e.g., clinical, regulatory).
- Your adherence to industry standards and regulatory requirements.

By providing a detailed account of a complex project like this, you'll demonstrate your technical expertise, problem-solving abilities, and understanding of the clinical oncology field.

statistical methods are used to analyze clinical trial data and evaluate the efficacy and safety

In oncology, several specialized statistical methods are used to analyze clinical trial data and evaluate the efficacy and safety of treatments. Here are a few notable methods, including Nadir, RECIST, and some other important approaches used in oncology studies:

1. Nadir Method

Nadir refers to the lowest point that a tumor marker or measurement reaches during treatment. It is often used in the context of tumor size or blood counts. For instance, in oncology, the nadir can indicate the point at which a tumor is at its smallest size following treatment before any potential regrowth.

- **Usage:** Monitoring nadir values helps in assessing the response to treatment and can be critical in adjusting therapy plans.
- **Calculation:** Nadir is calculated as the lowest measurement recorded over a specified period, often during the course of treatment.

2. RECIST (Response Evaluation Criteria in Solid Tumors)

RECIST is a standardized set of criteria for assessing tumor response to treatment.

- **RECIST 1.1:** The most current version, which includes guidelines for measuring tumor size and evaluating changes over time.
- **Categories of Response:**
- **Complete Response (CR):** Disappearance of all target lesions.
- **Partial Response (PR):** At least a 30% decrease in the sum of the diameters of target lesions.
- **Stable Disease (SD):** Neither sufficient shrinkage to qualify for PR nor sufficient increase to qualify for Progressive Disease (PD).
- **Progressive Disease (PD):** At least a 20% increase in the sum of the diameters of target lesions.

3. Kaplan-Meier Method

The **Kaplan-Meier method** is used to estimate survival probabilities over time in the presence of censored data.

- **Usage:** Commonly used to plot survival curves and compare survival rates between different treatment groups.
- **Calculation:** The Kaplan-Meier estimator calculates the probability of survival at different time points, taking into account the time until the event (e.g., death, progression) or censoring.

4. Cox Proportional Hazards Model

The **Cox proportional hazards model** is a regression model used to investigate the association between the survival time of patients and one or more predictor variables.

- **Usage:** Helps identify prognostic factors that affect survival.
- **Assumption:** Assumes that the hazard ratios between groups are constant over time.
- **Calculation:** Estimates the hazard ratio for each covariate, providing insights into their impact on survival.

5. Log-Rank Test

The **log-rank test** is used to compare the survival distributions of two or more groups.

- **Usage:** Evaluates the null hypothesis that there is no difference in survival between the groups.
- **Calculation:** Compares the observed number of events to the expected number under the null hypothesis across groups.

6. Immune-Related Response Criteria (irRC)

irRC are criteria designed to assess responses to immunotherapy treatments, which can differ significantly from responses to traditional chemotherapy.

- **Usage:** Accounts for unique patterns of response and progression seen with immunotherapy, such as delayed responses or initial tumor growth followed by shrinkage.
- **Categories:** Similar to RECIST but adapted to consider immune-related changes.

7. Time to Progression (TTP)

Time to Progression (TTP) measures the duration from the start of treatment until the disease starts to progress.

- **Usage:** Important endpoint in oncology trials to evaluate how long a treatment can keep the disease from worsening.
- **Calculation:** Based on the time until the documented progression of the disease or death due to disease progression.

8. Objective Response Rate (ORR)

Objective Response Rate (ORR) is the proportion of patients with a tumor size reduction of a predefined amount for a minimum time period.

- **Usage:** Evaluates the proportion of patients who have a significant reduction in tumor size, indicating treatment efficacy.
- **Components:** ORR includes both Complete Response (CR) and Partial Response (PR) rates.

9. Progression-Free Survival (PFS)

Progression-Free Survival (PFS) is the length of time during and after the treatment that a patient lives with the disease without it getting worse.

- **Usage:** A critical endpoint in oncology trials to assess the efficacy of new treatments.
- **Calculation:** The time from the start of treatment until the disease progresses or the patient dies from any cause.

10. Overall Survival (OS)

Overall Survival (OS) is the length of time from either the date of diagnosis or the start of treatment that patients diagnosed with the disease are still alive.

- **Usage:** Considered the gold standard endpoint in oncology trials.
- **Calculation:** Measures the time from the start of treatment until death from any cause.

These methods and criteria are essential for the robust analysis of oncology clinical trial data, enabling researchers to draw meaningful conclusions about the effectiveness and safety of cancer treatments.

macros for visualizing data with multiple timed events in clinical trials

Macros for visualizing data with multiple timed events in clinical trials, drawing from common practices in the field.

EventChart: A Macro to Visualize Data with Multiple Timed Events

Key Points:

1. **Purpose and Overview:**
- The EventChart macro is designed to create visual representations of multiple timed events for subjects in a clinical trial.
- It is particularly useful for displaying timelines and events such as adverse events, treatment periods, and other significant clinical milestones.

2. **Features:**
- **Horizontal Timelines:** Each subject is represented by a horizontal line, with time on the x-axis and the subject ID on the y-axis.
- **Event Markers:** Different events are marked with distinct symbols or colors to differentiate between types of events.
- **Customization:** The macro allows customization of the appearance of the chart, including marker types, colors, and labels.

3. **Data Requirements:**
- Input data should include subject IDs, event dates, and event types.
- The data must be pre-processed to ensure consistency in date formats and event coding.

4. **Macro Parameters:**
- Parameters typically include options for specifying the dataset, variables for subject IDs, event dates, event types, and various visual attributes.
- Examples of parameters:
- `DATASET=` specifies the input dataset.
- `IDVAR=` specifies the subject ID variable.
- `DATEVAR=` specifies the date variable for events.
- `EVENTVAR=` specifies the event type variable.

5. **Usage Examples:**
- The document likely provides examples of how to call the macro and generate an event chart.
- Examples might include different configurations to highlight how to use the macro for various scenarios, such as displaying treatment periods or adverse event timelines.

6. **Benefits:**
- Enhances the understanding of the temporal relationships between different clinical events.
- Facilitates the identification of patterns or trends that may not be obvious from tabular data alone.
- Supports better communication of complex clinical data to stakeholders.

7. **Applications:**
- Useful in various phases of clinical trials, especially in safety monitoring and efficacy assessments.
- Can be used for interim analysis to provide insights into ongoing trials.

8. **Technical Implementation:**
- The macro is likely written in SAS and includes detailed code snippets.
- Instructions on how to integrate the macro into a larger data analysis pipeline are provided.
- Tips for troubleshooting common issues and optimizing performance.

9. **Visualization Output:**
- The macro generates a graphical output, typically in the form of a PDF or a graphical window within SAS.

- Example outputs might show how different events are plotted over time for individual subjects, highlighting key clinical endpoints.

If you need more specific information or detailed examples, you might need to access the document directly through a different method or contact the authors for a copy. The general principles outlined above should provide a good foundation for understanding the utility and implementation of such a macro in clinical data visualization.

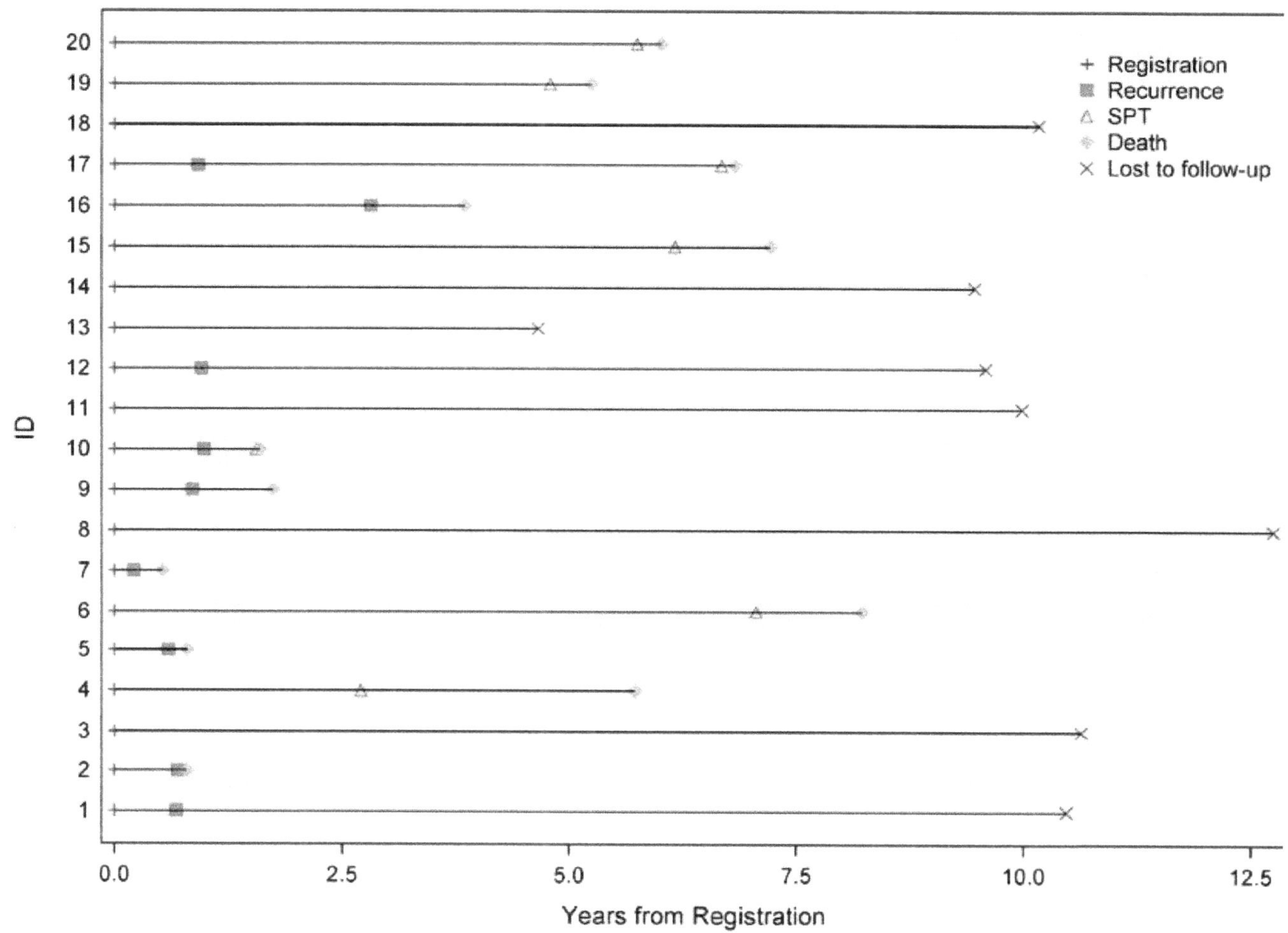

Figure 2. An Event Chart for an Oncology Study

CHAPTER LXV

Biomarkers role in oncology studies

Biomarkers play a crucial role in oncology studies by providing valuable information that can help in the diagnosis, prognosis, and treatment of cancer. Here are some key points on the role of biomarkers in oncology:

1. **Diagnosis and Early Detection**
- **Diagnostic Biomarkers:** These help in the early detection and accurate diagnosis of cancer. For example, PSA (Prostate-Specific Antigen) for prostate cancer and CA-125 for ovarian cancer.
- **Screening Tools:** Biomarkers can be used in screening programs to identify cancer in its early stages when it is more likely to be treatable.

2. **Prognosis**
- **Prognostic Biomarkers:** These biomarkers provide information about the likely course of the cancer. They can indicate how aggressive the cancer is and help predict the patient's overall outcome. For example, the presence of HER2 (Human Epidermal Growth Factor Receptor 2) in breast cancer can indicate a more aggressive disease and a poorer prognosis.

3. **Predicting Treatment Response**
- **Predictive Biomarkers:** These are used to predict how well a patient will respond to a particular treatment. For example, the presence of EGFR (Epidermal Growth Factor Receptor) mutations in non-small cell lung cancer can predict response to EGFR inhibitors.
- **Personalized Medicine:** Predictive biomarkers enable personalized treatment plans tailored to the individual's cancer biology, increasing the likelihood of treatment success and minimizing unnecessary side effects.

4. **Monitoring Disease Progression**
- **Disease Monitoring:** Biomarkers can be used to monitor the disease progression and response to treatment. For example, measuring the levels of circulating tumor DNA (ctDNA) can provide real-time insights into how well a patient is responding to therapy.
- **Detecting Recurrence:** Biomarkers can also help detect cancer recurrence at an early stage, allowing for timely intervention.

5. **Guiding Clinical Trials**
- **Patient Stratification:** Biomarkers can be used to stratify patients in clinical trials, ensuring that those who are most likely to benefit from a treatment are included. This can make trials more efficient and informative.
- **Endpoints and Surrogates:** Biomarkers can serve as endpoints or surrogate endpoints in clinical trials, providing early indications of treatment efficacy.

6. **Biomarker Types and Examples**
- **Genomic Biomarkers:** Include mutations, gene expression profiles, and chromosomal abnormalities. Examples: BRCA1/BRCA2 mutations in breast and ovarian cancers.
- **Proteomic Biomarkers:** Proteins whose expression levels correlate with disease state. Examples: HER2 in breast cancer.
- **Metabolomic Biomarkers:** Metabolic changes that reflect disease presence or progression. Examples: Altered levels of metabolites in urine or blood.
- **Epigenetic Biomarkers:** Changes in DNA methylation or histone modification patterns. Examples: Methylation of the MGMT gene in gliomas.

7. **Technological Advances**
- **Next-Generation Sequencing (NGS):** Has revolutionized the identification of genetic biomarkers, allowing for comprehensive profiling of cancer genomes.
- **Mass Spectrometry:** Used in proteomics to identify and quantify protein biomarkers.
- **Immunohistochemistry (IHC):** Used to detect protein biomarkers in tissue samples, such as HER2 in breast

cancer.

8. **Challenges and Future Directions**

- **Validation and Standardization:** There is a need for rigorous validation and standardization of biomarker assays to ensure accuracy and reproducibility.
- **Regulatory Approval:** Biomarkers must undergo stringent evaluation and approval processes before being used clinically.
- **Integration into Clinical Practice:** Effective strategies are needed to integrate biomarker testing into routine clinical practice, including considerations for cost and accessibility.

Biomarkers are integral to advancing the field of oncology by enhancing our understanding of cancer biology and improving patient care through more precise and personalized approaches. Their continued development and integration into clinical practice hold the promise of transforming cancer diagnosis and treatment.

CHAPTER LXVI

Statistical techniques are used to analyze efficacy endpoints

In clinical trials, various statistical techniques are used to analyze efficacy endpoints, depending on the type of data (normally distributed, non-normally distributed, or proportions). Here's a summary:

Statistical Techniques for Normally Distributed Measurements:
- **t-tests:** Used to compare the means of two groups.
- **Example:** Comparing the mean blood pressure reduction between two treatment groups.
- **Question:** "What statistical test would you use to compare the mean blood pressure reduction between two treatment groups?"
- **Answer:** "A t-test would be appropriate for comparing the mean blood pressure reduction between two groups."
   - **Analysis of Variance (ANOVA):** Used to compare the means of three or more groups.
- **Example:** Comparing the mean blood pressure reduction across three different treatment groups.
- **Question:** "How would you compare the mean blood pressure reduction across three different treatment groups?"
- **Answer:** "ANOVA would be used to compare the means across three or more groups."

Statistical Techniques for Non-Normally Distributed Measurements:
- **Wilcoxon or Mann-Whitney tests:** Used to compare the medians of two groups.
- **Example:** Comparing the median time to symptom relief between two treatments.
- **Question:** "What test would you use to compare the median time to symptom relief between two treatments if the data is not normally distributed?"
- **Answer:** "The Wilcoxon or Mann-Whitney test would be used to compare the medians of the two groups."

Statistical Techniques for Proportions:
- **Chi-Square Test:** Used to compare proportions (e.g., responders or survivors) between groups.
- **Example:** Comparing the proportion of patients who responded to treatment between two groups.
- **Question:** "How would you compare the proportion of patients who responded to treatment between two groups?"
- **Answer:** "The chi-square test would be used to compare the proportions between the two groups."
   - **Mantel-Haenszel Chi-Square Test:** Used for stratified or matched data to control for confounding variables.
- **Example:** Comparing the proportion of responders while controlling for age groups.
- **Question:** "Which test would you use to compare the proportion of responders between two treatments while controlling for age?"
- **Answer:** "The Mantel-Haenszel chi-square test would be appropriate for this comparison."
   - **Logrank Test:** Used to compare survival distributions between groups.
- **Example:** Comparing the survival times between two treatment groups.
- **Question:** "Which test would you use to compare survival times between two treatment groups?"
- **Answer:** "The logrank test would be used to compare survival times."
   - **Cox Proportional Hazards Test:** Used to explore the relationship between the survival of a patient and one or more predictor variables.
- **Example:** Assessing the impact of treatment, age, and gender on survival time.
- **Question:** "What statistical method would you use to assess the impact of multiple factors, like treatment and age, on survival time?"
- **Answer:** "The Cox proportional hazards test would be used to assess the impact of multiple predictors on survival time."

Summary of Key Points:
1. **Normal Distribution:**

- t-test for comparing two means.
- ANOVA for comparing three or more means.
    2. **Non-Normal Distribution:**
- Wilcoxon or Mann-Whitney tests for comparing medians.
    3. **Proportions (Binomial Distribution):**
- Chi-square test for comparing proportions.
- Mantel-Haenszel chi-square for stratified data.
- Logrank test for survival analysis.
- Cox proportional hazards for survival and multiple predictors.

CHAPTER LXVII

THE PRINCIPLE OF TESTING STATISTICAL SIGNIFICANCE

In clinical trials, hypotheses about treatment effects must be tested using statistical methods. Here are key points, followed by example questions and answers:

Key Points:

1. **Hypotheses and Data:**
- **Hypotheses:** Statements about the expected outcomes of the study (e.g., the effect of a treatment).
- **Assessment:** Hypotheses need to be tested with empirical data to confirm or refute them.

2. **Assumptions for Statistical Analysis:**
- **Representativeness:** The study sample should represent the entire population, meaning that if the trial is repeated, the results would be similar.
- **Consistency in Variation:** Similar trials should have the same standard deviation (SD) or standard error of the mean (SEM).

3. **Statistical Testing:**
- **Uncertainty:** Biological processes are variable, so statistics provide probabilities, not certainties.
- **Null Hypothesis (H0):** Assumes no effect or difference (e.g., the mean effect is zero).
- **Alternative Hypothesis (H1):** Assumes there is an effect or difference.

4. **Testing Differences:**
- **Comparing Means:** To test the effect of a treatment, compare the mean difference between the treatment and control groups against zero.

5. **Normal Distribution and SEM:**
- **Normal Distribution Graph:** Data can be depicted with a normal distribution, showing SEMs on the x-axis.
- **Null Hypothesis Graph:** A graph where the mean is zero (mean ± SEM = 0 ± 1) represents the null hypothesis.

Example Questions and Answers:

1. Hypothesis Testing

Question: What is the null hypothesis (H0) in a clinical trial testing a new drug?

Answer: The null hypothesis (H0) is that there is no difference in the mean effect of the new drug compared to the control, i.e., the mean effect is zero.

2. Assumptions in Statistical Analysis

Question: What assumption about the study sample is crucial for statistical analysis?

Answer: It is crucial to assume that the study sample is representative of the entire population, meaning that repeating the trial would yield similar results.

3. Consistency in Variation

Question: Why is it important to assume that similar trials will have the same standard deviation (SD) or standard error of the mean (SEM)?

Answer: This assumption ensures that the variability in the results is consistent across similar studies, allowing for accurate comparisons and conclusions.

4. Testing Differences Between Groups

Question: How can you simplify the comparison of two treatment groups in a study?

Answer: You can simplify the comparison by calculating the difference between the means of the two groups and testing whether this difference is significantly different from zero.

5. Interpreting a Normal Distribution Graph

Question: What does a normal distribution graph with SEMs on the x-axis represent in a clinical trial?

Answer: It represents the distribution of the data around the mean, showing the variability (standard error) and helping to visualize how far individual data points deviate from the mean.

6. Probability and Hypotheses

Question: What do statistical tests estimate in the context of hypotheses?

Answer: Statistical tests estimate the probability that the observed difference in the data is true and not due to chance, thereby testing the validity of the hypotheses.

CHAPTER LXVIII

Hypotheses are evaluated using statistical methods

In clinical trials, hypotheses are evaluated using statistical methods to determine if observed effects are genuine or due to chance. The following points highlight key concepts and methods used:

1. **Hypotheses and Data:**
- **Hypotheses:** Statements predicting an outcome (e.g., a new drug is effective).
- **Assessment:** Hypotheses are tested using empirical data to verify their validity.

2. **Assumptions for Statistical Analysis:**
- **Representativeness:** The study sample must accurately represent the population to ensure results are generalizable.
- **Consistency:** Similar studies should show consistent standard deviations (SD) or standard errors of the mean (SEM).

3. **Statistical Testing:**
- **Null Hypothesis (H0):** Assumes no effect or difference (mean difference = 0).
- **Alternative Hypothesis (H1):** Assumes there is an effect or difference.

4. **Comparing Means:**
- **t-test:** Compares the means of two groups to see if they are significantly different.
- **ANOVA:** Compares the means of three or more groups.

5. **Non-Parametric Tests:**
- Used when data do not follow a normal distribution (e.g., Wilcoxon or Mann-Whitney tests).

6. **Proportions:**
- **Chi-Square Test:** Compares proportions of outcomes between groups.
- **Logrank Test:** Used in survival analysis to compare survival distributions.
- **Cox Proportional Hazards:** Assesses the effect of several variables on survival.

1. Hypothesis Testing

Question: What is the null hypothesis (H0) in a clinical trial?

Answer: The null hypothesis (H0) is that there is no difference in the mean effect between the treatment and control groups (mean difference = 0).

2. Assumptions in Statistical Analysis

Question: Why is it important that a study sample is representative of the population?

Answer: It ensures that the study results are generalizable to the entire population, making the findings valid and reliable.

3. Consistency in Variation

Question: What assumption about standard deviation (SD) or standard error of the mean (SEM) is made in similar trials?

Answer: It is assumed that similar trials will have consistent SD or SEM, allowing for accurate comparisons and conclusions.

4. Comparing Means Between Groups

Question: How can you test if the means of two groups are significantly different?

Answer: By using a t-test to compare the means of the two groups.

5. Non-Parametric Tests

Question: When would you use a Wilcoxon test instead of a t-test?

Answer: A Wilcoxon test is used when the data do not follow a normal distribution.

6. Comparing Proportions

Question: What statistical test would you use to compare the proportion of patients who responded to treatment between two groups?

Answer: The chi-square test is used to compare proportions between two groups.

7. Survival Analysis

Question: What is the logrank test used for in clinical trials?

Answer: The logrank test is used to compare survival distributions between two or more groups.

8. Cox Proportional Hazards

Question: How do you assess the impact of multiple variables on survival time in a clinical trial?

Answer: By using the Cox proportional hazards model.

CHAPTER LXIX

Best Overall table logics

Table 14.2.1
Best Overall Response and Duration of Response by Investigator Assessment
Safety Population

	Statistics	+ nab-pac 100 mg/ m^2 (N=xx)	mg Int + nab-pac 75 mg/m^2 (N=XX)	Int+ nab-pac 75 mg/m^2 (N=XX)	Cont + nab-pac 75 mg/m^2 (N=XX)	pac 75 mg/m^2-Expansion (N=XX)	pac 75 mg/m^2-Total (N=XX)	All Patients (N=XX)
Best Overall Response								
Complete Response (CR)	N(%)	X(XX.X)	X(XX.X)	X(XX.X)	X(XX.X)	X(XX.X)	X(XX.X)	X(XX.X)
Partial Response (PR)	N(%)	X(XX.X)	X(XX.X)	X(XX.X)	X(XX.X)	X(XX.X)	X(XX.X)	X(XX.X)
Stable Disease (SD)	N(%)	X(XX.X)	X(XX.X)	X(XX.X)	X(XX.X)	X(XX.X)	X(XX.X)	X(XX.X)
Progressive Disease (PD)	N(%)	X(XX.X)	X(XX.X)	X(XX.X)	X(XX.X)	X(XX.X)	X(XX.X)	X(XX.X)
Not Evaluated (NE)	N(%)	X(XX.X)	X(XX.X)	X(XX.X)	X(XX.X)	X(XX.X)	X(XX.X)	X(XX.X)
Objective Response Rate (ORR confirmed; CR+PR)	N (%)	X(XX.X)	X(XX.X)	X(XX.X)	X(XX.X)	X(XX.X)	X(XX.X)	X(XX.X)
	95% CI [1]	XX.X, XX.X	XX.X, XX.X	XX.X, XX.X	XX.X, XX.X	XX.X, XX.X	XX.X, XX.X	XX.X, XX.X
Responders With Progression or Death	N (%)	X(XX.X)	X(XX.X)	X(XX.X)	X(XX.X)	X(XX.X)	X(XX.X)	X(XX.X)
Responders Censored	N (%)	X(XX.X)	X(XX.X)	X(XX.X)	X(XX.X)	X(XX.X)	X(XX.X)	X(XX.X)
Duration of Response (Months)	Median	XX.X	XX.X	X.X	XX.X	X.X	X.X	X.X
	95% CI [2]	X.X, XX.X	X.X, XX.X	X.X, X.X	X.X, XX.X	X.X, XX.X	X.X, X.X	X.X, X.X
	range	X.X, X.X+	X.X, X.X	X.X, X.X+	X.X, X.X	X.X, X.X+	X.X+, X.X	X.X, X.X+

Criteria for response assessment is RECIST 1.1.
Duration of Response is calculated only for confirmed responders and requires subsequent tumor assessments. DOR is measured from the date of first objective response (either CR or PR) to first documentation of disease progression or death due to any cause. For patients without disease progression or death, DOR will be censored at the last tumor assessment date. If there is no tumor assessment after the last date of response, the DOR will be censored at the date of response + 1 day.
'+' denotes a censored event.
[1] Confidence interval for ORR is based on Clopper-Pearson method.
[2] Confidence interval for median DOR is calculated based on Kaplan-Meier method.

/* Assuming you have data with information on response to treatment and tumor assessments */
   /* Calculate Duration of Response (DOR) */
data dor;
set your_data; /* Replace 'your_data' with the name of your dataset */
   /* Assuming 'response_date' is the variable containing the date of first objective response */
/* Assuming 'progression_date' is the variable containing the date of disease progression */
/* Assuming 'death_date' is the variable containing the date of death */
   /* Calculate DOR for confirmed responders */
if response_status = 'CR' or response_status = 'PR' then do;
DOR_start = response_date;
if progression_date ne . then DOR_end = progression_date;
else if death_date ne . then DOR_end = death_date;
else DOR_end = .; /* No progression or death */
/* Censoring for patients without progression or death */
if DOR_end = . then DOR_end = last_tumor_assessment_date + 1; /* Assuming 'last_tumor_assessment_date' is the variable for last tumor assessment */
DOR = DOR_end - DOR_start;
output;
end;
run;

/ Calculate confidence interval for Objective Response Rate (ORR) */*
proc freq data=your_data; / Replace 'your_data' with the name of your dataset */*
tables response_status / binomial method=clopperpearson;
run;
/ Calculate confidence interval for Median DOR using Kaplan-Meier method */*
proc lifetest data=dor method=km;
time DOR(!DOR_end);*
strata response_status;
run;

This SAS code performs the following tasks:

1. Calculates the Duration of Response (DOR) for confirmed responders, considering disease progression, death, and censoring.

2. Calculates the confidence interval for the Objective Response Rate (ORR) using the Clopper-Pearson method.

3. Calculates the confidence interval for the Median DOR using the Kaplan-Meier method.

Replace 'your_data' with the name of your actual dataset and adjust variable names accordingly based on your data structure.

Sure, here's a breakdown of the provided information:

1. **Criteria for response assessment (RECIST 1.1)**:

- RECIST 1.1 (Response Evaluation Criteria in Solid Tumors version 1.1) is the standard method used to assess responses to cancer treatment.

- It provides guidelines for measuring tumor size and defining response categories like complete response (CR), partial response (PR), stable disease (SD), and progressive disease (PD).

2. **Duration of Response (DOR)**:

- DOR is calculated only for confirmed responders, meaning those patients who have shown a positive response to treatment (either CR or PR).

- It is measured from the date of the first objective response to either the first documentation of disease progression or death due to any cause.

- For patients who do not experience disease progression or death, DOR is censored at the last tumor assessment date.

- If there is no tumor assessment after the last date of response, DOR is censored at the date of response plus one day.

3. **Censored Events**:

- The symbol '+' denotes a censored event. Censoring occurs when the event of interest (in this case, disease progression or death) has not occurred by the end of the study or observation period.

4. **Confidence Interval for Objective Response Rate (ORR)**:

- The confidence interval for ORR is based on the Clopper-Pearson method. This method provides a range estimate for the true ORR in the population.

5. **Confidence Interval for Median DOR**:

- The confidence interval for the median DOR is calculated based on the Kaplan-Meier method. This method estimates survival probabilities over time, in this case, the probability of maintaining response to treatment.

Each of these points outlines specific aspects of assessing treatment response and determining the duration of response in cancer patients, along with the statistical methods used to estimate confidence intervals for key metrics.

CHAPTER LXX

Kaplan–Meier Estimates of Progression–Free Survival and Overall Survival Table

```
                                              Table 14.2.2
                 Kaplan-Meier Estimates of Progression-Free Survival and Overall Survival
                                           Safety Population
```

Parameter/ Category	Statistics	pac 100 mg/ m^2 (N=xx) n(%)	Int + nab-pac 75 mg/m^2 (N=XX) n(%)	nab-pac 75 mg/m^2 (N=XX) n(%)	Cont + nab-pac 75 mg/m^2 (N=XX) n(%)	75 mg/m^2-Expansion (N=XX) n(%)	Int + mg/m^2-Total (N=XX) n(%)	All Patients (N=XX) n(%)
Progression-Free Survival (PFS)								
Events	N(%)	X(XX.X)	X(XX.X)	X(XX.X)	X(XX.X)	X(XX.X)	X(XX.X)	X(XX.X)
Censored	N(%)	X(XX.X)	X(XX.X)	X(XX.X)	X(XX.X)	X(XX.X)	X(XX.X)	X(XX.X)
PFS (months)								
	Median	XX.X	XX.X	XX.X	XX.X	XX.X	XX.X	XX.X
	95%CI	(XX.X-XX.X)	(XX.X-XX.X)	(XX.X-XX.X)	(XX.X-XX.X)	(XX.X-XX.X)	(XX.X-XX.X)	(XX.X-XX.X)
	range	X.X, X.X	X.X, X.X	X.X, X.X	X.X, X.X	X.X, X.X	X.X, X.X	X.X, X.X
Overall Survival (OS)								
Events	N(%)	X(XX.X)	X(XX.X)	X(XX.X)	X(XX.X)	X(XX.X)	X(XX.X)	X(XX.X)
Censored	N(%)	X(XX.X)	X(XX.X)	X(XX.X)	X(XX.X)	X(XX.X)	X(XX.X)	X(XX.X)
OS (months)								
	Median	XX.X	XX.X	XX.X	XX.X	XX.X	XX.X	XX.X
	95%CI	(XX.X-XX.X)	(XX.X-XX.X)	(XX.X-XX.X)	(XX.X-XX.X)	(XX.X-XX.X)	(XX.X-XX.X)	(XX.X-XX.X)
	range	X.X, X.X	X.X, X.X	X.X, X.X	X.X, X.X	X.X, X.X	X.X, X.X	X.X, X.X

Per RECIST 1.1 criteria PFS event is death or radiographic progression, and the PFS time is calduated in months from the first dose of either component of the study therapy until the first observation of disease progression.
Kaplan-Merier survival methods will be used to obtain the survial parameters for both OS an PFS.

Progression-Free Survival (PFS) using the RECIST 1.1 criteria and Kaplan-Meier survival methods:

```
/* Assuming you have data with information on response to treatment and tumor assessments */
    /* Calculate Progression-Free Survival (PFS) */
data pfs;
set your_data; /* Replace 'your_data' with the name of your dataset */
    /* Assuming 'progression_date' is the variable containing the date of disease progression */
/* Assuming 'death_date' is the variable containing the date of death */
/* Assuming 'first_dose_date' is the variable containing the date of the first dose of study therapy */
    /* Calculate PFS */
PFS_start = first_dose_date;
if progression_date ne . then PFS_end = progression_date;
else if death_date ne . then PFS_end = death_date;
else PFS_end = .; /* No progression or death */
PFS_months = intck('month', PFS_start, PFS_end, 'c'); /* Calculate PFS in months */
output;
run;
    /* Calculate Kaplan-Meier survival estimates for Overall Survival (OS) */
proc lifetest data=your_data; /* Replace 'your_data' with the name of your dataset */
time OS*(!death_date);
```

run;
    /* Calculate Kaplan-Meier survival estimates for Progression-Free Survival (PFS) */
proc lifetest data=pfs method=km;
time PFS_months*(!PFS_end);
run;

This SAS code now includes the following:

1. Calculation of Progression-Free Survival (PFS) according to RECIST 1.1 criteria, considering disease progression, death, and censoring.

2. Calculation of PFS time in months from the first dose of either component of the study therapy until the first observation of disease progression.

3. Calculation of Kaplan-Meier survival estimates for Overall Survival (OS) based on the time to death.

4. Calculation of Kaplan-Meier survival estimates for Progression-Free Survival (PFS) based on the PFS time in months.

Adjust variable names and data structure based on your specific dataset.

1. **RECIST 1.1 Criteria for Progression-Free Survival (PFS)**:

- According to RECIST 1.1 criteria, events defining disease progression for PFS include either death or radiographic progression.

- PFS time is calculated in months from the first dose of either component of the study therapy until the first observation of disease progression.

- This means that the clock for measuring PFS starts ticking from the time the patient receives the first dose of treatment until disease progression is observed, either radiographically or through death.

2. **Kaplan-Meier Survival Methods for OS and PFS**:

- Kaplan-Meier survival analysis is a statistical method used to estimate survival probabilities over time in medical research.

- It's commonly used to analyze time-to-event data, such as time to death or disease progression.

- In this context, Kaplan-Meier survival methods will be used to obtain survival parameters for both Overall Survival (OS) and Progression-Free Survival (PFS).

- These methods provide estimates of survival probabilities at different time points, allowing for comparison between different treatment groups or patient populations.

These points outline how RECIST 1.1 criteria define progression-free survival and how Kaplan-Meier survival methods will be applied to estimate survival probabilities for both OS and PFS in the context of the study or clinical trial.

CHAPTER LXXI

Compliance in oncology

Compliance in oncology studies typically refers to the extent to which patients adhere to the prescribed treatment regimen and follow study protocols. Here's a breakdown of compliance in oncology studies:

1. **Treatment Adherence**:
- Compliance involves patients taking the prescribed medications as instructed by their healthcare providers.
- In oncology studies, treatment adherence is crucial for evaluating the efficacy and safety of experimental therapies. Patients who do not comply with treatment regimens may skew study results.

2. **Protocol Adherence**:
- Patients in oncology studies are often required to follow specific protocols regarding treatment administration, follow-up visits, imaging scans, and laboratory tests.
- Compliance with study protocols ensures that data collected during the trial are accurate and reliable.

3. **Monitoring and Support**:
- Oncology studies typically include measures to monitor patient compliance, such as patient diaries, pill counts, or electronic medication monitoring devices.
- Healthcare providers may offer support and education to help patients understand the importance of adherence and manage treatment-related side effects.

4. **Impact on Study Outcomes**:
- Non-compliance can have significant implications for study outcomes. For example, patients who miss doses or skip appointments may experience treatment failure or adverse events that could affect the overall results of the study.
- It's essential for researchers to monitor and address compliance issues proactively to ensure the integrity of the study data.

5. **Factors Affecting Compliance**:
- Various factors can influence patient compliance in oncology studies, including treatment-related side effects, logistical challenges (such as transportation to medical appointments), psychological factors (such as anxiety or depression), and socioeconomic factors (such as access to healthcare or financial constraints).
- Understanding these factors can help researchers develop strategies to improve compliance and support patients throughout the study.

Overall, compliance in oncology studies is critical for maintaining the validity and reliability of research findings and ensuring that patients receive optimal care and support during the course of the study.

Compliance (%) = (Total capsules taken in a cycle/Total capsules planned on Day 1 in a cycle)*100

Note: Patients administered at least one dose in the cycle are counted as exposed during that cycle

CHAPTER LXXII

What are the key parameters used to assess dose intensity and exposure duration

1. **Cumulative Doses (mg):**
- Represents the total sum of all doses received within each treatment cycle.
- Provides an aggregate measure of the amount of medication administered to a patient during a specific period.

    2. **Cumulative Exposure Duration (weeks):**
- Calculates the total duration of exposure to ORIC-101 within a treatment cycle.
- Derived from the difference between the end date and start date of ORIC-101 treatment in a cycle, divided by 7 to convert to weeks.

    3. **Dose Intensity (DI) (mg/week):**
- Indicates the rate at which medication is administered per week.
- Calculated by dividing Cumulative Doses in a cycle by Cumulative Exposure Duration in weeks.

    4. **Planned Dose Intensity (PDI) (mg/week):**
- Represents the intended rate of medication administration per week as per the treatment plan.
- Obtained by dividing the cumulative planned dose in a cycle by the planned exposure duration in weeks.

    5. **Relative Dose Intensity (RDI) (%):**
- Provides a measure of the actual treatment intensity compared to the planned intensity.
- Calculated as a percentage by dividing DI by PDI and multiplying by 100.
- Offers insight into how closely patients adhere to the planned treatment regimen and whether adjustments are necessary to maintain therapeutic efficacy.

CHAPTER LXXIII

Adverse events role in oncology efficacy statistics

Adverse events play a crucial role in oncology efficacy statistics as they provide essential information about the safety profile and tolerability of a treatment regimen. Here's how adverse events influence oncology efficacy statistics:

1. **Safety Profile Assessment**:
- Adverse events are systematically monitored and recorded during clinical trials and real-world clinical practice.
- The type, severity, and frequency of adverse events provide insights into the safety profile of a treatment.
- Efficacy statistics must consider adverse events to ensure that any observed benefits are not outweighed by potential risks or harm to patients.

2. **Dose Modification and Treatment Discontinuation**:
- Severe or intolerable adverse events may lead to dose modifications or discontinuation of treatment.
- These modifications can impact treatment efficacy by altering the dose intensity or duration of therapy.
- Efficacy analyses often account for dose modifications and treatment discontinuations to assess the overall impact on patient outcomes.

3. **Quality of Life Considerations**:
- Adverse events can significantly impact patients' quality of life by causing discomfort, pain, or functional impairment.
- Assessing treatment efficacy requires considering not only clinical outcomes but also patients' subjective experiences and quality of life measures.
- Adverse event data contribute to a comprehensive understanding of treatment efficacy by incorporating patient-reported outcomes and functional assessments.

4. **Balancing Efficacy and Safety**:
- Oncology efficacy statistics must balance the benefits of treatment with its potential risks and adverse effects.
- Statistical analyses may evaluate efficacy endpoints in the context of specific adverse events or safety concerns.
- Risk-benefit assessments help clinicians and regulatory agencies make informed decisions about treatment recommendations, approvals, and labeling.

In summary, adverse events are integral to oncology efficacy statistics as they inform the safety profile, treatment tolerability, and overall risk-benefit balance of therapeutic interventions. Integrating adverse event data into efficacy analyses ensures a comprehensive evaluation of treatment outcomes and supports evidence-based clinical decision-making in oncology practice.

CHAPTER LXXIV

Solid Tumor Lesion, Lesions

1. **Solid Tumor Lesion**:
- A solid tumor lesion refers to an abnormal growth of cells that form a lump or mass in tissues or organs of the body.
- These tumors can occur in various parts of the body, including the breast, lung, colon, prostate, and brain, among others.
- Solid tumors are characterized by the uncontrolled proliferation of cells that can invade surrounding tissues and potentially spread to other parts of the body (metastasis).
2. **Pathology of Solid Tumor Lesions**:
- The pathology of solid tumor lesions involves the examination of tissue samples (biopsies) under a microscope to determine the characteristics of the tumor cells.
- Pathologists assess factors such as the tumor's histological type, grade, size, margins, and presence of specific biomarkers or genetic mutations.
- This information helps oncologists diagnose the type and stage of cancer, predict its behavior and prognosis, and guide treatment decisions.

CHAPTER LXXV

Why is planned treatment used for statistics in oncology efficacy programming?

1. **Consistency and Standardization**:
- Planned treatment ensures consistency by evaluating all patients according to the initially intended treatment regimen outlined in the study protocol.
- This standardization minimizes bias and facilitates valid comparisons across study participants.

2. **Preservation of Randomization**:
- Analyzing efficacy based on planned treatment preserves the integrity of randomization, ensuring that patient characteristics are evenly distributed across treatment arms.
- This helps maintain the comparability of treatment groups and supports the validity of statistical inference.

3. **Adherence to Intent-to-Treat Principle**:
- Planned treatment aligns with the intent-to-treat principle, allowing for the inclusion of all randomized patients in the analysis, regardless of adherence or protocol deviations.
- This approach ensures that the analysis reflects the real-world scenario and provides a comprehensive understanding of treatment effects.

4. **Clinical Relevance and Interpretability**:
- Results based on planned treatment provide insights into the anticipated outcomes of the intended treatment regimens.
- This enhances clinical relevance and interpretability, as clinicians can better understand the expected efficacy of the studied interventions.

5. **Regulatory Compliance and Scientific Standards**:
- Adherence to using planned treatment in efficacy analyses meets regulatory requirements and scientific standards.
- It ensures the credibility and acceptance of study findings within the scientific community and facilitates the regulatory approval process.

CHAPTER LXXVI

Population used for efficacy analysis

The population used for efficacy analysis in clinical trials typically includes participants who meet specific eligibility criteria and have received at least one dose of the study treatment. Here are the key points regarding the population used for efficacy analysis:

1. **Inclusion Criteria**:
- Participants included in the efficacy analysis must meet the predefined inclusion criteria outlined in the study protocol.
- These criteria may include factors such as age, gender, disease stage, histology, biomarker status, and prior treatment history.
- Inclusion criteria ensure that the study population is representative of the target patient population and allows for meaningful interpretation of efficacy outcomes.

2. **Randomized Treatment Assignment**:
- Efficacy analysis is typically conducted based on the treatment assignment randomized at the start of the trial.
- Participants are analyzed according to their allocated treatment arm, whether it be the experimental treatment, standard of care, or placebo.

3. **Intent-to-Treat (ITT) Population**:
- The ITT population includes all randomized participants who have received at least one dose of the study treatment, regardless of adherence or protocol deviations.
- ITT analysis maintains the benefits of randomization and provides a conservative estimate of treatment efficacy by including all participants as originally assigned, preserving the trial's internal validity.

4. **Per-Protocol (PP) Population**:
- In addition to ITT analysis, efficacy outcomes may be analyzed in the per-protocol population, which includes participants who adhere strictly to the study protocol without major protocol deviations.
- PP analysis provides insights into the efficacy of the treatment under optimal conditions but may introduce bias due to the exclusion of non-adherent participants.

5. **Subgroup Analyses**:
- Efficacy analysis may involve subgroup analyses to explore treatment effects in specific patient subpopulations.
- Subgroup analyses may focus on demographic factors, disease characteristics, biomarker status, or other relevant stratification factors identified a priori.

Overall, the population used for efficacy analysis in clinical trials is carefully selected based on predefined criteria, and the analysis is conducted in accordance with the principles of randomization and intention-to-treat to ensure the validity and generalizability of the study findings.

6. **DLT (Dose-Limiting Toxicity) Population**:
- In oncology clinical trials, the DLT population comprises participants who experience predefined toxicities or adverse events during the dose-escalation phase of the study.
- DLTs are adverse events that are considered significant and potentially dose-related, warranting careful monitoring during the early stages of treatment.
- Participants experiencing DLTs may have their treatment dose reduced or delayed, or they may be withdrawn from the study altogether.
- The analysis of the DLT population provides valuable insights into the safety and tolerability of the investigational treatment at various dose levels.
- Understanding the DLT profile helps determine the maximum tolerated dose (MTD) or recommended phase II dose (RP2D) for subsequent phases of the trial and informs dosing recommendations for future studies or clinical practice.

CHAPTER LXXVII

CMH table explantion

```
TINKER Pharmaceuticals Inc.
                                                                                    Page 1 of 1
                                         Table 4
           Number and Percentage of Clinical Responders Evaluated on Day 28 Using a CMH Test
                                       ITT Population
________________________________________________________________________________________________
Definition / rate                                              DRUG A              Placebo
    Statistic                                                  (N=28)              (N=30)
________________________________________________________________________________________________

Improvement of 2 or more point on clinical status
    n/N' (%)                                                XX /XX (XX.X)       XX /XX (XX.X)
    Risk (higher is better) difference                         XX.XX
    95% CI for risk difference (vs. placebo) [a]           (XX.XXX,XX.XXX)
    Adjusted relative risk (vs. placebo) [b]                   XX.XX
    95% CI for adjusted relative risk (vs. placebo) [b]    (X.XXXX,X.XXXX)
    CMH p-value (vs. placebo) [c]

________________________________________________________________________________________________

% = 100 x n/N', where N' is the number of subjects with non-missing values. CMH = Cochran-Mantel-Haenszel. CI = Confidence Interval.
[a] The 95% CI of risk difference is based on the Wald test.
[b] Adjusted relative risk and 95% CI are based on the ratio of responder rates for DRUG A versus placebo, stratified by sites.
[c] p-value is based on CMH test for association between treatment and responder rate, stratified by sites.
```

1. **Percentage Calculation**:

- The formula for calculating a percentage is: % = (100 x n) / N', where 'n' is the number of subjects with a specific characteristic or outcome, and 'N' is the total number of subjects.
- The denominator 'N' is adjusted to 'N'' to account for subjects with non-missing values, ensuring that missing data do not skew the calculation.

2. **CMH (Cochran-Mantel-Haenszel)**:

- CMH is a statistical method used to analyze categorical data, particularly in the context of stratified analysis.
- It adjusts for potential confounding variables (such as study sites) by stratifying the data before conducting statistical tests or estimations.

3. **Confidence Interval (CI)**:

- A confidence interval provides a range estimate for a population parameter (e.g., risk difference, relative risk) based on sample data.
- It quantifies the uncertainty associated with the estimate and indicates the precision of the result.
- The 95% CI, as mentioned, indicates that there is a 95% probability that the true population parameter lies within the calculated interval.

4. **Wald Test**:

- The Wald test is a statistical test used to assess the significance of estimated parameters in regression models or hypothesis testing.

- In this context, the 95% CI of the risk difference is based on the Wald test, indicating that it relies on the estimated parameters and their standard errors.

    5. **Adjusted Relative Risk**:

- Adjusted relative risk compares the risk of a specific outcome (e.g., responder rates) between different treatment groups while controlling for potential confounding factors.

- In this case, the adjusted relative risk compares the responder rates for tradipitant versus placebo, with stratification by study sites to account for potential site effects.

    6. **CMH Test**:

- The CMH test assesses the association between categorical variables (e.g., treatment and responder rate) while controlling for confounding variables through stratification.

- In this context, the p-value based on the CMH test indicates the significance of the association between treatment (tradipitant versus placebo) and responder rate after adjusting for site effects.

These explanations provide a clearer understanding of the statistical methods and interpretations involved in the analysis of clinical trial data, particularly in assessing treatment effects and associations.

    1. **Percentage Calculation**:

```
/* Assuming 'n' is the number of subjects with a specific characteristic or outcome */
/* Assuming 'N' is the total number of subjects */
    data example;
n = 50; /* Number of subjects with the characteristic */
N = 100; /* Total number of subjects */
percentage = (100 * n) / N;
run;
```

    2. **Confidence Interval (CI)**:

```
/* Assuming 'estimate' is the point estimate */
/* Assuming 'std_error' is the standard error of the estimate */
    proc means data=your_data mean std;
var estimate std_error;
run;
```

    3. **Adjusted Relative Risk (ARR)**:

```
/* Assuming 'responder_rate_tradipitant' is the responder rate for tradipitant */
/* Assuming 'responder_rate_placebo' is the responder rate for placebo */
/* Assuming 'site' is the variable representing study sites */
    proc freq data=your_data;
tables treatment*site / chisq relrisk;
run;
```

    4. **CMH Test**:

```
/* Assuming 'treatment' is the variable representing treatment groups */
/* Assuming 'responder' is the variable representing responder status */
/* Assuming 'site' is the variable representing study sites */
    proc freq data=your_data;
tables treatment*responder*site / chisq cmh;
run;
```

CHAPTER LXXVIII

Wald test

The Wald test is commonly used in statistical hypothesis testing to assess the significance of estimated parameters, particularly in regression models. Here's how you can conduct a Wald test using SAS:

```
/* Assuming you have fitted a regression model */
   proc reg data=your_data;
model dependent_variable = independent_variable;
run;
   /* Assuming you want to perform a Wald test for a specific parameter */
   proc reg data=your_data;
model dependent_variable = independent_variable;
test independent_variable;
run;
```

In this SAS code:

- Replace `your_data`, `dependent_variable`, and `independent_variable` with the names of your dataset, dependent variable, and independent variable, respectively.
- The `proc reg` procedure is used to fit a regression model.
- The `model` statement specifies the regression model, where `dependent_variable` is regressed on `independent_variable`.
- The `test` statement is used to perform the Wald test for a specific parameter (in this case, `independent_variable`).
- The Wald test assesses the null hypothesis that the coefficient of `independent_variable` is equal to zero, indicating no effect on the dependent variable.

Adjust the code according to your specific regression model and hypothesis testing requirements.

CHAPTER LXXIX

Kaplan–Meier Method table

```
                              Table 5
          Analysis of Time to First Opioid Use Using Kaplan-Meier Method
                            ITT Population
          ________________________________________________________________

                            Placebo                  Active
          Statistics
                            (N = xxx)                (N = xxx)
          ________________________________________________________________

          Kaplan-Meier Method


          Mean (SE)         XX.X (XX.X)              XX.X (XX.X)
          Median            XXX.X                    XXX.X
          Q1 - Q3           XXX.X - XXX.X            XXX.X - XXX.X
          p-value[a]                                 0.xxxx
          ________________________________________________________________

          Patients with no use will be censored at the time of discharge.
          [a]p-value were provided by log-rank test for treatment comparison.
```

1. **Censoring of Patients with No Use at Time of Discharge**:

- In survival analysis, censoring occurs when the event of interest (such as death or disease progression) has not occurred by the end of the study or observation period.

- Patients who have not experienced the event of interest by the time of discharge from the study are considered censored.

- Censoring at the time of discharge is a common practice in clinical studies, especially in longitudinal studies or trials with varying follow-up periods.

- By censoring patients at the time of discharge, the analysis accounts for the fact that their outcomes are unknown beyond that point, thus ensuring the integrity of the survival analysis.

2. **P-Values Provided by Log-Rank Test for Treatment Comparison**:

- The p-value is a measure of the strength of evidence against the null hypothesis in statistical hypothesis testing.

- In the context of survival analysis, the log-rank test is a commonly used statistical test to compare survival curves between different groups or treatments.

- The log-rank test assesses whether there is a significant difference in survival probabilities between the groups being compared.

- The p-value provided by the log-rank test indicates the probability of observing the observed difference in survival between groups if there were no true difference.

- A small p-value (typically < 0.05) suggests that there is evidence to reject the null hypothesis of no difference in survival, indicating a significant difference between the groups being compared.

- The p-value from the log-rank test is often reported in survival analysis to assess the efficacy of different treatments or interventions in clinical studies.

```
/* Assuming you have a dataset named 'your_data' with the relevant variables */
    /* Calculate Mean, Standard Error, Median, First Quartile, and Third Quartile */
proc means data=your_data mean std median q1 q3;
var variable_of_interest; /* Replace 'variable_of_interest' with the name of your variable */
run;
    /* Perform Log-Rank Test for Treatment Comparison */
proc lifetest data=your_data method=logrank;
```

time time_variable; / Replace 'time_variable' with the name of your time-to-event variable */*
strata treatment_variable; / Replace 'treatment_variable' with the name of your treatment variable */*
run;

   - Replace ``your_data`` with the name of your dataset.
- Replace ``variable_of_interest`` with the name of the variable for which you want to calculate the mean, SE, median, Q1, and Q3.
- Replace ``time_variable`` with the name of your time-to-event variable, and ``treatment_variable`` with the name of your treatment variable in the log-rank test.

This code will provide you with the mean, SE, median, Q1, and Q3 using `proc means`. Additionally, it will perform a log-rank test for treatment comparison using `proc lifetest`. Adjust the variable names and dataset according to your specific data and analysis requirements.

CHAPTER LXXX

Estimate the hazard ratio and its 95% confidence interval (CI) using Cox regression:

Estimate the hazard ratio and its 95% confidence interval (CI) using Cox regression:
   1. **Hazard Ratio (HR)**:
- The hazard ratio is a measure of the relative risk of experiencing an event (e.g., death, disease progression) between two groups.
- It quantifies the instantaneous risk of an event occurring in one group compared to another, over time.
- In Cox regression, the hazard ratio is estimated based on the proportional hazards assumption, which assumes that the hazard functions of the compared groups are proportional over time.
   2. **95% Confidence Interval (CI)**:
- The 95% confidence interval provides a range of values within which the true hazard ratio is likely to fall with 95% confidence.
- It indicates the precision of the estimated hazard ratio and helps assess the uncertainty associated with the point estimate.
   3. **Cox Regression**:
- Cox regression, also known as proportional hazards regression, is a statistical method used to model the relationship between survival time and one or more predictor variables.
- It estimates the hazard ratio by assessing how the hazard function changes as a function of the predictor variables while assuming proportional hazards.

   Here's how you can perform Cox regression analysis in SAS to estimate the hazard ratio and its 95% CI:

```
/* Assuming you have a dataset named 'your_data' with the relevant variables */
   /* Perform Cox Regression Analysis */
proc phreg data=your_data;
model time_to_event*censor(1) = predictor_variable / ties=efron;
/* Replace 'time_to_event' with the name of your time-to-event variable,
'censor' with the censoring indicator variable,
and 'predictor_variable' with the predictor variable(s) of interest */
/* The 'ties=efron' option specifies the Efron method for handling tied event times */
/* Add 'strata' statement if there are stratification variables */
run;
```

   In this SAS code:
- Replace ``your_data`` with the name of your dataset.
- Replace ``time_to_event`` with the name of your time-to-event variable.
- Replace ``censor`` with the censoring indicator variable.
- Replace ``predictor_variable`` with the predictor variable(s) you want to include in the Cox regression model.

   The output of the Cox regression analysis will include the estimated hazard ratio and its 95% CI, along with other relevant statistics.

CHAPTER LXXXI

Mixed-effects model for repeated measures (MMRM)

mixed-effects model for repeated measures (MMRM)
   1. **LS Means**:
- LS means, or least squares means, represent the average response across treatment groups after adjusting for covariates in the model.
- They provide estimates of the mean response at each level of categorical variables, accounting for the effects of other variables in the model.
- LS means are often used to compare treatment groups while controlling for covariates and other factors.
   2. **Confidence Intervals (CIs)**:
- CIs provide a range of values within which the true population parameter (e.g., mean response) is likely to fall with a certain level of confidence (e.g., 95% confidence).
- In this context, CIs for LS means indicate the uncertainty associated with the estimated mean response for each treatment group.
   3. **P-Values**:
- P-values indicate the statistical significance of differences between treatment groups or the significance of the effects of predictors in the model.
- They quantify the evidence against the null hypothesis of no difference or no effect.
- In MMRM analysis, p-values are commonly used to assess the significance of treatment effects, time effects, and interaction effects.
   4. **Mixed-Effects Model for Repeated Measures (MMRM)**:
- MMRM is a statistical method used to analyze longitudinal or repeated measures data, such as data collected over multiple time points.
- It accounts for within-subject correlation and handles missing data more effectively compared to traditional methods like repeated measures ANOVA.
- MMRM allows for the inclusion of both fixed effects (e.g., treatment group, disease type, time) and random effects (e.g., subject-specific intercepts) in the model.
- The model estimates fixed effects parameters (such as treatment group effects) and provides adjusted estimates of means over time (LS means), along with associated CIs and p-values.

Here's how you can perform MMRM analysis in SAS:

```
/* Assuming you have a dataset named 'your_data' with the relevant variables */
    proc mixed data=your_data;
class treatment_group disease_type week;
model response_variable = treatment_group|week disease_type|week baseline baseline*week / solution;
random intercept / subject=subject_id;
run;
```

In this SAS code:
- Replace `'your_data'` with the name of your dataset.
- Replace `'response_variable'` with the name of your response variable.
- Adjust the `class` statement to include the categorical variables in your model (e.g., treatment group, disease type, week).
- Specify the fixed effects (e.g., treatment group, disease type, week, interactions) and covariates (e.g., baseline) in the `model` statement.

- Use the `random` statement to specify any random effects (e.g., subject-specific intercept) if applicable.
- The `solution` option in the `model` statement requests LS means estimation.
- The output will include LS means, CIs, and p-values based on the specified MMRM model. Adjust variable names and data structures based on your specific dataset and analysis requirements.

CHAPTER LXXXII

LS means LS mean difference

LS mean difference refers to the difference between the least squares means (LS means) of two or more groups or levels of a categorical variable.

LS means represent the estimated average response for each group after accounting for other variables in the model, such as covariates and interaction terms.

LS mean differences are useful for comparing treatment effects or group differences while adjusting for potential confounders.

Here's how you can calculate LS mean differences using SAS:

```
/* Assuming you have a dataset named 'your_data' with the relevant variables */
   /* Calculate LS Means and LS Mean Differences */
proc mixed data=your_data;
class treatment_group;
model response_variable = treatment_group / solution;
lsmeans treatment_group / adjust=tukey cl diff;
run;
```

In this SAS code:
- Replace `'your_data'` with the name of your dataset.
- Replace `'response_variable'` with the name of your response variable.
- Adjust the `class` statement to include the categorical variable for which you want to calculate LS means and differences (e.g., treatment_group).
- The `lsmeans` statement requests LS means estimation for the specified variable.
- The `adjust=tukey` option performs pairwise comparisons of LS means using the Tukey adjustment method to control the family-wise error rate.
- The `cl diff` option requests confidence limits for the LS mean differences.
- The output will include LS means and LS mean differences along with confidence intervals. Adjust variable names and data structures based on your specific dataset and analysis requirements.

p-values Demographic tables

In statistical analysis, p-values are used to determine the significance of associations or differences between groups.

Table 2 Subject Demographics -Sex and Race (Safety Population)

Category	Statistic	DRUG A (N=3)	DRUG B (N=3)	P-value
Gender	Male	3(100)	0	0.014
	Female	0	3(100)	
Race	Asian	0	1 (33.3)	1.000
	Black or african american	0	1 (33.3)	
	White	2 (66.7)	1 (33.3)	
	Other	1 (33.3)	0	

When analyzing demographics such as sex and race, p-values can help assess whether there are statistically significant differences in the distribution of these variables among groups or treatment arms.

Here's how you can use p-values to analyze demographics like sex and race using SAS:

```
/* Assuming you have a dataset named 'your_data' with the relevant demographic variables */
   /* Perform Chi-Square Test for Sex */
proc freq data=your_data;
tables sex / chisq;
run;
   /* Perform Chi-Square Test for Race */
proc freq data=your_data;
tables race / chisq;
run;
```

In this SAS code:

- Replace ``your_data`` with the name of your dataset.
- The `proc freq` procedure is used to perform frequency analysis.
- The `tables` statement specifies the variables for which you want to calculate frequencies and conduct the chi-square test.
- The `chisq` option in the `tables` statement requests the chi-square test for assessing the association between the demographic variable and other categorical variables.
- The output will include p-values indicating the significance of associations between sex/race and other categorical variables in your dataset.

<u>Interpreting the results:</u>

- A small p-value (typically < 0.05) indicates that there is evidence to reject the null hypothesis of no association, suggesting that there may be a statistically significant difference in the distribution of sex or race among groups.
- Conversely, a large p-value suggests that there is insufficient evidence to reject the null hypothesis, indicating that there may not be a statistically significant difference in the distribution of sex or race among groups.

By analyzing p-values for demographics such as sex and race, researchers can assess whether these variables are associated with other variables of interest in their dataset, helping to identify potential confounding factors or subgroup differences. Adjust variable names and data structures based on your specific dataset and analysis requirements.

CHAPTER LXXXIV

Improvement rate at a specific time

To calculate the improvement rate at a specific time, you can subtract the survival rate from 1.

This approach assumes that the survival rate represents the proportion of individuals who have not experienced the event of interest (e.g., death, disease progression) up to that point in time.

Subtracting this rate from 1 gives you the proportion of individuals who have experienced the event by that time, representing the improvement rate.

/ Assuming you have a dataset named 'your_data' with the relevant survival data */*
   / Calculate Survival Rate */*
proc lifetest data=your_data method=kaplanmeier;
time time_variable;
event event_variable;
run;
   / Calculate Improvement Rate */*
data improvement_rate;
set your_data;
/ Assuming 'survival_rate' is the variable representing survival rate */*
/ Calculate Improvement Rate at Time t */*
improvement_rate_at_t = 1 - survival_rate_at_t;
run;

In this SAS code:
- Replace ``your_data`` with the name of your dataset.
- Replace ``time_variable`` with the name of your time-to-event variable.
- Replace ``event_variable`` with the name of your event indicator variable (1 for event occurrence, 0 for censored).
- The `proc lifetest` procedure is used to calculate the survival rate using the Kaplan-Meier method.
- The `time_variable` specifies the time-to-event variable, and the `event_variable` specifies the event indicator variable.
- The `data` step calculates the improvement rate at a specific time ('t') by subtracting the survival rate at that time from 1.
- The output dataset `improvement_rate` will contain the improvement rate at the specified time point.

CHAPTER LXXXV

25th percentile, 75th percentile, median, and Kaplan–Meier estimates with 95% confidence intervals.

calculate the 25th percentile, 75th percentile, median, and Kaplan-Meier estimates with 95% confidence intervals.

1. **Percentiles:**
- Percentiles represent specific points in a dataset below which a certain percentage of observations fall. For example, the 25th percentile (also known as the first quartile) represents the value below which 25% of the observations lie.

2. **Median**:
- The median is the middle value of a dataset when it is ordered from least to greatest. It represents the value below and above which 50% of the observations lie.

3. **Kaplan-Meier Estimates**:
- Kaplan-Meier estimates are used to estimate survival probabilities over time in survival analysis.
- They provide a non-parametric estimate of the survival function, which represents the probability of surviving beyond a certain time point.

4. **95% Confidence Intervals (CI)**:
- Confidence intervals provide a range of values within which the true population parameter (e.g., survival probability) is likely to lie with a certain level of confidence (e.g., 95% confidence).
- They quantify the uncertainty associated with the estimated parameter.

```
/* Assuming you have a dataset named 'your_data' with the relevant survival data */
    /* Calculate Percentiles, Median, and Kaplan-Meier Estimates */
proc lifetest data=your_data method=kaplanmeier;
time time_variable;
event event_variable;
output out=km_estimates pctlpts=(25 50 75) median=0.5 ci=(lower upper);
run;
    /* Display Kaplan-Meier Estimates and Confidence Intervals */
proc print data=km_estimates;
var time_variable survival_est lower upper;
title 'Kaplan-Meier Estimates with 95% CI';
run;
```

Explanation of SAS code:
- Replace ``your_data`` with the name of your dataset.
- Replace ``time_variable`` with the name of your time-to-event variable.
- Replace ``event_variable`` with the name of your event indicator variable (1 for event occurrence, 0 for censored).
- The `proc lifetest` procedure calculates Kaplan-Meier estimates of survival probabilities.
- The `pctlpts` option specifies the percentiles to calculate (25th, 50th, and 75th percentiles for median and quartiles).
- The `median` option specifies to calculate the median survival time.
- The `ci` option specifies to calculate confidence intervals for the estimates.
- The `output` statement stores the Kaplan-Meier estimates, percentiles, and confidence intervals in an output dataset named `km_estimates`.
- The `proc print` procedure displays the Kaplan-Meier estimates along with their confidence intervals.

Adjust variable names and data structures based on your specific dataset and analysis requirements. This code will provide you with Kaplan-Meier estimates at the specified percentiles (25th, 50th, and 75th), along with the median and their associated 95% confidence intervals.

CHAPTER LXXXVI

What is correlation and what is positive and negative correlation

Certainly! Here's an explanation of correlation along with SAS code to compute the correlation coefficient and interpret positive and negative correlations:

    1. **Correlation**:
- Correlation measures the strength and direction of the linear relationship between two continuous variables.
- The correlation coefficient, denoted by 'r', ranges from -1 to 1.
- A positive value of 'r' indicates a positive correlation, where both variables tend to increase or decrease together.
- A negative value of 'r' indicates a negative correlation, where one variable tends to increase while the other decreases.

    2. **Positive Correlation**:
- In a positive correlation, an increase in one variable is associated with an increase in the other variable.
- The correlation coefficient 'r' is close to 1 for a strong positive correlation.
- Example: In SAS, let's say we want to compute the correlation between study time and exam scores. We expect a positive correlation, meaning that as study time increases, exam scores also tend to increase.

    3. **Negative Correlation**:
- In a negative correlation, an increase in one variable is associated with a decrease in the other variable.
- The correlation coefficient 'r' is close to -1 for a strong negative correlation.
- Example: We might want to compute the correlation between temperature and heating costs. We expect a negative correlation, as higher temperatures are associated with lower heating costs.

    Here's the SAS code to compute and interpret correlations:

```
/* Assuming you have a dataset named 'your_data' with variables 'variable1' and 'variable2' */
    /* Compute Correlation Coefficient */
proc corr data=your_data;
var variable1 variable2;
/* Replace 'variable1' and 'variable2' with your variables of interest */
run;
```

    Explanation of SAS code:
- Replace `'your_data'` with the name of your dataset.
- Replace `'variable1'` and `'variable2'` with the names of the variables for which you want to compute the correlation coefficient.
- The `proc corr` procedure computes the correlation coefficient between the specified variables.
- The `var` statement specifies the variables of interest.
- The output includes the correlation coefficient ('r'), which can be interpreted as follows:
- Positive correlation: 'r' close to 1.
- Negative correlation: 'r' close to -1.
- No correlation: 'r' close to 0.

    This SAS code helps you calculate and interpret correlations between variables, aiding in understanding the relationships and patterns in your data. Adjust variable names and data structures based on your specific dataset and analysis requirements.

CHAPTER LXXXVII

What is P-value and why P-value required (To compare the variable values in two different groups)

The p-value is a statistical measure used in hypothesis testing to determine the strength of evidence against the null hypothesis. In general, the null hypothesis represents the default assumption that there is no effect or no difference between groups, while the alternative hypothesis suggests that there is an effect or difference.

The p-value indicates the probability of obtaining the observed data, or more extreme data, assuming that the null hypothesis is true. A low p-value (< 0.05) suggests that the observed data is unlikely to have occurred if the null hypothesis is true, leading to the rejection of the null hypothesis in favor of the alternative hypothesis. On the other hand, a high p-value (> 0.05) suggests that the observed data is likely to occur even if the null hypothesis is true, leading to the failure to reject the null hypothesis.

In the context of comparing variable values in two different groups:
- The null hypothesis often states that there is no difference between the two groups (e.g., no difference in means, proportions, etc.).
- The alternative hypothesis suggests that there is a difference between the groups.
- The p-value associated with a statistical test (e.g., t-test, chi-square test) quantifies the likelihood of observing the data if there is no true difference between the groups.
- If the p-value is sufficiently low, it provides evidence against the null hypothesis, indicating that there is a statistically significant difference between the groups.

In summary, the p-value is required to assess the significance of differences between groups and to make informed decisions about whether these differences are likely to be due to chance or reflect true underlying differences in the population.

Oncology clinical trials shift tables

In oncology clinical trials, shift tables are commonly used to summarize shifts in categorical variables, particularly adverse events (AEs), laboratory abnormalities, or other safety-related outcomes. Shift tables provide a concise summary of the changes or shifts from baseline to post-baseline measurements for each category or severity level of an event.

Here are different types of shift tables used in efficacy and oncology:

1. **Adverse Event (AE) Shift Tables**:
- These tables summarize shifts in the severity or grade of adverse events observed in clinical trials.
- Categories often include mild, moderate, severe, and life-threatening events, as well as events leading to death or discontinuation.
- The table shows the number and percentage of patients who experience shifts in severity from baseline to post-baseline assessments.

2. **Laboratory Abnormality Shift Tables**:
- These tables summarize shifts in laboratory parameters such as blood chemistry, hematology, or urinalysis results.
- Categories typically include normal, mild, moderate, and severe abnormalities, based on predefined reference ranges or criteria.
- The table presents the number and percentage of patients who experience shifts in abnormality severity from baseline to post-baseline measurements.

3. **Vital Sign Shift Tables**:
- These tables summarize shifts in vital sign measurements such as blood pressure, heart rate, temperature, or respiratory rate.
- Categories may include predefined ranges for normal, low, high, or clinically significant values.
- The table displays the number and percentage of patients with shifts in vital sign measurements from baseline to post-baseline assessments.

4. **Efficacy Shift Tables**:
- In efficacy analysis, shift tables may summarize shifts in response categories or disease status.
- Categories could include complete response, partial response, stable disease, progressive disease, or improvement in disease severity.
- The table presents the number and percentage of patients with shifts in response or disease status from baseline to post-treatment assessments.

5. **Duration of Shifts**:
- Some shift tables also include information on the duration of shifts, indicating how long patients remained in a particular category or severity level after the initial shift occurred.
- Duration data can provide insights into the persistence of treatment-related effects or the resolution of adverse events over time.

6. **Shifts by Treatment Group**:
- Shift tables may stratify shifts by treatment group to compare the occurrence and severity of events between different treatment arms.
- Comparing shift patterns across treatment groups helps evaluate the safety and efficacy profile of each treatment regimen and identify potential differences in treatment effects.

7. **Shifts Over Time**:
- Longitudinal shift tables track shifts in categorical variables over multiple time points, allowing for the assessment of temporal trends and changes in event frequency or severity throughout the study duration.
- Analyzing shifts over time provides a comprehensive understanding of the dynamic nature of treatment-related

effects and disease progression.

   8. **Cumulative Shifts**:

- Cumulative shift tables aggregate data across multiple visits or assessment periods to summarize the overall incidence and severity of shifts over the entire study duration.

- Cumulative shift tables help capture the cumulative burden of adverse events or changes in efficacy outcomes, considering all available data points.

   9. **Shifts by Baseline Characteristics**:

- Shift tables may analyze shifts in categorical variables based on baseline characteristics such as age, sex, disease stage, or biomarker status.

- Stratifying shift analyses by baseline characteristics allows for the identification of subgroups that may be more susceptible to certain treatment effects or disease-related changes.

   10. **Safety and Tolerability Assessment**:

- Shift tables play a crucial role in safety and tolerability assessments by summarizing treatment-emergent adverse events and changes in laboratory parameters.

- These tables inform clinical decision-making by providing clinicians, investigators, and regulatory authorities with a clear overview of treatment-related risks and benefits.

CHAPTER LXXXIX

Different types of figures specific to oncology

Different types of figures specific to oncology research:
  1. **Kaplan-Meier Plot**:
- A Kaplan-Meier plot displays survival probabilities over time for different groups of patients in oncology studies.
- It is commonly used to visualize survival outcomes, such as overall survival or progression-free survival, in response to different treatments or interventions.
  2. **Forest Plot**:
- A forest plot presents the effect sizes and confidence intervals of multiple studies or subgroups within a meta-analysis.
- In oncology research, forest plots are often used to compare treatment effects across various studies or to evaluate the impact of prognostic factors on outcomes.
  3. **Waterfall Plot**:
- A waterfall plot illustrates the change in tumor size or response to treatment for individual patients in oncology clinical trials.
- It provides a visual representation of treatment responses, with bars showing the magnitude and direction of change in tumor measurements.
  4. **Swimmer Plot**:
- A swimmer plot depicts the survival status and time to event (e.g., progression, death) for individual patients over time.
- In oncology, swimmer plots are used to visualize patient outcomes, treatment duration, and disease progression patterns.
  5. **Receiver Operating Characteristic (ROC) Curve**:
- An ROC curve evaluates the diagnostic accuracy of a binary classifier (e.g., a biomarker or imaging test) in distinguishing between two outcomes (e.g., presence or absence of cancer).
- It is commonly used in oncology to assess the sensitivity and specificity of diagnostic tests or predictive models.
  6. **Spider Plot**:
- A spider plot, also known as a radar plot, displays multiple variables on a circular grid, with each axis representing a different variable.
- In oncology, spider plots can be used to compare multiple treatment outcomes or biomarker profiles across different patients or subgroups.
  7. **Mutation Landscape Plot**:
- A mutation landscape plot visualizes the distribution and frequency of genetic mutations across different genes or genomic regions in cancer patients.
- It provides insights into the mutational landscape of tumors and can help identify recurrent mutations or driver genes.
  8. **Chord Diagram**:
- A chord diagram represents relationships or connections between different entities (e.g., genes, pathways) in a circular layout, with ribbons connecting related entities.
- In oncology research, chord diagrams can illustrate gene-gene interactions, pathway crosstalk, or co-occurrence patterns of mutations in cancer genomes.
  9. **Heatmap with Clustering**:
- A heatmap with clustering combines a heatmap with hierarchical clustering techniques to visualize similarities or differences between samples (e.g., patients, tumors) based on multiple variables.
- It can reveal patterns of gene expression, protein expression, or molecular profiles in cancer datasets.

<u>10. **Response Surface Plot**</u>:

- A response surface plot visualizes the relationship between multiple continuous variables (e.g., drug dose, treatment duration) and a response variable (e.g., tumor size, survival probability) in oncology studies.
- It helps identify optimal treatment regimens or dose-response relationships for maximizing treatment efficacy and minimizing toxicity.

swimmer plot

A swimmer plot is a type of graph used in oncology research to visualize individual patient data over time, particularly in clinical trials or observational studies. It displays the survival status and time to event (such as disease progression or death) for each patient on a horizontal timeline. Each patient is represented as a horizontal line or "swimmer," with events indicated by symbols or markers along the line.

    1. **Explanation**:

- In a swimmer plot, each patient's line starts at the time of study entry and progresses horizontally to the time of the event (e.g., progression or death) or to the last follow-up time if the event has not occurred.

- Events such as progression or death are marked along each patient's line, providing a visual representation of their clinical course over time.

- Swimmer plots allow for the comparison of patient outcomes, treatment durations, and disease progression patterns in oncology studies.

    2. **SAS Code**:

```sas
/* Assuming you have a dataset named 'your_data' with patient-level survival data */
   /* Sort the dataset by patient ID and time to event */
proc sort data=your_data;
by patient_id time_to_event;
run;
   /* Create a swimmer plot using PROC SGPLOT */
proc sgplot data=your_data noautolegend;
/* Plot each patient's survival status over time */
scatter x=time_to_event y=patient_id / markerattrs=(symbol=circlefilled);
/* Connect points for each patient */
series x=time_to_event y=patient_id / group=patient_id lineattrs=(thickness=2);
/* Add reference lines for events (e.g., progression, death) */
refline x=0 to max_time / axis=x lineattrs=(pattern=dash) label=('Event');
/* Customize plot appearance */
yaxis display=(noline noticks) label='Patient ID';
xaxis label='Time to Event';
title 'Swimmer Plot of Patient Survival';
run;
```

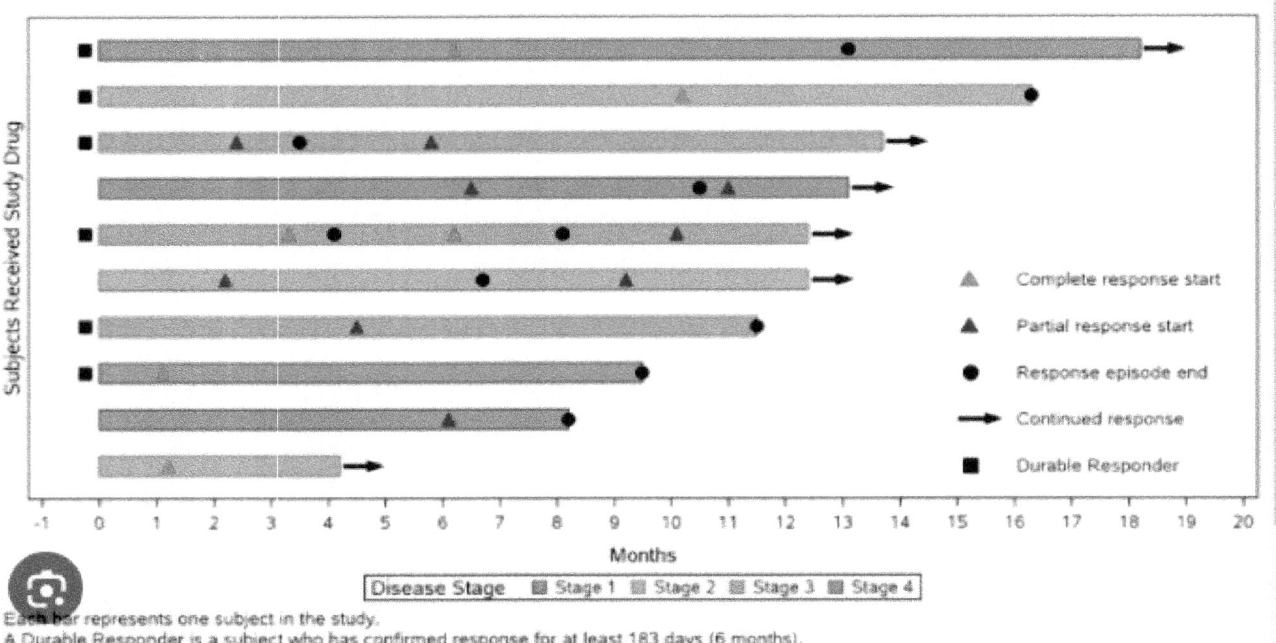

In this SAS code:

- Replace ``your_data`` with the name of your dataset containing patient-level survival data.

- Ensure the dataset is sorted by patient ID and time to event to maintain the correct order of observations.

- The `scatter` statement plots markers for each event occurrence (e.g., progression, death) at the corresponding time point for each patient.

- The `series` statement connects the markers for each patient, creating the swimmer plot.

- Reference lines (`refline`) can be added to mark specific events or time points of interest along the x-axis.

- Customize the appearance of the plot using options such as axis labels, titles, and line attributes.

This SAS code generates a swimmer plot to visualize individual patient survival data over time in an oncology study. Adjust variable names, data structures, and plot customization according to your specific dataset and analysis requirements.

spider plot

In oncology research, a spider plot, also known as a radar plot or spider chart, is a graphical tool used to compare multiple variables or parameters across different categories or groups. It consists of multiple axes radiating from a central point, with each axis representing a different variable. The data for each category are plotted as points or lines on the respective axes, and the overall pattern or shape of the plot helps visualize patterns or differences between categories.

1. **Explanation**:

- A spider plot is particularly useful in oncology for comparing multiple treatment outcomes, biomarker profiles, or patient characteristics across different treatment groups, disease subtypes, or time points.
- Each axis of the spider plot represents a relevant variable or parameter, such as treatment response criteria, biomarker expression levels, or clinical endpoints.
- The values for each variable are scaled and plotted along the corresponding axis, and the resulting plot provides a visual representation of the relative performance or characteristics of each category.

2. **SAS Code**:

```
/* Example SAS code to create a spider plot */
/* Create sample data */
data spider_data;
input Category $ Response Biomarker1 Biomarker2 Biomarker3;
datalines;
Group1 0.8 0.6 0.7 0.5
Group2 0.6 0.7 0.5 0.8
Group3 0.5 0.8 0.6 0.7
;
run;
    /* Create spider plot using PROC SGPLOT */
proc sgplot data=spider_data;
radar category=Category values=(Response Biomarker1 Biomarker2 Biomarker3);
keylegend / location=inside position=right;
title 'Spider Plot of Treatment Responses and Biomarker Profiles';
run;
```

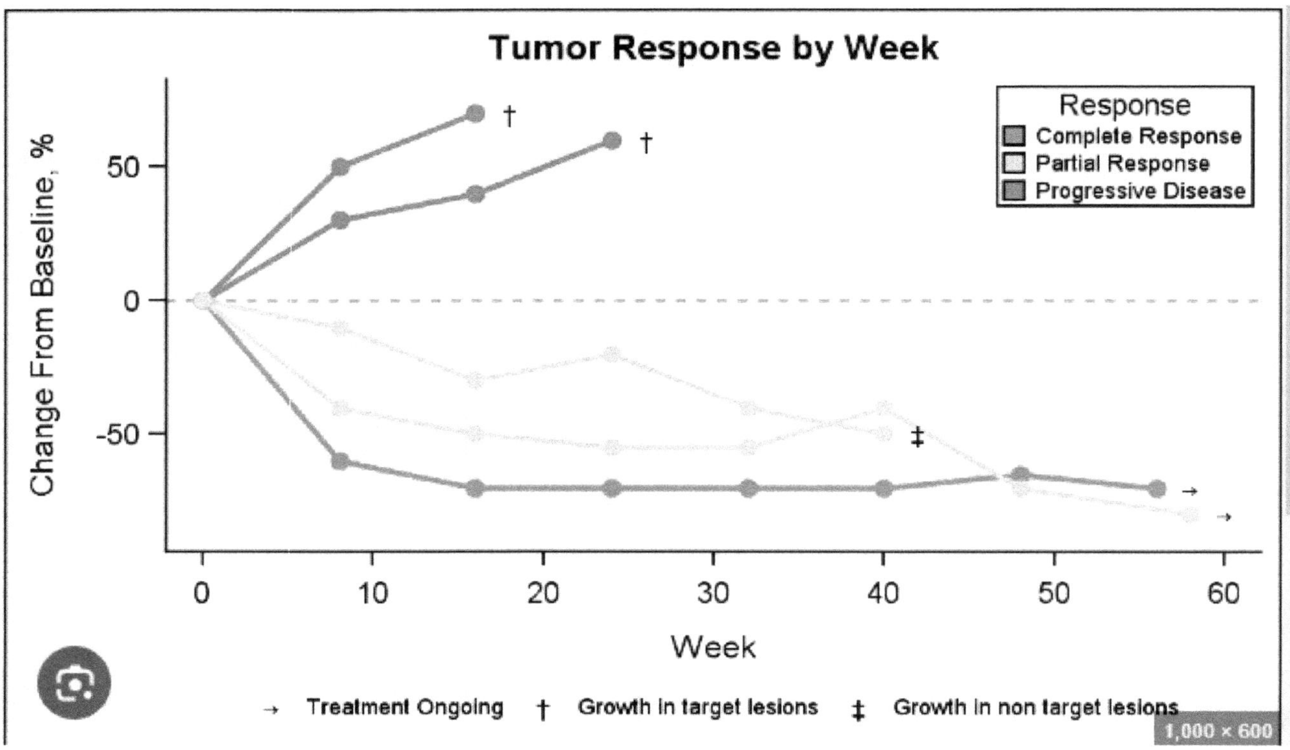

In this SAS code:

- We create sample data (`spider_data`) containing different treatment groups (`Category`) and their corresponding responses and biomarker profiles.
- The `radar` statement in `PROC SGPLOT` is used to create the spider plot, with `Category` as the categorical variable and `Response` and `Biomarker1` to `Biomarker3` as the variables plotted on the axes.
- The `keylegend` statement adds a legend to the plot for better interpretation.
- Finally, we provide a title for the plot.

Adjust the variable names, data structures, and plot customization according to your specific dataset and analysis requirements. This SAS code generates a spider plot to compare treatment responses and biomarker profiles across different categories or groups in oncology research.

How do statisticians determine the most suitable statistical method for analyzing clinical data?

The choice of statistical method, such as PROC ANOVA, PROC GLM, PROC MIXED, PROC TTEST, or PROC FREQ, to analyze clinical data depends on several factors, including the research question, the type of data, the study design, and the underlying assumptions of the statistical model. Statisticians typically consider the following criteria when selecting the appropriate method:

1. **Research Question**:
- Statisticians consider the specific research question being addressed by the analysis. Different statistical methods are suitable for different types of research questions, such as comparing means, assessing associations, predicting outcomes, or exploring patterns in categorical data.

2. **Type of Data**:
- The type of data collected in the study (e.g., continuous, categorical, binary) influences the choice of statistical method. For example, ANOVA and GLM are commonly used for continuous data, while PROC FREQ is used for categorical data.

3. **Study Design**:
- The study design, including factors such as the number of treatment groups, repeated measures, and the presence of covariates, informs the choice of statistical method. For example, PROC ANOVA is suitable for comparing means across multiple groups, while PROC MIXED is used for repeated measures or longitudinal data.

4. **Assumptions**:
- Statisticians assess whether the assumptions of the chosen statistical method are met based on the characteristics of the data. For example, ANOVA and GLM assume homogeneity of variance and normally distributed residuals, while PROC TTEST assumes independent samples and equal variances.

5. **Sample Size**:
- The size of the sample affects the choice of statistical method and the reliability of the results. Some methods may require larger sample sizes to achieve adequate statistical power.

6. **Software Capabilities**:
- The availability of specific statistical procedures within the chosen software platform also influences the choice of method. Statisticians select methods that are implemented in the software they are using and are compatible with their data format.

7. **Previous Research**:
- Statisticians may review previous research studies with similar objectives or data characteristics to determine which statistical methods have been commonly used and validated in similar contexts.

By considering these factors, statisticians can select the most appropriate statistical method to analyze clinical data, ensuring accurate and reliable interpretation of study findings. It's essential to choose a method that aligns with the specific requirements and assumptions of the research study to obtain valid and meaningful results.

Writing an efficacy dataset according to CDISC (Clinical Data Interchange Standards Consortium) standards, specifically in the ADaM

Writing an efficacy dataset according to CDISC (Clinical Data Interchange Standards Consortium) standards, specifically in the ADaM (Analysis Data Model) format, involves organizing and documenting the clinical trial data to facilitate statistical analysis and regulatory submission. Here's a general outline of how to write an efficacy dataset specification in ADaM format:

1. **Introduction**:
- Provide an overview of the dataset, including its purpose, scope, and intended use.
- Describe any relevant standards or guidelines (e.g., CDISC SDTM, ADaM) followed in dataset creation.

2. **Dataset Structure**:
- Specify the structure of the efficacy dataset, including the variables to be included and their attributes.
- Define the primary analysis dataset(s) for efficacy endpoints, such as efficacy analysis dataset (ADSL) or analysis dataset for a specific analysis (e.g., ADLB for longitudinal data).

3. **Variable Definitions**:
- Define each variable included in the dataset, including variable names, labels, formats, and descriptions.
- Specify the origin of each variable (e.g., derived from SDTM datasets, derived from other ADaM datasets, or derived directly from source data).

4. **Derived Variables**:
- Document any derived variables or transformations performed on the raw data to generate analysis-ready variables.
- Clearly define the logic or algorithms used to derive each variable, ensuring transparency and reproducibility.

5. **Analysis Population**:
- Define the analysis population(s) to be included in the dataset, such as the intent-to-treat (ITT) population, per-protocol population, or safety population.
- Specify any inclusion/exclusion criteria or rules for defining the analysis population(s).

6. **Timepoints and Analysis Periods**:
- Define the timepoints and analysis periods relevant to the efficacy analysis, including baseline assessments, follow-up visits, and endpoint assessments.
- Specify the timing and frequency of data collection for each variable.

7. **Statistical Analysis**:
- Describe the statistical methods or analyses to be performed using the dataset, including primary and secondary efficacy endpoints, subgroup analyses, sensitivity analyses, and statistical models.
- Specify any statistical programming code or algorithms required to generate analysis datasets or perform statistical analyses.

8. **Dataset Validation**:
- Outline data validation checks and quality control procedures to ensure the accuracy, completeness, and consistency of the dataset.
- Define validation criteria for key variables, outliers, missing data, and inconsistencies.

9. **Documentation**:
- Provide detailed documentation for the dataset, including annotated case report forms (CRFs), data validation plans, data review listings, and analysis documentation.
- Ensure compliance with regulatory requirements and standards for dataset documentation and submission.

10. **Review and Approval**:
- Establish procedures for dataset review, validation, and approval by cross-functional teams, including statisticians,

clinical programmers, data managers, and study sponsors.

Warnings that are considered ignorable

When executing efficacy procedures in SAS, there may be certain warnings that are considered ignorable, meaning they do not significantly impact the validity or reliability of the analysis results. These warnings are typically related to data issues, computational precision, or statistical assumptions. Here are some examples of ignorable warnings in SAS efficacy procedures:

1. **Missing Values**:
- Warnings related to missing values or incomplete data in variables used in the analysis.
- Ignorable if missing data occur infrequently or are appropriately handled in the analysis (e.g., using appropriate imputation methods).

2. **Convergence Issues**:
- Warnings related to convergence issues in iterative estimation algorithms (e.g., in PROC GLM, PROC LOGISTIC).
- Ignorable if the model still converges to a reasonable solution or if alternative convergence criteria are satisfied.

3. **Heteroscedasticity**:
- Warnings related to heteroscedasticity (unequal variance) in residuals or model errors (e.g., in PROC GLM, PROC MIXED).
- Ignorable if the assumptions of homogeneity of variance are not critical for the analysis or if robust standard errors are used.

4. **Collinearity**:
- Warnings related to multicollinearity (high correlation between predictor variables) in regression models.
- Ignorable if the presence of collinearity does not substantially affect the interpretation or inference of the regression coefficients.

5. **Small Sample Size**:
- Warnings related to small sample sizes or low frequencies in categorical variables.
- Ignorable if the sample size is still adequate for the intended analysis or if sensitivity analyses are conducted to assess the robustness of results.

6. **Round-off Errors**:
- Warnings related to round-off errors or numerical precision issues in computations.
- Ignorable if the errors are negligible relative to the scale of the data or if alternative methods are used to improve numerical stability.

7. **Model Fit**:
- Warnings related to model fit statistics or goodness-of-fit measures not meeting predefined thresholds.
- Ignorable if the overall model fit is still acceptable based on other criteria or if the warning is due to minor deviations from assumptions.

While these warnings may be considered ignorable in certain contexts, it is essential to carefully assess their implications for the specific analysis and ensure that they do not compromise the validity or reliability of the results. Ignoring warnings should be done judiciously, and sensitivity analyses or alternative approaches may be warranted to confirm the robustness of the findings.

P–value of 0.05

A p-value of 0.05 is a commonly used threshold in hypothesis testing, particularly in the context of null hypothesis significance testing (NHST). When conducting statistical tests, the p-value represents the probability of observing the data, or more extreme data, assuming that the null hypothesis is true. In other words, it quantifies the strength of evidence against the null hypothesis.

Here's what a p-value of 0.05 indicates:

1. **Interpretation**:

- If the p-value is less than or equal to 0.05 (i.e., p ≤ 0.05), it suggests that the observed data are unlikely to occur if the null hypothesis is true.

- This result is often interpreted as providing sufficient evidence to reject the null hypothesis in favor of the alternative hypothesis.

- In practical terms, it implies that there is a statistically significant difference, effect, or association present in the data.

2. **Statistical Significance**:

- A p-value of 0.05 is commonly used as a threshold for statistical significance, indicating that the observed result is unlikely to be due to random chance alone.

- However, it's important to note that statistical significance does not necessarily imply practical or clinical significance. It only indicates the presence of a statistically detectable effect.

3. **Type I Error Rate**:

- Using a significance level (alpha) of 0.05 means accepting a 5% risk of committing a Type I error, also known as a false positive.

- This means that there is a 5% chance of incorrectly rejecting the null hypothesis when it is actually true.

4. **Caution**:

- While a p-value of 0.05 is commonly used, it should not be viewed as a rigid cutoff or threshold. The interpretation of p-values should be considered in conjunction with other factors, such as effect size, study design, and clinical relevance.

- Results with p-values slightly above or below 0.05 should be interpreted cautiously and in the context of the specific research question and study design.

Overall, a p-value of 0.05 is often used as a guideline for determining statistical significance, but it should be interpreted thoughtfully and in conjunction with other relevant information.

Type I Error and Type II Error

Type I Error and Type II Error are two types of errors that can occur in hypothesis testing:
   1. **Type I Error**:
- Type I Error, also known as a false positive, occurs when the null hypothesis is incorrectly rejected when it is actually true.
- In other words, a Type I Error happens when we conclude that there is a significant effect or difference in the data when there isn't one.
- The probability of committing a Type I Error is denoted by α (alpha) and is typically set as the significance level in hypothesis testing (e.g., α = 0.05).
   2. **Type II Error**:
- Type II Error, also known as a false negative, occurs when the null hypothesis is incorrectly accepted when it is actually false.
- In other words, a Type II Error happens when we fail to detect a significant effect or difference in the data when there actually is one.
- The probability of committing a Type II Error is denoted by β (beta).
   Here's a comparison between the two types of errors:
   - **Type I Error**:
- Null hypothesis is true, but we reject it.
- Probability denoted by α (alpha).
- Often associated with the risk of false positives.
- Example: Concluding that a new drug is effective when it actually has no effect.
   - **Type II Error**:
- Null hypothesis is false, but we fail to reject it.
- Probability denoted by β (beta).
- Often associated with the risk of false negatives.
- Example: Failing to detect that a new drug is effective when it actually has an effect.
   Both Type I and Type II errors are important considerations in hypothesis testing, and researchers aim to minimize the probability of both errors. However, there is typically a trade-off between Type I and Type II errors: reducing one type of error often increases the risk of the other. The balance between Type I and Type II errors is influenced by factors such as sample size, effect size, and the chosen significance level (α).

Sample size Population and Standard Deviation

Sample size, population, and standard deviation are fundamental concepts in statistics:

 1. **Sample Size**:
- Sample size refers to the number of observations or data points included in a sample, which is a subset of the larger population.
- It is denoted by n and plays a crucial role in determining the precision and reliability of statistical estimates and inferences.
- A larger sample size generally provides more accurate estimates of population parameters and reduces the margin of error in statistical analyses.

 2. **Population**:
- Population refers to the entire group of individuals, items, or units that are of interest to a researcher and from which a sample is drawn.
- It encompasses all possible observations that could be made and is often too large or impractical to study in its entirety.
- Population parameters, such as the mean, variance, or proportion, represent summary measures of the entire population.

 3. **Standard Deviation**:
- Standard deviation (SD) is a measure of the dispersion or variability of a set of values around their mean.
- It quantifies the average distance between each data point and the mean of the dataset.
- A larger standard deviation indicates greater variability or spread of the data points around the mean, while a smaller standard deviation indicates less variability.
- The formula to calculate the standard deviation depends on whether the data represents a sample or a population. For a sample, it is typically denoted by s, while for a population, it is denoted by σ.

In summary, sample size represents the number of observations in a sample, population refers to the entire group of interest, and standard deviation measures the variability of data points around their mean. These concepts are essential for designing studies, conducting statistical analyses, and making inferences about populations based on sample data.

statistical programming in oncology challenges

Statistical programming in oncology presents unique challenges due to the complexity of clinical trial data, the evolving nature of oncology research, and the stringent regulatory requirements in drug development. Some of the challenges faced by statistical programmers in oncology include:

1. **Complexity of Data**:
- Oncology clinical trial data often include complex longitudinal data, survival data, biomarker data, and imaging data, which require specialized analytical techniques and programming skills.
- Dealing with missing data, censoring, and time-to-event endpoints (e.g., progression-free survival, overall survival) adds to the complexity.

2. **Data Integration and Standardization**:
- Integrating data from multiple sources, such as electronic health records, laboratory results, imaging studies, and patient-reported outcomes, can be challenging due to differences in data formats, structures, and quality.
- Ensuring adherence to CDISC (Clinical Data Interchange Standards Consortium) standards, such as SDTM (Study Data Tabulation Model) and ADaM (Analysis Data Model), is essential for regulatory submission.

3. **Advanced Statistical Methods**:
- Oncology studies often require the application of advanced statistical methods, such as mixed-effects models, time-to-event analyses, Bayesian methods, and machine learning algorithms, to address complex research questions and endpoints.
- Implementing these methods requires deep understanding and expertise in statistical theory and programming languages such as SAS or R.

4. **Regulatory Compliance**:
- Meeting regulatory requirements set by agencies such as the FDA (Food and Drug Administration) and EMA (European Medicines Agency) is crucial in oncology drug development.
- Ensuring data integrity, traceability, and reproducibility of analyses, as well as generating submission-ready outputs and documentation, are essential for regulatory compliance.

5. **Interdisciplinary Collaboration**:
- Effective collaboration between statisticians, clinical researchers, data managers, regulatory affairs professionals, and other stakeholders is essential for designing studies, analyzing data, interpreting results, and making informed decisions in oncology research.
- Communication skills and the ability to translate technical concepts into actionable insights are crucial for successful collaboration.

6. **Data Privacy and Security**:
- Protecting patient privacy and ensuring data security are paramount in oncology research, especially when dealing with sensitive health information and genomic data.
- Compliance with data protection regulations (e.g., GDPR in Europe) and implementing robust data governance practices are essential for maintaining confidentiality and integrity.

Statistical programmers role in efficacy and oncology programming

Statistical programmers play a crucial role in efficacy and oncology programming in SAS, contributing to the analysis, interpretation, and reporting of clinical trial data. Here are the key roles and responsibilities of statistical programmers in efficacy and oncology programming:

1. **Data Preparation and Integration**:
- Collect, validate, and integrate clinical trial data from multiple sources, including electronic case report forms (eCRFs), laboratory results, and imaging data.
- Ensure data quality and consistency, perform data cleaning, and address any anomalies or discrepancies in the data.

2. **Statistical Analysis**:
- Implement statistical analysis plans (SAPs) developed by statisticians, including the analysis of efficacy endpoints, safety data, and exploratory analyses.
- Conduct statistical analyses using SAS procedures such as PROC GLM, PROC MIXED, PROC LOGISTIC, PROC LIFETEST, and PROC PHREG for continuous, categorical, survival, and time-to-event endpoints.

3. **Programming and Automation**:
- Write and execute SAS programs to generate analysis datasets, perform statistical analyses, and produce analysis outputs, including tables, listings, and figures (TLFs).
- Develop and implement macros, scripts, and automation tools to streamline programming processes, improve efficiency, and ensure consistency across analyses.

4. **Documentation and Reporting**:
- Prepare documentation for statistical programming activities, including annotated SAS code, data specifications, and programming validation plans.
- Generate analysis outputs and statistical summaries for clinical study reports (CSRs), regulatory submissions, and scientific publications, ensuring compliance with regulatory standards and guidelines.

5. **Validation and Quality Control**:
- Perform validation checks and quality control (QC) procedures to verify the accuracy, completeness, and integrity of analysis datasets and programming outputs.
- Review and validate statistical programs and outputs produced by other team members to ensure consistency and adherence to programming standards.

6. **Collaboration and Communication**:
- Collaborate closely with cross-functional teams, including statisticians, clinical researchers, data managers, and regulatory affairs professionals, to support study design, analysis planning, and interpretation of results.
- Communicate effectively with team members and stakeholders to clarify requirements, address programming challenges, and ensure alignment with project timelines and objectives.

7. **Continuous Learning and Development**:
- Stay updated on advancements in statistical methodologies, regulatory guidelines, and industry best practices in efficacy and oncology programming.
- Participate in training programs, workshops, and professional development activities to enhance technical skills, domain knowledge, and programming proficiency.

By fulfilling these roles and responsibilities, statistical programmers contribute to the successful conduct of clinical trials, the generation of high-quality evidence in oncology research, and the advancement of treatments for cancer patients.

why you are looking for job change?

Firstly, be clear about your reasons for changing jobs. Is it a step in career progression after you have learned all that you could in your current job, or are you resigning under unpleasant circumstances? Either way, the key to answering right is to sound positive, be crisp and concise, and definitely not beat around the bush if it's the latter case. Some concrete reasons can be:

   - A search for newer opportunities and challenges
- A chance to work in a larger, more established organization or alternately a smaller start-up with greater responsibilities/learning curve
- Shift in work domain

Ah, this is a great (and very common) question. To begin, your interviewer is looking to see your response to determine your character. As a candidate, you should never use this question to bash your current or previous employer. Nor should you use this question to make yourself look bad by saying something like, "I just couldn't handle it," or "I didn't like my co-workers." The best response is: "I am looking for the experience that can prepare me better for my future as a [specific role]. I have been told that your company is known for developing people professionally..." etc.